"Thoroughly researched and highly readable, this volume will instruct, entertain and fascinate the reader. Unlike Zhukov's memoirs, which tantalizingly end with his recall from Germany in 1946, Spahr's book is a balanced, full-length biography covering Zhukov's exciting postwar political and military careers, his enduring struggle to establish his place in Russian history and the final bittersweet years. I highly recommend this book to the specialist, the layman or the general reader who enjoys a fast-moving, quality biography."

Col. Otto P. Chaney, USA (Ret.)
Military Review

"Spahr has written a far more textured account of Marshal Zhukov than has heretofore been available, offering new insights into Stalin's wartime command, military operations, and also the partisan struggles among political and military elites during Khrushchev's rule. Its challenge to several longstanding interpretations makes it an important book."

Lt. Gen. William E. Odom, USA (Ret.)

"Examines Zhukov's often abrasive command style [and] explains Zhukov's overbearing handling of his subordinates without excusing the flaw. . . . The author skillfully traces the ebb and flow of Zhukov's power and prestige after World War II; the sudden fall from grace in 1946 at Stalin's hand; the return to power in 1953; and the final political "exile" of Zhukov ordered by Khruschev in 1957. Particularly noteworthy is Spahr's description of the events surrounding the arrest of the chief of the secret police, Lavrentii Beria, in which Zhukov played a greater role than most historians have previously portrayed."

—*Assembly*

Bust of Marshal Zhukov presented to Admiral William Crowe, at that time chairman of the U.S. Joint Chiefs of Staff, on the occasion of his visit to a Soviet military academy named in honor of the marshal.

ZHUKOV

THE RISE AND FALL OF A GREAT CAPTAIN

William J. Spahr

PRESIDIO

Published by Presidio Press
505 B San Marin Drive, Suite 300
Novato, CA 94945

Printing History
First published in cloth by Presidio Press in 1993
This paperbound edition published in 1995

Library of Congress Cataloging-in-Publication Data

Spahr, William J., 1921–
    Zhukov : the rise and fall of a great captain / William J. Spahr
      p.   cm.
    ISBN 0-89141-469-X (cloth)
    ISBN 0-89141-551-3 (paper)
    1. Zhukov, Georgii Konstantinovich, 1896–1974. 2. Marshals—
Soviet Union—Biography. 3. World War, 1939–1945—Soviet Union.
4. Soviet Union—History—1939–1945. I. Title.
DK268.Z52S6 1993
940.54'0092—dc20
[B]   92-42332
                                             CIP

Maps courtesy of Government Printing Office, Washington, D.C.

Typography by ProImage
Printed in the United States of America

To my wife and best friend Barbara, for all her help in this and so many other things.

CONTENTS

LIST OF MAPS

ACKNOWLEDGMENTS

Although this book will be considered a monograph, it could not have been written without the assistance, advice and support of many people whom it is my pleasure to thank.

My friend and classmate, Bill Scott, and his wife, Harriet, helped me to keep abreast of the numerous articles about Zhukov which have been appearing in the Soviet press since the advent of glasnost'. They have also given me access to their collection of Soviet military writings which I believe surpasses any other in this country.

To my old friend, David Murphy, I owe my interest in things Soviet in the first place. He has continued to provide me with articles of interest when they pass through his broad field of view.

Several of my fellow parishioners at Grace Episcopal Church in Alexandria, Virginia, including William Bryson, who struggled with an amateur who owns a word-processor; Richard Farkas and Julie Glass, who advised about such things as the maps and the photographs; Jean Reed, who advised on contemporary military terminology; Katherine Elder, who suggested where I might find a publisher; and Barbara Morris, who provided moral support.

Joan Griffin has done a scrupulous job of editing the manuscript and attempted to polish the prose. She should not be faulted if she did not make a silk purse out of a sow's ear.

For the maps, I would like to thank the Office of the Chief of Military History of the U.S. Army and the U.S. Government Printing Office.

The translation from Pindar's *Isthmians* 7: 26–30, is reprinted by permission of the publishers from *The Invention of Athens: The Funeral Oration in the Classical City* by Nicole Loraux, Harvard University Press: Cambridge, Mass., copyright 1986 by the President and Fellows of Harvard College.

Of course, I take responsibility for any errors and the judgments of people and events that have been made in the text.

Source Note

The principal source for this biography is the memoirs of Marshal Zhukov, *Vospominaniia i razmyshleniia* (Reminiscences and reflections) which were published in 1969 by Novosti. This work was widely criticized in the Free World as a transparent attempt to, among other things, refurbish the tarnished image of Josef Stalin. It was also disappointing in that Zhukov ended his story in 1946 after he had returned from Germany. In the Soviet Union, despite the absence of official enthusiasm for the work and what to knowledgeable citizens were obvious signs of censorship, the first edition sold out immediately. Since then there have been nine subsequent Russian editions and the work has been translated into seventeen foreign languages.

In 1990, the 10th Russian edition was published in three volumes. It includes, according to its publishers, the material that was excised from the original manuscript. The 10th edition also includes and notes the insertions that Zhukov was required to accept if the book was to be published. Except where indicated otherwise, the 10th edition is the source cited as *Memoirs*.

The sources for the story of Zhukov's life after 1946 until his death in 1974 are mainly the recollections of family, old colleagues, friends, and journalists. These of course are anecdotal and sometimes contradictory. In 1992, *Molodaia Gvardiia* (Young Guard) published a biography entitled *Zhukov* by the Russian historian N. N. Iakovlev, using these sources and some from the archives of the former Soviet Ministry of

Defense. The work, which provides additional details of Zhukov's life and times, unfortunately does not have what the Russians call a "scientific apparatus," that is, it does not attribute its sources. Also, because it is apparently written to inspire youthful readers, it is silent on some of the more controversial episodes in the marshal's life.

Vladimir Karpov has written extensively and added much to the available information on Zhukov's post-1946 problems. He has had access to the transcript of the expanded plenary session of the Communist Party Central Committee of October 1957. That session, chaired by Nikita Khrushchev, sent Zhukov to his final exile. Karpov found the evidence presented against Zhukov to be unconvincing, but his account of what he found in the transcript seems to be incomplete. The publication of Khrushchev's rambling reminiscences has had the effect of clouding up an already murky affair.

All translations are by the author. The Library of Congress transliteration system has been used throughout the text except where certain names of individuals and places have a generally accepted transliteration not in accord with that system, e.g., Moscow for *Moskva*, Dnieper for *Dnepr*.

INTRODUCTION

I cannot keep silent;
for I hear the sound of the trumpet,
the alarm of war.
Jeremiah 4:19

Perhaps no one of the prominent Soviet military leaders of World War II has received more attention in the current rewriting of Soviet history than Georgii Konstantinovich Zhukov. The policy of *glasnost'* has permitted the exposure of the considerable revisions that his memoirs underwent prior to their publication in 1969. The conditions of glasnost' have also allowed the revelation of the details of episodes in Zhukov's career not covered in his memoirs—his military exile in 1946, his disgrace in 1957, and his enforced silence and isolation until his death in 1974.

From the German invasion in June 1941 until Soviet troops smashed their way into Berlin in May 1945, the name of Zhukov was intimately connected with a series of victories in important land battles that changed the course of the Second World War in Europe. But from 1946 until 1953 he was banished to the command of secondary military districts. Then, following the death of the dictator Josef Stalin, Zhukov seemingly recovered his position, becoming Minister of Defense and the first military professional to become a member of the Soviet Politburo. His new prominence did not continue for long. In 1957 Stalin's successor, Nikita Khrushchev, accused Zhukov of Bonapartism and removed him from his party and government positions, forcing him into early retirement and isolation.

From then until his death in 1974, the old soldier was concerned with ensuring that his version of the great events in which he had played such an important part would some day be available to historians. The deposal of Khrushchev in 1964 seemed to provide the opportunity. Here, again, he found that the ruling political figures were not willing to permit him to reveal fully the number and extent of the military errors and misjudgments that Stalin had made before and during the war. He also found that they were unwilling to share too much public attention with an aging hero. Nor were some of his former military colleagues willing to forgive or forget the real and imagined hurts that he had inflicted on them, often in the heat of battle.

The manner in which the one-party state that was the Soviet Union treated its most famous military leader appears to have been the result of a combination of factors: a leadership never confident of its own legitimacy to an extent that bordered on paranoia; the personal jealousy that his renown seems to have inspired in the political and the military leadership; the antipathy he engendered in some of his subordinates because of his style of military leadership; and the jackal-like attitudes of many officers who, encouraged by the influence and guidance of the Main Political Administration of the Soviet Army and Navy, sniped at and criticized him once they found it politic to do so. It is noteworthy that there appears to be no credible evidence that Zhukov ever openly opposed or plotted to subvert the policies of his civilian political masters.

That he was allowed to live out his life in comfortable isolation was in large measure due to the fame that he achieved as a result of his World War II victories. Scores of experienced, capable officers whose background and training were at least equal to that of Zhukov were executed in the great purges of 1937-1938. Lesser numbers were killed in subsequent years. No credible evidence has ever been revealed to establish that the victims were threats to the Soviet state or its leadership. That Zhukov survived was a minor miracle.

The new information has not been entirely positive in its contribution to an appraisal of Zhukov as a commander and as a man, and future revisions to Russian military historiography may again attempt to denigrate the military achievements of this great soldier. However, although some of the further details of the life and career of this extraordinary leader may eventually appear, the main outlines are sufficiently clear, so that we can now proceed with confidence on the writing of a balanced and more accurate biography.

I

EARLY YEARS, 1896–1918

The Soviet Army's most renowned soldier during World War II was born on the 1st of December 1896, in the village of Strelkovka, Kaluga Province, about 200 kilometers south of Moscow. His father was an impoverished shoemaker-peasant; his mother was a physically powerful woman who at times lifted 180-pound sacks of grain to supplement the family income. At an early age he demonstrated his own physical prowess, his stubbornness, and his determination to excel. At the age of ten he completed the local parochial school with praise. The same year, 1906, his father, who spent considerable time separated from his family, working in Moscow, was banished from the city for participation in the disorders of 1905. When he was eleven, Zhukov was apprenticed to his mother's brother, a successful Moscow furrier who did not allow the relationship to soften the conditions of service—the young lad worked fifteen- or sixteen-hour days and slept on the workshop floor. Despite these harsh working conditions, Zhukov, with the assistance of a cousin, continued his studies, took courses at night, and successfully passed equivalency examinations for the city elementary school system. He also became a "submaster furrier" at age fifteen, thereby earning ten rubles a month.*

---

*Zhukov has written that he was born on 19 November 1896 (old style). According to conversion rules his birthday in the current calendar should be 1 December and is so indicated in several Soviet reference books. However, he apparently celebrated it on 2 December and it is so recorded on the place where his ashes were placed in the

1

Zhukov's political attitudes during this period, as he recollected them, had not been shaped. He recalled the poverty of his parents and the destitute condition of his native village. But furriers were apolitical, had no trade union, and were concerned mainly with accumulating sufficient capital to open their own shops. In this they differed sharply from factory workers: "from the real proletariat by their petit bourgeois ideology and by the absence of strong proletarian solidarity."[1]

Zhukov admitted that he did not fully understand political questions, but he claims to have recognized clearly the different interests that were being defended by the newspapers of the day, including those of the Bolsheviks. He considered volunteering for service at the outbreak of World War I, but was dissuaded by a politically wise older worker. When he was conscripted in 1915, at age nineteen, he did not experience any special enthusiasm because he had already seen many unfortunate cripples return from the front, while he perceived the sons of the rich as living high and without care. Nevertheless, when drafted he was ready to fight honorably for Russia.[2]*

The young conscript Zhukov had lived for almost eight years in the heart of Moscow. His job had enabled him to travel to Nizhnii Novgorod (formerly Gorki, most recently again Nizhnii Novgorod) on the Volga and into the Ukraine. Although his family still lived in a village, the level of his education, his urban experiences, and his trade made it unlikely that he would ever return to village life. His trade and the economic and political views of the people in it also made it unlikely that he would have become involved in the working class movement.

In spite of his long stay in the city, his natural physical gifts remained intact and, perhaps because of them, he was selected for the cavalry. On the basis of his performance as a recruit he was selected for noncommissioned officer training in the spring of 1916. He recalled that he had not wanted to enter the training command but a friendly

---

Kremlin wall. Zhukov was christened Egor and continued to be called that by those who knew him in his youth. He began to be called Georgii at about 15 years of age. His first wife frequently called him "George."

*Zhukov decided to serve even though his master offered to arrange a deferment for health reasons. This offer was deleted from the first nine editions. Zhukov, *Memoirs* 1: pp. 63, 64.

noncommissioned officer who had been at the front convinced him that the training was an opportunity to postpone exposure to the dangers of combat. He did not arrive at the front until August 1916. Three months later, in October, he was wounded and evacuated but not until he had received two crosses of St. George (one for capturing a German officer) and had been promoted from an acting to a full-fledged noncommissioned officer.[3]

On return to duty in December 1916, Zhukov was assigned as an instructor to the noncommissioned officer training command, where he came to sense the general disaffection that was spreading throughout the army. Although he again admits that he poorly understood political questions, he considered that "peace, land and freedom could only be given to the Russian people by the Bolsheviks and no one else. This, as much as my capabilities would allow, I impressed on my soldiers, for which I was rewarded by them."[4] His reward was to be elected, immediately after the February Revolution, chairman of his squadron's soldiers committee and delegate to the regimental council. Zhukov reports that at that time the regimental council was Bolshevik. In May, however, after the departure of an otherwise unidentified Iakovlev who was the Bolshevik head of the regimental council, SRs (Social Revolutionaries) and Mensheviks who supported the Provisional Government took control, and some units transferred their loyalty to the Ukrainian nationalist, Simon P. Petliura. Zhukov's squadron committee, consisting mainly of residents of Moscow and Kaluga, issued an order demobilizing the unit and sending all of its troops home. Zhukov himself was forced to hide for several weeks from Ukrainian nationalist officers. On 30 November 1917 he returned to Moscow. For the next two months Zhukov rested with his mother and father. When he decided to join the Red Guards he fell ill with typhus, from which he did not fully recover until August 1918. He volunteered at that time for service in the 4th Cavalry Regiment of the 1st Moscow Cavalry Division.[5]

The details of this critical period in Zhukov's life are sparse, and his description of it raises some questions. It appears that the squadron committee issued an unauthorized order which, in effect, resulted in a mass desertion and that Zhukov may have been hiding from more than Ukrainian nationalists. His ability to stay out of action for almost nine months in his native village also suggests a certain indecision on his part about which side he was going to support in the military events that were exploding all around him. Later in life he would speculate that if he had become a commissioned officer before the revolution he might have opposed it and spent the rest of his life in foreign exile.[6] However, questions about this interlude were probably obvious to those who became Zhukov's enemies later in his career. If the answers had been in any way compromising they certainly would have been used against him.

NOTES

1. Georgii K. Zhukov, *Vospominaniia i razmyshleniia,* 10th edition (Moscow: Novosti, 1990) (hereinafter *Memoirs*) 1: pp. 11–21, 62.
2. Vladimir Karpov, "Marshal Zhukov, ego soratniki i protivniki v gody voiny i mira" (Marshal Zhukov, his comrades in arms and opponents in the years of war and peace) in *Znamia,* no. 10 (1989): p. 11. Hereinafter "Soratniki." M. M. Pilikhin, "Moi brat Georgii Zhukov" (My brother Georgii Zhukov) in Mirkina and Iarovikov, *Marshal Zhukov: Polkovodets i chelovek* (Marshal Zhukov: great captain and man) (Moscow: Novosti, 1988), 1: p. 17. Ella Zhukova, "Interesy otsa" (My father's interests) in Ibid., p. 53.
3. Zhukov, *Memoirs* 1: 75. A biographical article on Zhukov in *Voenno-Istoricheskii Zhurnal* (The Military Historical Journal) (hereinafter *VIZh*), no. 11, (1966): p. 31, reported that Zhukov received two crosses of St. George and two medals for "repeated bravery in battles with the Germans."
4. Zhukov, *Memoirs* 1: 75, 76.
5. Ibid., pp. 77, 78.
6. K. M. Simonov, "Zametki k biografii G. K. Zhukova" (Notes for a biography of G. K. Zhukov) (hereinafter "Zametki") in *VIZh,* no. 12 (1987): p. 47.

II

In the Red Army during the Civil War, 1918–1921

Zhukov began his formal political education in the Red Army as one of five "sympathizers" in his squadron who were visited twice weekly by the secretary of the regimental Party buro and the political commissar. During these sessions the Party workers talked about the internal and external situation, measures being taken by the Party at the front, and the Bolshevik version of the history of the revolution. On 1 March 1919 he was accepted as a member of the Communist Party and after that

> all of my thoughts, strivings, actions, I have tried to subordinate to the duties of a member of the Party, and when matters have come to a conflict with enemies of the motherland, I, as a Communist, remembered the requirement of our Party to be an example of selfless service to my people.[1]

During this period, Zhukov came into contact with the commissar of the 1st Moscow Cavalry Division, who coincidentally bore the same given and family names—Georgii Vasil'evich Zhukov—and whose military-political biography made a lasting impression on him. The commissar had served in the Tsarist cavalry for ten years, had become a member of the Party in 1917, and had led a significant portion of his regiment into the Red Army—a career in many ways similar to his own. In discussing his namesake, Zhukov defined the duties of the commissar as he conceived it in those early days of the Soviet Army:

The work of a commissar included not only propaganda and agitation, but first of all providing a personal combat example, manner of action, and conduct. A commissar was required to know all operational instructions, to participate in the development of orders, (the deciding word remained with the commander in questions of an operational character), to study military matters carefully. Usually, before battle the commissars gathered the political workers and the Communists, explained to them the unit's mission and themselves went to the most dangerous and decisive areas of the battlefield. The rank and image of the commissar of the time of the Civil War was deservedly pervaded with glory.[2]

On one occasion, Commissar Zhukov asked Red Army soldier Zhukov if he would care to transfer to political work but the latter refused, saying that he preferred to remain with the line troops.

These recollections of Zhukov's first contacts with a political commissar during his early years in the Red Army may be seen as the basis of his attitude toward the military political apparatus of which he was to run afoul later in his career. First, he was convinced that his political indoctrination, conducted twice weekly by the two full-time Party workers in the regiment, was adequate. The content of the sessions was unquestionably political enlightenment and in Zhukov's evaluation it was sufficient, so sufficient that Zhukov reported, "To this day I remember [them] with gratitude."

The numerical strength of the Party apparatus in the army would also become an important issue later. The small number of professional Party workers in Zhukov's regiment—two—was a reflection of their scarcity throughout the army, somewhat more than 7,000 political commissars who depended on the Party cells in the army and the navy to link more than 50,000 Communists in a force of more than 1,800,000.[3]

Finally, there was the image of Commissar Zhukov, who was experienced and capable militarily, in addition to being fluent and literate politically. Was this the image of an ideal commissar Zhukov was to retain throughout his career? From his own experience he realized that educational work was probably sufficient to inspire Red Army soldiers to perform their duties in a manner that met military and political standards. There were no sessions of criticism and self-criticism, during which young officers and soldiers examined the short-comings of their superiors.

The 1st Moscow Cavalry Division was assigned to Mikhail Frunze's 4th Army as it faced the forces of Admiral Aleksandr V. Kolchak in the southern Urals in the spring of 1919. Zhukov's first Red Army combat action occurred at Shipovo, a village about 80 kilometers west of Ural'sk, in mid-June 1919. There, Zhukov recalled, his 4th Cavalry Regiment engaged in a desperate sabre-slashing engagement with a White Cossack unit. During the battles around Ural'sk the young Red Army trooper had an opportunity to see and hear Frunze, one of the famous commanders of the Civil War and future Commissar of Defense.

In the fall of 1919, the 4th Cavalry Regiment was engaged south of Tsaritsyn (later Stalingrad, now Volgograd), where Zhukov was wounded by hand grenade fragments in his left leg and side in a skirmish with what he described as "White Kalmyks." The wounds so weakened him that, following treatment in a field hospital (where he again contracted typhus), he was given a month's convalescence leave which he spent at home.

Following his leave, in January 1920 Zhukov was ordered to attend a Red Army commanders' course in Riazan', where he remained until July 1920. Then the student commanders were formed into a provisional regiment and moved via Moscow to Krasnodar where they were sent into action against the forces of Baron Petr N. Vrangel. Zhukov did not participate in the final defeat of Vrangel in the Crimea because the more experienced officer candidates in the provisional regiment were declared to have completed their training and transferred as officer replacements to units that had suffered severe combat losses. Zhukov was assigned to the 14th Separate Cavalry Brigade, then engaged in mopping-up operations against remnants of Vrangel's troops. By December 1920, Zhukov was in command of a squadron against the "army" of Antonov, which Zhukov described as made up mainly of unreconciled Social Revolutionaries whose goal was the overthrow of the Bolshevik regime. To liquidate this opposition the Soviets assembled a force of over 40,000 troops in the Tambov region in the spring of 1921, commanded by Mikhail N. Tukhachevskii, whom Zhukov met during a visit to the brigade. Zhukov also encountered Ieronim P. Uborevich,

Tukhachevskii's deputy, in the course of this campaign. Operations against Antonov were often small unit cavalry actions, which were tests of a commander's ability to lead by personal example. In these clashes Zhukov had his mount shot from under him on two occasions and was saved from death or capture both times by his political commissar.[4]

NOTES

1. Zhukov, *Memoirs* 1: 95.
2. Ibid., p. 97.
3. Ibid., p. 95.
4. Ibid., pp. 100–116.

III

THE PEACETIME ARMY, 1922-1936

After the conclusion of the Civil War, Zhukov remained in the Red Army—whether by choice or by Party order is not clear from his memoirs. He cites a Party decision of February 1921 which halted the demobilization of Party members from the army, but does not indicate whether the order affected his personal plans. Outside of the army his skills were in the fur trade or in tilling the soil, neither of which seemed to promise much for the future in the Soviet state in 1921. On the other hand he had shown aptitude for military life, and the situation that faced the Soviets at the time seemed to demand continuous attention to national defense. There was probably little doubt in Zhukov's mind that he wanted to continue to serve.

Zhukov's success as a Red Army commander during the years between the end of the Civil War and the start of World War II was achieved by the same determined, independent effort to improve his knowledge that he displayed in achieving a basic education as a youth in Moscow. He recognized the shallowness of his knowledge of military strategy and tactics, and he reports that, having been advanced to regimental command in 1923 at age 26, he decided to add three or four hours of independent study to his long work day.[1] In 1924, he was given the opportunity to attend a one-year training course for cavalry commanders in Leningrad. Characteristically, at the end of the course, he and three of his fellow officer-students elected to return to their units in Minsk, 963 kilometers away, on horseback. On the seventh day after their departure from Leningrad they were met in Minsk by members of their regiments and local civilians:

Using our spurs, at a field gallop, we rode up to the tribune and reported to the garrison commander and the chairman on the city council. . . . We were greeted with an ovation.[2]

About this time, he received a short leave of absence and visited his mother and sister. His father had died in 1921. He observed:

The village was poor, the people poorly clothed, the number of head of cattle had declined sharply and for many there were none left after the bad harvest of 1921. But, what was surprising, with rare exception no one complained. The people understood the postwar difficulties correctly. The kulaks and traders kept aloof. Evidently they still hoped for a return to former times, especially after the proclamation of the New Economic Policy.[3]

Zhukov returned to his regiment after his schooling, confident and self-reliant in questions of military and political training and of his ability to command the regiment. In the winter of 1926, he became the first commander in his division to be designated an *edinonachal'nik* (a one-man commander).

This designation was a result of one of the most important of the military reforms of 1925, a reform considered possible because the nucleus of the Red Army commanders were now representatives of the working class. The Red Army had continued to use the system developed during the Civil War. Military units were often commanded by officers from the old army and navy who were usually not Party members. Party members were assigned as military commissars to observe and control the commander's activities. All orders required the signature of both the commander and the military commissar. Even so, one-man command was installed carefully, "considering in each case the peculiarities of a given unit, the specifics of a given region, the characteristics of the commander and the commissar, etc."[4]*

Zhukov dismissed the objections that one-man command could lead to a diminution of the influence of the Party in the Army. For him,

---

*Presumably, it was on such occasions that Zhukov's record in the Revolution would have received a thorough screening and any negative aspects exposed.

the role of the Party was strengthened and not weakened when the commander was a Party member: his responsibility to the Party was increased for all aspects of the performance of his unit, discipline was improved, and the level of combat readiness was raised.[5] It is notable that, even in an edited and censored version of his memoirs, Zhukov's emphasis was on discipline and combat readiness; the ideological function of the army as a "school of communism" was not mentioned.

Zhukov received his last formal military schooling in late 1929 and early 1930 at a short course in Moscow preparing officers for command of larger units.[6] Upon his return to his regiment he was promoted to command a brigade subordinate to the 7th Samara Cavalry Division, commanded by Konstantin Konstantinovich Rokossovskii, whom Zhukov was to encounter often during his subsequent service. Excerpts from some of Zhukov's efficiency reports are available, and they stress his energy, decisiveness, and the excellence of the unit he was commanding. Two reports recommended his promotion. But these reports also noted character traits that would appear again and again in the future and would stain his military reputation. The first written performance evaluation in his personnel file, dating from 1922, noted that he sometimes was insolent in his relations with his political officer. Rokossovskii noted in 1930 that he was "painfully proud." In 1931, Budennyi observed "excessive rigidity and crudity" in his dealings with his subordinates.[7]

In February 1931, at thirty-four years of age, Zhukov was ordered to Moscow for duty as assistant to the Inspector of Cavalry of the Red Army, Semen M. Budennyi—the "legendary commander" of the 1st Cavalry Army in the Civil War.[8]* In 1966, Rokossovskii recalled this transfer as a forced one, caused by complaints from Zhukov's subordinates in the brigade against his "unfounded strictness and even crudeness. . . . Attempts to bring pressure on the brigade commander were unsuccessful."[9] Zhukov in other words was "kicked upstairs," a solution to a personnel problem not unknown in other armies.

---

*Zhukov comments in his memoirs that he did not meet Budennyi for the first time until the spring of 1927. Because of Zhukov's service with the cavalry during the Civil War it is often assumed mistakenly that he served with Budennyi and the 1st Cavalry Army.

Arriving in Moscow in 1931, after almost twelve continuous years of duty with troops, Zhukov was an officer with a promising future, judging by his assignment, the available efficiency reports, and his designation as a one-man commander. (His reputation for strictness may have been a plus in the Red Army of that era.) Zhukov had developed firm ideas about how to achieve results in the competitive atmosphere that is characteristic of peacetime military service. One was his willingness to devote considerable time and energy to independent study. In particular, he was attracted to the study of tactics:

Special attention was given to field tactical training of the units, the command element, the staff and the regiment as a whole. I must say that of all military disciplines I liked tactics most and always worked at it with special pleasure. As is known, an army is an instrument of war, it exists for armed combat with the enemies of the Motherland, and for this combat it must first of all be prepared tactically. In the opposite case it will be forced to learn in the course of battles, taking large losses at the same time.[10]

Next to tactical training, or perhaps along with it, Zhukov stressed physical training. "All we former soldiers knew better than anyone else that only hardened, strong soldiers are capable of bearing the weight of war. The success of the unit as a whole depends on the physical condition of each soldier." Zhukov himself constantly engaged in equestrian sports.[11]

He admitted that he made some mistakes and may have been excessively demanding on his subordinates—not always restrained and patient.

This or that careless work in the conduct of a serviceman upset me. Some didn't understand that, and I, in my turn, evidently was not sufficiently indulgent toward human weakness. Of course, now these errors have become more obvious; having experience teaches much. However, even now I consider that no one is given the right to enjoy life because of the labor of another. And this is especially important for military people to realize, who must on the battlefield, without regard for their lives, be the first to defend the Motherland.[12]

The political side of his duties received relatively little mention, simply that as a "one-man commander I understood more fully the leading organizing role of the Party in the structuring and the early activity of the units of the Red Army."[13]*

During his early service Zhukov had encounters with such well-known Red Army commanders as Mikhail Vasil'evich Frunze, Mikhail Nikolaevich Tukhachevskii, Vitalii Markovich Primakov, Vasilii K. Bliukher, Ieronim Petrovich Uborevich, and Aleksandr Il'ich Egorov, all of whom (with the exception of Frunze, who died on the operating table in 1925), would become victims of the purges of 1937–1938. He also had direct contact with younger officers who would serve with him in the future. K. K. Rokossovskii, I. Kh. Bagramian, and Andrei I. Eremenko attended the Advanced Cavalry Course with him in 1925–1926. Primakov headed the course when the students arrived in 1925. Rokossovskii later became commander of his division, and Semen K. Timoshenko was Zhukov's corps commander in 1926 when he was installed as a one-man commander.[14] His service as an assistant to the inspector of cavalry enabled him to see and to be seen by the high command of that period. He became personally acquainted with Tukhachevskii, who was at that time a first deputy commissar of defense, with Kliment E. Voroshilov, the commissar of defense, and, of course, his direct superior, S. M. Budennyi.

Of these acquaintances the latter two were to prove almost immediately significant because of Zhukov's assignment to the 4th Cavalry Division, which had been named in honor of Voroshilov. This division, one of the veteran divisions of Budennyi's 1st Cavalry Army, had fallen to a low state of combat readiness, causing the Belorussian Military District commander, Uborevich, to ask Voroshilov to replace the division commander. Budennyi was given the task of finding a new commander and chose Zhukov in the spring of 1933.

---

*Three months after Zhukov's arrival in Moscow he was elected secretary of the Party buro of all the inspectorates of the Combat Training Directorate. According to his friend, Aleksandr Mikhailovich Vasilevskii, who arrived in Moscow for service with the Directorate of Combat Training at about the same time, Zhukov required all of the officers in the Party organization to toe the line regardless of rank. Konstantin Simonov, "Besedy s Marshalom A. M. Vasilevskim" (conversations with Marshal A. M. Vasilevskii) in *Znamia*, no. 5 (1988): p. 96.

Applying the methods that had proven successful in his previous assignments, Zhukov quickly restored the division to its former competence. He called together the Party *aktiv* (the most prominent and active members of the division's Party organization) and determined that the general decline in the division was the result of insufficient political work and military training. The division had been transferred recently to an area where the housing and training facilities were almost nonexistent and had devoted most of its training time to the construction of facilities. To accomplish both the task of restoring the division's combat readiness and providing the necessary facilities, Zhukov set aside certain days for construction, but spent most of the time on tactical training in the field and physical training. He also managed to get significantly more help from the military district headquarters than had been furnished previously.[15] This was an early manifestation of another of Zhukov's repertoire of problem-solving methods: he never hesitated to ask his superiors for help. Having served in Moscow, he realized that the military district commander also bore a share of the responsibility for the condition of units in his command.

Zhukov does not describe the political work the division did for the next four years under his command. Instead he describes interesting occurrences on field exercises and maneuvers and, of course, the various honors and compliments paid the division and its commander by such visitors and inspectors as Budennyi, Voroshilov, Uborevich, and Timoshenko. In 1935, the division and its commander were awarded the Order of Lenin, recognizing that it had become one of the best divisions in the army.[16]

Another aspect of his service with the 4th Cavalry Division that shaped Zhukov's attitude toward younger officers later in his career was the difficult conditions in which the family of even the division commander had to live.

We arrived at Slutsk during the spring thaw. At the station there was thick mud and in getting into the carriage my wife* left her

---

*Zhukov married Aleksandra Dievna Zuikova, a village schoolteacher, in 1920. His first daughter, Era, was born in 1928. Era Zhukova, "Otets" (My father), in Mirkina and Iarovikov, *Marshal Zhukov: Polkovodets* 1: pp. 30, 45.

galoshes in the mud more than once. Sitting on my shoulders, Era [his daughter] asked: Why are there no sidewalks as we have in Sokol'niki [an area of Moscow]? I answered her: Here there will also be sidewalks and a beautiful square, but only later. . . . I and my family were housed temporarily in an 8-square-meter room.[17]

In 1936 Zhukov suffered a severe attack of brucellosis, which was attributed to drinking contaminated milk while on a field exercise. He was hospitalized in Minsk and Moscow for seven or eight months. While he was in Moscow his family stayed with his cousin M. M. Pilikhin and his wife.[18]

NOTES

1. Zhukov, *Memoirs* 1: 134.
2. Ibid., pp. 140, 141.
3. Ibid., p. 142.
4. Iurii P. Petrov, *Partiinoe stroitel'stvo v Sovetskoi armii i flote (1918–1961)* (Party structuring in the Soviet army and fleet 1918–1961), (Moscow: Voenizdat, 1964), 186 (hereinafter *Partiinoe stroitel'stvo*).
5. Zhukov, *Memoirs* 1: 144.
6. *VIZh*, no. 11 (1966): p. 32. In fn. 3 on this page it is denied that Zhukov ever received any military training in Germany. This fiction may have been started by the German Field Marshal Gerd von Rundstedt who in an interview with B. H. Liddell Hart remarked that Zhukov had studied with von Seeckt in about 1921–1923. B. H. Liddell Hart, *The German Generals Talk* (New York: Morrow, 1948), p. 222.
7. Karpov, "Soratniki" in *Znamia*, no. 10: p. 16. *VIZh*, no. 11 (1966): p. 32. The full text of the last two fitness reports was printed in *VIZh*, no. 5 (1990): pp. 22, 23.
8. The reference to Budennyi is Zhukov's. *Memoirs* 1: 148; his assignment to Moscow, Ibid., pp. 160, 169.
9. N. G. Pavlenko, "Razmyshleniia o sud'be polkovodtsa" (Reflection on the fate of a Great Captain), in *VIZh*, no. 10 (1988): p. 17. (Hereinafter "Razmyshleniia")
10. Zhukov, *Memoirs* 1: 146.
11. Ibid., p. 147.
12. Ibid., p. 153.
13. Ibid., p. 152.
14. Ibid., pp. 145, 152.
15. Ibid., pp. 186–192.
16. Ibid., pp. 184–205. Karpov, "Soratniki" in *Znamia*, no. 10: p. 24.
17. Zhukov, *Memoirs* 1: p. 187.
18. M. M. Pilikhin, "Moi brat Georgii Zhukov" (My brother Georgii Zhukov) in Mirkina and Iarovikov, *Marshal Zhukov: Polkovodets*, pp. 22, 23.

IV

THE PURGES, 1937–1938

During 1937, the purges reached the Red Army after the February–March plenum of the Central Committee, during which Stalin accused the security organs of being "several years behind" in exposing "enemies of the people." The military was singled out by Molotov and accused of being unwilling to participate in the struggle. A campaign was initiated immediately after the plenum to expose the "counterrevolutionary fascist organization" in the armed forces, and in the ensuing months thousands of military leaders, including political officers, were imprisoned and many were shot. The effect of these arrests and investigations can be judged by Iurii Petrov's calculation that, already in 1937, 60 percent of the commanders of infantry regiments, divisions, and corps were new; 40 percent in equivalent tank units; and 20 percent in aviation units. It is now admitted that more than 40,000 officers were "suppressed" during the purges.[1]

In the first nine editions of Zhukov's memoirs these tragic events were passed over in two short paragraphs—a total of seven lines, two complete sentences.[2] There was no mention of his own difficulties during this period. Zhukov, in this and many other places in the book as it was first published, had to choose between accepting the censor's deletions (and the politicians' insertions) or forego seeing the book published in his lifetime. When the book was first published in 1969, Soviet politics was within the period the Soviets now call the time of "stagnation" (*zastoi*) when the Brezhnev regime decided that discussion of Stalin's crimes would be muted.[3]

In the tenth edition, the unexpurgated original version, Zhukov, in his recollections of the military comrades of his prewar service, made a point of recalling those who had become victims of Stalin's crimes: Marshal Bliukher, "slandered and without proof accused of hostile activity and destroyed"[4]; Primakov, "destroyed in 1937"[5]*; Batorskii, "tragically died in 1937"[6]; Danilo Serdich, "died tragically in 1937"[7]; Sedyakin, "tragically died in 1938."[8] Tukhachevskii was referred to several times: Zhukov's regret that Tukhachevskii was not there in 1941; his opinion that Tukhachevskii played the leading role in the scientific and technical work in the Commissariat of Defense; his being told that Tukhachevskii did not praise Stalin because the dictator had unjustly accused him of responsibility for the defeat before Warsaw in 1920; and his description of Tukhachevskii's warnings in 1936 of the threat from Nazi Germany as a "voice crying in the wilderness." All of these references were deleted from the first nine editions.[9]

During the turbulent years 1937 and 1938, Zhukov commanded the 3rd Cavalry Corps for seven months and was then offered command of the 6th Cavalry Corps, which included in its units his former command—the 4th Cavalry Division. In the first editions of the memoirs these transfers are ascribed simply to changes in assignments for the former commanders.[10] It was not surprising that "personnel turbulence" (to use the U.S. Army term) occurred during this period. And it seemed plausible that Zhukov had somehow avoided the fate of so many others. However, in the tenth edition the details are provided of Zhukov's difficulties during this incredibly tragic period in the history of the Soviet armed forces.

After Danilo Serdich, the Serbian veteran of the 1st Cavalry Army and commander of the 3d Cavalry Corps, was arrested in 1937 as an

---

*Primakov headed the cavalry commanders course that Zhukov attended in 1926. During the Civil War he rose to the command of the 1st Cavalry Corps of Chervonnyi Cossacks in the Ukraine. During the Soviet-Polish War in 1920, Budennyi accused Primakov of criminal conduct because of his inactivity and unresponsiveness during an operation. Budennyi demanded his court martial but the recommendation was never acted on. Primakov was the first victim arrested in preparation for the 1937 trial of Tukhachevskii and others. His confession was obtained on 8 May 1937 after he had been in prison since August 1936. On 21 May, he named Tukhachevskii as the head of the plot to remove Stalin and install Trotskii as head of the Soviet government. *Izvestiia TsK KPSS,* no. 4 (1989): pp. 47, 48.

"enemy of the people," Zhukov was called to Minsk and interviewed by the newly appointed member of the Military Council of the Belorussian Military District, Filip I. Golikov. Golikov questioned Zhukov closely about which of the arrested officers he knew and was friendly with. Zhukov responded that he knew well Uborevich and several of the corps commanders including K. K. Rokossovskii. He also said that he had been friendly with Rokossovskii and Serdich and continued to believe that they were patriots and honest Communists. Zhukov sensed that Golikov was not satisfied with these answers.

Golikov told Zhukov that the commissar of the 3rd Cavalry Corps had reported that in his dealings with subordinates Zhukov was sharp to the point of crudity and did not appreciate fully the role and significance of political workers. Zhukov responded that he was only sharp with those who had a lackadaisical attitude toward their duty. He defended his attitude toward political workers in similar terms. Golikov then stated that there was information that Zhukov's wife, with his knowledge, had had their second daughter Ella baptized. Zhukov denied the allegation.

Following this unpleasant interview, the acting Military District commander, V. M. Mulin, entered and told Zhukov that the district Military Council proposed to nominate him as the new commander of the 3d Cavalry Corps. When Golikov insinuated an underlined copy of the report on Zhukov to Mulin, the latter read it quickly, found it unconvincing, and said that someone should talk to its author. Zhukov was ordered to return to his division and await Moscow's decision.[11]

It took more than a month for a favorable decision to be received from Moscow. Zhukov suspected that Golikov, who apparently gave more credence to the negative report than Mulin, had communicated to the high command a negative opinion on Zhukov's reliability. Zhukov, however, claims that he was in no hurry to take a higher command because the NKVD (*Narodnyi Komissariat Vnutrennikh Del*—the People's Commissariat of Internal Affairs) seemed to be conducting an especially active hunt for senior officers at the time. "They hardly succeeded in moving a man to a high position, when you next looked, he had been arrested as an 'enemy of the people' and the poor devil was wasting away in the basements of the NKVD."[12]

When he eventually took command of the corps, Zhukov found that in the majority of its units the level of combat and political preparation had fallen sharply. This he attributed directly to the effect of the arrests on morale and discipline. Demanding commanders found themselves the targets of demagogues who tried to attach the label of "enemy of the people" to them. Zhukov, as was his manner, admitted that he intervened in these cases directly and sharply; he would agree later that in a number of cases he used excessive sharpness. Certain "unprincipled" subordinates reported to Golikov and to the NKVD on the "hostile training of cadres" conducted by the commander of the 3d Cavalry Corps, Zhukov.[13]

As an example of the impact of all this, Zhukov describes how one of his division commanders, aware of the decline of discipline and general performance of his division, called him in despair to report that a meeting of the division Party organization was to be held that night to discuss the division commander's performance. The division commander was convinced that the meeting would find him unworthy, expel him from the Party, and that his expulsion would clear the way for his arrest the next day by the NKVD. Zhukov agreed to attend the meeting, which proceeded along familiar paths. The division commander was accused of having close relations with various "enemies of the people," the most prominent of whom was Uborevich, the executed former commander of the Belorussian Military District. In addition, according to the complainants, the division commander was insensitive in his dealings with subordinates and was too demanding in the level of performance he required of them. The discussion lasted three hours, and no one spoke in defense of the commander. The acting corps commissar seemed to support those who were attempting to oust the commander from the Party. Zhukov was given the floor last. He cited his long friendship with the commander, and asserted that he was a sensitive comrade, an honest Communist, and a sterling commander. As to his association with Uborevich and other "enemies of the people," he reasoned that no one yet knew the reasons for their arrests so how could this Party meeting get ahead of the competent organs that were presumably investigating the entire affair? As to the other questions, Zhukov concluded that they were minor and were not questions of principle; the division commander would draw the appropriate conclusions from the criticism. Zhukov's speech carried the day. The meeting soon ended, and with tears in his eyes the division commander thanked Zhukov.[14]

This division commander, V. E. Belokoskov, survived the purges and the Second World War, and ended his military career as a deputy minister of defense.[15]

Shortly after this episode, Zhukov was offered and accepted command of the 6th Cavalry Corps, which included among its subordinate units the 4th Cavalry Division, the unit he had commanded for four years. The vacancy occurred because of the transfer of the corps commander, E. I. Goriachev, to the Kiev Special Military District. To provide an illustration of the prevailing climate, Zhukov relates the fate of Goriachev. Faced with the ordeal of a Party meeting and the accusation that he had ties with Uborevich and the other "enemies of the people," and not wishing "to undergo the repressions of the organs of state security," he committed suicide.[16] The reference to the suicide of Goriachev was deleted from the first nine editions.

Zhukov accepted the transfer readily, but one suspects that he was influenced by the knowledge that certain elements in the 3d Cavalry Corps were ready to exploit his next political mistake. However, the transfer did not shield him from a showdown similar to that experienced by many other senior officers. Zhukov's inquisition was conducted by the combined Party aktiv of the 4th Cavalry Division, the 3d and the 6th Cavalry Corps. The Party organizations of those units were prepared to make complaints about matters that were months if not years old. Approximately eighty Communists assembled for the process, which began with the declarations of those critical of Zhukov's command style, his excessive crudity, his conservative promotion policies, and his relationships with Uborevich (with whom he had dined privately) and other enemies of the people.

The chief of the political section of the 4th Cavalry Division, S. P. Tikhomirov, who had served with Zhukov several years, gave what Zhukov assessed as a "tacking" speech, avoiding a direct answer to questions of where Zhukov had been wrong and where he had been correct. His testimony, considering that he had served with Zhukov so long, was damaging in that he did not give his former commander a clear-cut endorsement.

In the end, Zhukov had to speak for himself. He began by acknowledging he at times lost his restraint when dealing with those who were slack in their performance of duty. He admitted that as a Communist he was obligated to help with good counsel and not demonstrate tension. As to dining with Uborevich, he questioned who in the audience knew before the trial that Uborevich was an "enemy of the people." Good relations between seniors and their subordinates should be the goal of all Communists as long as one was not aware of suspicions of disloyalty. As to his attitude toward political officers, Zhukov said that he was opposed to those officers who wanted to be "good uncles" to the troops at the expense of unit efficiency and discipline.

The group decided to end further discussion of Zhukov and his fitness to command and to accept his explanation. But for Zhukov the matter did not end there. According to his later recollection, he realized immediately where matters were heading when the Uborevich matter was raised. When he left the conference he sent a telegram to Voroshilov and Stalin. He received no answer, but afterwards he was left in peace. Zhukov also admits that he never forgave his former political officer, Tikhomirov, for his waffling speech, and even years later when Zhukov was minister of defense did not answer his letters.[17]

As a corps commander, Zhukov began the study of operational-strategic questions to help him in his current assignment and to enhance his future prospects. He admits that his understanding of Marxist-Leninist theory was acquired when the occasion presented itself on individual questions, without any attempt at systematic study. This was the case with other commanders and, although the Party provided an opportunity to learn, many did not put forth the individual effort. Zhukov was aware of the need to understand political questions but it did not come easily to him—especially Karl Marx's *Capital* and the philosophic works of Lenin. In his own mind it was more important to understand Lenin's tactics and strategy.[18]

At the end of 1938, Zhukov was offered the post of deputy commander for cavalry of the Belorussian Military District. His duties included supervising the training of all cavalry units in the district and those separate tank brigades designated to support the cavalry. In the event of war he was to command a horse-mechanized group consisting of four or five cavalry divisions, three or four separate tank brigades, and other support units. Although he did not want to leave the corps, he was attracted by the opportunity to command a large operational formation. He was succeeded as corps commander by A. I. Eremenko, whom he had known at the cavalry command course in 1924–1925. In a remark his editor may have considered gratuitous and the censor considered unacceptable, he noted that people did not like Eremenko because he was conceited and an idolator [of Stalin?]. It did not appear in the first nine editions.[19]

NOTES

1. Petrov, *Partiinoe stroitel'stvo,* pp. 299–300.
2. Zhukov, *Memoirs,* 1st ed., p. 152.
3. Maria Zhukova, "Korotko o Staline" (In brief about Stalin) in *Pravda,* 20 January 1989, p. 3. The Party name for this period was the campaign to "liquidate the distortions in the struggle with the personality cult." Pavlenko, "Razmyshleniia," *VIZh,* no. 11: p. 19.
4. Zhukov, *Memoirs,* 10th ed., 1: p. 137.
5. Ibid., p. 138.
6. Ibid., p. 140.
7. Ibid., p. 152.
8. Ibid., p. 176.
9. Ibid., pp. 180, 182.
10. Zhukov, *Memoirs,* 1st ed., p. 152.
11. Zhukov, *Memoirs,* 10th ed., 1: pp. 221–223.
12. Ibid., p. 224.
13. Ibid., p. 225.
14. Ibid., pp. 225, 226.
15. Ibid., p. 227.
16. Ibid.
17. Ibid., pp. 231–234. N. Svetlishin, "Marshal Zhukov: Krutye stupeni sud'by" (The abrupt steps of fate) in *Sovetskii Voin,* no. 8 (1988): p. 14.
18. Zhukov, *Memoirs* 1: pp. 234, 235.
19. Ibid., p. 237.

V

HALHIN GOL, 1939

Zhukov's stay at the Belorussian Military District Headquarters was brief. In early June 1939, Zhukov was ordered to report to Voroshilov without explanation. He and his wife thought that he might be on his way to prison or worse. Once there, he was ordered by Voroshilov to fly to Chita and thence to Tamsagbulag in Mongolia. His mission was to report on the situation and take command, if necessary, of the Soviet and Mongolian troops who were defending against a Japanese incursion across the Mongolian-Manchurian border which had penetrated almost to the Halhin Gol (river).[1]

Zhukov's successful execution of this mission, driving the Japanese back to the recognized border, was to win him fame, promotion to the rank of General of the Army, the gold star of a Hero of the Soviet Union, and command of the Kiev Military District. Most important of all, it brought him to Stalin's attention. Many years after the event, Zhukov added another reason that Halhin Gol was an important turning point in his life. The victory there enabled him to cast away "all the slander and the accusations that had been assembled against me in the previous years some of which I knew and some of which I figured out."[2]

Zhukov's solution to the problem at Halhin Gol was characteristic of his method of military problem-solving, while the Soviet military-political leadership adopted command arrangements that typified the Stalin style of directing military operations far from Moscow. On arriving at Tamsagbulag, headquarters of the 57th Special Corps, Zhukov found that the headquarters was located 120 kilometers from the scene of the action and that the corps commander had not visited the area. After a personal reconnaissance, Zhukov recommended to Moscow that the Soviet-Mongolian positions on the right bank of the Halhin Gol be held while a counterattack was prepared to drive the Japanese back across the border. To accomplish this, Zhukov requested additional aviation, not less than three infantry divisions, artillery reinforcements, and one tank brigade. These proposals were accepted and Zhukov was given command of the force, which was to be called the 1st Army Group.[3]*

Shortly after Zhukov made these recommendations, G. I. Kulik, then a member of the Main Military Council and chief of the Main Artillery Directorate,[4] who was also in the area as an artillery instructor, ordered the bulk of the Soviet and Mongolian troops on the east (right) bank of the Halhin Gol withdrawn across the river for reinforcement and regrouping. Zhukov protested this move and was supported by Voroshilov in Moscow. Later, Kulik returned to Moscow and reported that an additional five to seven divisions were needed to prevent the Japanese from reaching Chita. Voroshilov again overruled Kulik, "rebuked him for being panicky and rejected all of his baseless proposals."[5]

Zhukov also had to deal with advice from G. M. Shtern, then commander of the Transbaikal Military District, headquartered in Chita. Under the peculiar command chain established by Stalin and Voroshilov, Shtern was responsible for the logistics support of Zhukov's troops but was only authorized to assume command if military action were to break out in another sector and grow into a war. On the third day of the Soviet August offensive, Shtern became alarmed over the losses being suffered by the Soviet left wing, which was attempting to envelop the Japanese from the north while Soviet forces in the south tried to join them in the Japanese rear and complete the encirclement. He advised Zhukov to halt the offensive for two or three days, allow the troops to regroup, and then continue the offensive. Zhukov rejected his advice, saying that to halt the offensive would increase Soviet losses ten times. Shtern, apparently after verifying that he had no command authority over Zhukov, withdrew his recommendation.[6] The result was

---

*This Soviet designation should not be confused with a U.S. Army Group, which is a group of armies. The Soviet equivalent of a U.S. Army Group was a *Front.* An *armeiskaia gruppa* in the Soviet Army was a temporary combined arms unit established to accomplish a particular mission. Such a group was often called an operational group during World War II.

a complete Soviet victory over the Japanese, who were driven over the border with heavy losses.

The Japanese force that Zhukov defeated consisted of two infantry divisions, each of almost 25,000 men plus supporting troops and aircraft. The Japanese tank brigade was used only once, losing almost a hundred tanks to Soviet artillery as they attacked over the only available tank approach, presumably without adequate air and artillery support. The Soviets calculated Japanese and Manchurian losses, in what Zhukov later characterized as "a serious reconnaissance in force,"[7] at 61,000 killed, wounded, and captured. Soviet and Mongolian losses were more than 18,500 killed and wounded.[8] Zhukov believed that this outcome later predetermined the restrained conduct of the Japanese on the eastern borders of the Soviet Union during the Soviet-German war.[9] Zhukov, as well as other Soviet commentators, rarely acknowledged that the Japanese restraint may have also been due to the fact that they were fighting a major war with the United States from December 1941 until 1945.

The campaign at Halhin Gol demonstrated that serious shortcomings existed in the preparedness of the Soviet territorial divisions. Created after the Civil War, these divisions consisted of a small cadre of regular soldiers and officers, supplemented by local personnel of military service age who underwent periodic training with the unit. In emergencies the entire unit could be called up. The 82d Rifle Division, a territorial division, was one of the units sent to reinforce Zhukov. When it was committed, it attempted to flee the battlefield after some Japanese artillery salvos; and it took all available staff personnel to halt the unit and reposition it on the Mongolian steppe. Zhukov relieved the division commander and gradually over a month and a half retrained the division to perform on the battlefield.[10]

The success at Halhin Gol also gave Zhukov his first interview with Stalin. The impression was a powerful one:

Returning to the Hotel Moskva, I could not get to sleep for a long time being under the influence of a conversation with members of the Politburo. The appearance of I. V. Stalin, his quiet voice, the concreteness and the depth of his judgments, his knowledge of military questions, the attention with which he heard the report, made a great impression on me.[11]

Considering Zhukov's state of mind at the time, having just returned to the capital in triumph, this was probably only a slightly exaggerated statement of his attitude toward the dictator. Zhukov was then not yet 43 years old.

Only in the tenth edition do we find that the comment on Stalin's knowledge of military questions had been inserted by an editor. And, reinstated was Zhukov's speculation about why there was so much talk that Stalin was a terrible person. In 1939, Zhukov did not want to believe anything bad about Stalin.[12] The editors also deleted Stalin's criticism of Voroshilov for the sad performance of the Soviet Army in the war with Finland. Timoshenko had replaced Voroshilov in May 1939 and Stalin noted that a number of corrective measures were being taken.[13]

NOTES

1. M. V. Zakharov claimed that he recommended Zhukov for the post. M. V. Zakharov, "Nakanune vtoroi mirovoi voiny" (On the eve of the Second World War) in *Novaia i Noveishaia Istoriia,* no. 5 (September–October, 1970): p. 22. (Hereinafter referred to as "Nakanune.")
2. K. M. Simonov, "Zametki k biografii G. K. Zhukova" (Notes for a biography of G. K. Zhukov) in *VIZh,* no. 6 (1987): p. 54. (Hereinafter referred to as "Zametki.")
3. Zhukov, *Memoirs* 1: 242, 243.
4. See page 66 for information on Marshal Kulik.
5. Zakharov, "Nakanune," p. 22.
6. Simonov, "Zametki," in *VIZh,* no. 6: p. 53.
7. Ibid., p. 50.
8. *Sovetskaia voennaia entsiklopediia* (The Soviet military encyclopedia) (Moscow: Voenizdat, 1976–1980) (hereinafter *SVE*) 8: p. 354.
9. Simonov, "Zametki," in *VIZh,* no. 6: p. 51.
10. Ibid., p. 53.
11. Zhukov, *Memoirs,* 1st ed., p. 184.
12. Zhukov, *Memoirs,* 10th ed., 1: 273.
13. Ibid., p. 272.

VI

In the High Command, 1940–1941

Zhukov's next assignment was command of the Kiev Special Military District—the largest and one of the strategically most important military districts in the Soviet Union. At the same time he was promoted "out of turn" to General of the Army.[1]

Zhukov's stay in Kiev was also to be a short one. Here again he devoted the major portion of his time and energy to field training, command post exercises, and various war games. One of the outstanding divisions in the district was the 99th Rifle Division, which was chosen to perform a demonstration exercise for the new defense minister, Marshal Timoshenko. The division was presented as an example in the military press for all phases of its performance. Its commander was praised for his command competence and the high standards he maintained in developing an outstanding division. Naturally, the commander, Andrei A. Vlasov,* received a fitness report that corresponded to the results he had achieved.

The major event of Zhukov's tour of duty in Kiev was the "liberation" campaign conducted by troops of the Kiev Special Military District in Bessarabia and northern Bukovina in the summer of 1940. For this

---

*A. A. Vlasov went on to command the 37th Army during the defense of Kiev in 1941, the 20th Army in the defense of Moscow, and the 2nd Shock Army in 1942. At that time he was captured by the Germans and eventually turned against Stalin. He commanded the Russian Liberation Army in its futile attempt to combat Bolshevism in 1944 and 1945. Vlasov was captured by the Soviet army in May 1945 and hanged on 2 August 1946.

32

operation the Southern Front was created under Zhukov's command, consisting of three armies, two from the Kiev Military District and one from the Odessa Military District. In the course of occupying what the Soviets claimed was territory illegally seized by Romania during the Civil War, the Romanians, in violation of their agreement with the Soviets, attempted to remove railroad rolling stock, factory equipment, and other supplies as they evacuated the area. To halt this, Zhukov had two airborne brigades dropped to block the bridges over the river Prut, which formed part of the new boundary between the two countries. He also dispatched two tank brigades to link up with the paratroopers. The effect of the sudden appearance of the parachutists and the tanks, which arrived almost simultaneously, caused panic in the withdrawing Romanian troops. Officers abandoned their units and their equipment and the Royal Romanian Army presented a sad spectacle to the onrushing Soviets.

The next day Stalin called to ask what was going on. The Romanian ambassador had protested that the Soviet command had violated the agreement by using airborne troops and airborne tanks to disperse the Romanian army. When Zhukov explained what had happened— that the sudden appearance of the parachute troops and the tanks had caused the panic-stricken Romanians to conclude that the tanks had been transported by air—Stalin laughed and told him to gather the discarded weapons and to guard the captured equipment. Stalin said he would direct the Ministry of Foreign Affairs to protest the affair to the Romanians.

There is no indication, as this episode is described by Zhukov, that he had cleared his actions with Moscow in advance. If the Romanians were in fact removing property belonging to the Soviet government, time was of the essence. Nevertheless, for a newly appointed military district commander to risk an international incident was a demonstration of initiative and self-confidence that at that period in Soviet history, with the purges still ongoing, was rarely seen. Zhukov had given Stalin another reason to remember his name.

Soviet censors found reason to delete these events from the first nine editions of the Zhukov memoirs. One can only speculate that they found this evidence of Zhukov's brashness and his willingness to face Stalin at this early stage in his career too precocious, particularly when compared to the overwhelming evidence that other high ranking officers built their careers by pleasing the dictator.

This campaign remained in Rokossovskii's memory because his role in it, as one of Zhukov's subordinates, was his first duty following his release from prison in 1940.* Zhukov had requested Stalin to release Rokossovskii to his command, and with the support of Timoshenko it had been accomplished. Rokossovskii was assigned to command the 5th Cavalry Corps, the same unit he had commanded prior to his arrest. By requesting his release and accepting him in his command, Zhukov was, in effect, taking responsibility for Rokossovskii's loyalty to the regime. Released officers were not given constructive credit on the promotion lists for the time spent in prison, even if they had been wrongfully accused and convicted.[2]

While in Kiev, Zhukov was joined by another classmate from the Advanced Cavalry Course of 1925, I. Kh. Bagramian. Bagramian had been retained at the Academy of the General Staff as an instructor after completing the course in 1938. To escape from his assignment as an instructor, Bagramian wrote Zhukov in the summer of 1940 asking for any available assignment. Zhukov secured his transfer but may have had motives beyond those of cronyism and the desire to secure the services of an Academy-trained officer. Recognizing that his own fundamental military education was weak, he requested that Bagramian bring with him materials available at the Academy on offensive operations.[3] Zhukov, as the Soviet commander with the most recent successful combat experience, had been ordered in September 1940 to prepare a report on the theme "The character of contemporary offensive operations" for a December presentation to a conference of the senior command element in Moscow.

Bagramian provides a retrospective impression of Zhukov in 1940. He found him little changed physically after 15 years—if anything he was even more solidly built than in his younger days. His success had

---

*Rokossovskii, who had risen to corps command, was retired in July 1937, arrested in August, and released in March 1940. He acted as an inspector during the "liberation campaign" of July 1940 that was in progress when he reported to Zhukov. Rokossovskii then reassumed command of the 5th Cavalry Corps. His former subordinate, Zhukov, whom he had "kicked upstairs" in 1931, was now his military district commander. K. K. Rokossovskii, *Soldatskii dolg* (A soldier's duty), 5th ed., p. 3.

not surprised Bagramian because "he was unconditionally the bright-est and most gifted personality" of all the important pre-war military leaders.[4] He differed from some in that he was not only gifted mili-tarily but also had a strong character and was merciless to dishonest people. However, his strictness to subordinates, thanks to a superior mind and a developed intellect, rarely turned into the open crudity that was characteristic of a number of military leaders of that time. He was a threat only to loafers.[5]

With Bagramian's help, Zhukov's report was finished on schedule and a draft was sent to Moscow for approval by 1 November. Two weeks later Zhukov was informed that the report was approved for presentation.

The conference ordered by the Central Committee took place as planned in Moscow at the end of December 1940. In attendance were the military district and field army commanders and their chiefs of staff, the chiefs of all the military academies, professors, chiefs of the central direc-torates, and the directing element of the General Staff. Members of the Politburo were also present during the entire conference. It was held against a backdrop of German military successes in the west: the relatively easy occupation of Norway and Denmark; the lightning conquest of France; and the expulsion of British forces from the continent. The Red Army during the same year had been humiliated in Finland. If Stalin had hoped that Hitler would be engaged for years in the west, he now had to face the reality that only a nonaggression pact stood between him and Hitler.

Zhukov recalled that his presentation was well received, that his listeners made a number of valuable suggestions and critical comments. One of the sharpest critics was P. L. Romanenko, a veteran of the Spanish Civil War and an ardent supporter of the massed employment of tanks. Zhukov was to remember his critic fondly in 1942 when he gave him command of the 5th Tank Army during the counterattack at Stalingrad. Given the success of the German mechanized and armored forces in Poland and France, the question of the deployment and employment of such forces by the Soviet Army received extended discussion and almost unanimous support; one who was opposed was Marshal Kulik. The narrower questions of the composition, march order, and resupply of mechanized exploitation forces and the details of organizing air support were discussed extensively.[6]

Following the conference, a nine-day, two-sided war game was scheduled, but before it began Stalin saw fit to humiliate his minister of defense, Semen K. Timoshenko, in the presence of the game's participants. Timoshenko had made his concluding remarks and ended the conference the previous day without awaiting Stalin's comments. When Timoshenko tried to explain that he had sent him an advance copy of his remarks, Stalin angrily told him that he was not obligated to read everything that was sent him. Turning to the members of the Politburo who were present, Stalin asked, "How are we going to correct Timoshenko?" Molotov, speaking for the Politburo, answered,

> We have to oblige Timoshenko to analyze your comments on the theses more seriously and taking them into consideration present the Politburo, in a couple of days, a draft of a directive to the forces.[7]

The Politburo agreed unanimously with Molotov's proposal.

Stalin, having demonstrated his authority, asked about the war game—who was commanding the "blue" side (the enemy) and who was commanding the "red" side (the Soviet forces). After warning Timoshenko not to release the participants without his permission, Stalin dismissed the generals like a pack of disobedient school boys. Zhukov observed that this was a different Stalin from the one he had seen when he returned from Halhin Gol. The generals returned from the Kremlin in a depressed state of mind.[8]

The war game was played with two scenarios. In the first scenario Zhukov played the commander of the attacking "blue" side. The defenders were led by D. G. Pavlov who played the commander of the "red" Western Front. G. M. Shtern played the commander of the "red" Southwestern Front. The focus of the exercise was on what the Soviets called the western strategic axis, which stretched from East Prussia to the Pripiat' Marshes. Zhukov developed his operations plan using data on the German forces furnished by the Soviet General Staff, reflecting the latest German operational methods. His "offensive" moved along the routes that the Germans would use in June 1941. The configuration of the border, he recalled, drove him to the same solutions to the problem of planning the offensive that the Germans arrived at six months later. Even though the game's directors artificially restrained the movement of the "blue" forces, they had reached Baranovichi in Belorussia when the game ended.[9]*

In the second scenario Zhukov again commanded the "west" side, defending a fortified area against the "east" as it forced a crossing of the Vistula and attempted to encircle the "western" defenders. In this scenario, as in the first, Zhukov managed to thwart the "easterners."

The critique of the exercise was conducted in the Kremlin in the presence of Stalin and other members of the Politburo. It was held one day early on Stalin's order, and the timing apparently found Kirill A. Meretskov, then chief of the General Staff, unprepared. His fumbling attempt to summarize the results of the conference and the war game provoked Stalin to take over the critique. According to Zhukov, Stalin was already disgusted because the "red" forces had not performed well. He also questioned the superiority in forces that the Germans had been given at the start of the game. He was told, possibly by F. I. Golikov, who had become head of the Main Intelligence Directorate (GRU) in July 1940,[10]** that the German forces used in the game corresponded to German capabilities and were based on a realistic calculation of the forces that could be concentrated for the main effort. This was the reason for the blue success in the game,[11] a response that did not satisfy the dictator. When D. G. Pavlov, then the actual commander of the Belorussian Military District, reported on his role in the game, Stalin interrupted to ask him directly the reasons for the failures of the red side. Pavlov attempted to make light of the question, saying that such things happen in war games. To which Stalin replied that a military district commander should be able to find the correct decision in any situation but that this had not happened in the game.[12]

---

*The Germans actually reached Baranovichi on the 26th of June 1941, four days after they launched their offensive and by 1430 that day were attacking through Baranovichi on their way to Minsk approximately 150 kilometers away. Heinz Guderian, *Panzer Leader* (New York: Ballantine, 1961), p. 130.

**As head of the GRU, Golikov was responsible for furnishing the intelligence data on the German forces. His only recorded contribution to the prewar game conference was to deny the assertion of one of the critics of Zhukov's presentation that it was based on the capabilities and views of the 1932–34 period. His denial suggests that current intelligence data was reflected in Zhukov's presentation.

Zhukov raised the question of the fortified areas in western Belorussia being too close to the border, especially in the vicinity of Belostok, where the border formed a salient which the Germans could easily pinch off. This irritated Pavlov, who thought that Zhukov was criticizing him and his district. Voroshilov reminded Zhukov sharply that the configuration had been approved by the Main Military Council and that the construction was being supervised by a former chief of the General Staff, B. M. Shaposhnikov. Stalin asked a couple of questions, but his reaction to Zhukov's brash sally into sensitive forbidden territory was not recorded. Many of the military felt, before and after the German attack, that the new fortifications were constructed too close to the border, but they were overruled by Stalin who, for political reasons, wanted to defend the newly occupied territories in the west as far forward as possible. According to Zhukov, they were also guided by the "notorious" slogan, "We will not give one inch of our land to anyone."[13]

Certain aspects of this episode deserve emphasis as a basis for understanding Soviet political-military relations at that time. The participation of the highest political leadership in what a western observer would have considered a technical military conference was characteristic of the system. The military leadership that Stalin was to assume during World War II was based on his experience in the Civil War and such competence in military affairs as could be acquired over the years in sessions such as this one. During these sessions the entire military high command was under scrutiny. Their ability to present and to defend their proposals was measured by Stalin and his associates. They were also being measured, much more subjectively to be sure, as to their devotion to the leader and their potential to betray him. In these conditions, Stalin's closest associates such as Viacheslav M. Molotov, Georgii M. Malenkov, and Lavrentii P. Beriia, who thought they had divined the dictator's leanings on a particular question, would feel more confident to speak out than professional military men, who were accustomed to a structured environment and not used to speaking in the dictator's presence.

That Zhukov, although a relative newcomer to the high command, did not hesitate to speak out on this occasion is an indication of the confidence he felt in his own abilities and ideas. With this confidence and his admitted demanding and critical attitude, he must have begun, subconsciously perhaps, to evaluate those in the high command, both military and civilian, with whom he would be working. He found many of them wanting in terms of professional ability and intellectual honesty. These findings would be reinforced in the course of the crises of 1941 and 1942.

Another attitude that can be posited is that Zhukov developed an aversion to unstructured meetings in which uninformed and unsupported opinions could prevail, depending on the relationship of the speaker to Stalin. According to Bagramian, Zhukov's character did not permit him to approach an objective indirectly but only head-on.[14] The strategies and tactics of the upper levels of the Soviet state were bound to be difficult to master for an individual of Zhukov's temperament and background.

NOTES

1. *VIZh*, no. 11 (1966), p. 33.
2. Zhukov, *Memoirs* 1: 275–277. K. K. Rokossovskii, *Soldatskii dolg* (A soldier's duty) 5th ed. (Moscow: Voenizdat, 1988), p. 3. Zhukov related his role in Rokossovskii's release in a letter to the writer, Vasilii Sokolov, in 1963. V. Sokolov, "Slovo o Marshale Zhukove" (A word about Marshal Zhukov) in S. S. Smirnov, *Marshal Zhukov: Kakim my ego pomnim* (Marshal Zhukov: As we remember him) (Moscow: Politizdat, 1988), p. 210. (Hereinafter *Marshal Zhukov.*)
3. I. Kh. Bagramian, "Zapiski nachal'nika operativnogo otdela" (Notes of the chief of the operations section), in *VIZh*, no. 1 (1967): p. 50. Hereinafter "Zapiski."
4. Ibid.
5. Ibid.
6. V. Ivanov and K. Cheremukhin, "O knige 'V nachale voiny'" (On the book *In the beginning of the war*), in *VIZh*, no. 6 (1965): pp. 73, 74. S. P. Ivanov in his *Shtab armeiskii, shtab frontovoi* (Army staff, Front staff) (Moscow: Voenizdat, 1990), pp. 420, 421, reports on Zhukov's enthusiasm in 1942 for his erstwhile critic and also comments that the episode reflects favorably on Zhukov's ability to accept criticism.
7. Zukhov, *Memoirs* 1: p. 291, 292.
8. Ibid., p. 292.
9. Simonov, "Zametki," in *VIZh*, no. 9: p. 50.
10. Ivanov and Cheremukhin, "O knige" (see note 6), p. 74.
11. Simonov, "Zametki," in *VIZh*, no. 9: p. 50.
12. Zhukov, *Memoirs* 1: p. 294.
13. Ibid., pp. 294, 295. Simonov, "Zametki," in *VIZh*, no. 9: p. 50. Karpov, "Soratniki" in *Znamia*, no. 11: pp. 112, 113. V. Anfilov, "U Zhukova, v Sosnovke" (With Zhukov at Sosnovka) in *Krasnaia Zvezda* (KZ), 27 April 1992, p. 3.
14. Bagramian, "Zapiski," p. 51.

VII

CHIEF OF THE GENERAL STAFF

The day after the critique, Stalin called Zhukov in and told him that the Politburo had decided to appoint him chief of the General Staff, relieving Meretskov. Zhukov protested that he had always been in the line and never on the staff. Stalin responded by saying that the matter had been decided. In postwar conversations with the author, Konstantin Simonov, Zhukov returned to the topic. In addition to the absence of staff experience, Zhukov felt that by his nature he was more suited to be a commander than a staff officer.

Although Zhukov had read Shaposhnikov's work *Mozg armii* (The brain of the army)* when he attended the courses for the high command staff of the Red Army in 1929–30, he was under no illusions about the role of the General Staff in the Soviet state. He considered the title and the suggestion that the General Staff should be considered the "brain" of the army more applicable to the Tsarist Army than to the Red Army. The "brain" of the Red Army was the Central Committee of the Communist Party and had been from the first days of its existence. Not one decision on an important military question had been made without the participation of the Central Committee.[1]

---

*Shaposhnikov's work, which was published in 1927 and 1928, reviewed the activities of the Austrian General Staff in the period from 1906 through 1918. His analysis of the 3,000-page memoir of the chief of the Austrian General Staff during that period and the role of the European General Staffs in the period before the outbreak of the war was considered by some to provide a series of recommendations for a General Staff of the Red Army, which did not have one at that time.

Zhukov assumed his duties on the 1st of February 1941,* less than five months before the German attack.[2] He took charge of a General Staff that was trying to cope with the expansion of the armed forces to meet Hitler's potential threat in the west, the administrative and logistic problems of the new territories added to the western borders in 1940, the changes in training and doctrine required to correct the deficiencies revealed in the Finnish War, the tensions caused by the everpresent threat of continuing purges, and the anticipation of the policy and operational changes that the fourth chief in less than four years would bring.

He had been in place slightly more than a month when on 8 March a Party-government decision was issued defining the roles and functions of the Commissariat of Defense. The new directive confirmed that the chief of the General Staff was to be a deputy to the commissar of defense, S. K. Timoshenko, and that the General Staff was to be the executive agency for the Commissariat. In addition to its traditional functions of operations, planning, organization, and mobilization, the General Staff included directorates (*upravleniia*) having staff supervision over military rail and highway networks and troop movements (*voennye soobshcheniia*), organizing rear services and supply, troop staffing, and military topography. There were also departments (*otdely*) supervising fortified areas and cadres, and a general department dealing with administrative matters. It should be noted that control over military intelligence, one of the traditional functions of a general staff, was not included in the responsibilities of the pre–World War II Soviet General Staff. The Main Intelligence Directorate was directly under the minister of defense, Marshal Timoshenko. The head of the directorate, now F. I. Golikov, often reported directly to Stalin, to Timoshenko's irritation, and Timoshenko was never certain that he was being furnished all the available intelligence.[3]

In the second half of 1940 the number of military personnel on the staff was doubled and the number of civilians tripled. The General Staff

---

*Characteristically, one of his last acts as commander of Kiev Military District was to conduct a tactical and operational tutorial for senior military leaders of the district from January 17 to 21, 1941. These sessions were also attended by Party and government leaders of the Ukraine.

was acknowledged to be the most important institution within the Commissariat of Defense, and its chief was accorded the right to participate in governmental decision-making concerning the armed forces.[4]*

One of the urgent tasks that Zhukov faced almost immediately was the expansion of the armored and mechanized forces of the Red Army. The General Staff completed its plan in February, but it was not until March that Stalin decided to proceed with the formation of the twenty mechanized corps that the staff requested. However, Zhukov admits that the staff overestimated the capabilities of the Soviet tank construction industry. To fully supply the requirement for tanks, 32 thousand tanks were required, of which 16.6 thousand were new types. It was impossible to build that many under any conditions and particularly in light of existing shortages of technical and command personnel. By the beginning of the war less than half of the planned corps were equipped.[5]

The story was the same with the plans to modernize and increase the numbers of artillery, engineer, signal, railroad, and highway troop units in the force. A decision to reorganize and rearm the Air Force taken in late 1940 envisioned the formation of 106 new air regiments; by May of 1941, only 19 regiments had been formed and almost fully equipped. The Soviet economy could not satisfy such demands in the period of time that remained before the German onslaught.

In responding to a critical remark by Admiral N. G. Kuznetsov in his memoirs that he could not find common ground with Zhukov nor could the chief of the Naval Staff, I. S. Isakov, Zhukov disclaimed any responsibility for the condition of the Soviet Navy on the eve of the war. He writes that he was not invited by Stalin to participate in discussions of naval matters.[6] From an organizational point of view, one could surmise that Stalin did not intend that the Red Army high command would interact with the Soviet Navy at the commissariat

---

*Zakharov, on the matter of the chief of staff's authority to participate in decisions concerning the armed forces, wrote "the chief . . . was allotted the right to join the government for deciding questions of the Commissariat of Defense." The three previous chiefs of the General Staff were: A. I. Egorov, purged in 1937; B. M. Shaposhnikov, relieved in 1940 after being right about the forces required to win the war with Finland; and K. A. Meretskov, relieved in January 1941. M. V. Zakharov, "Stranitsy istorii sovetskoi vooruzhennykh sil nakanune Velikoi Otechestvennoi Voiny 1939–1941" (Pages of the history of the Soviet armed forces on the eve of the Great Fatherland War 1939–1941) in *Voprosy Istorii*, no. 5 (May 1970): p. 39.

(ministerial) level. In 1938, when the Main Military Council was established, a separate Main Naval Council was created, headed by Andrei A. Zhdanov, which considered naval matters and made recommendations to the Defense Committee chaired by Molotov. The final authority, of course, for all matters, military as well as naval, rested with Stalin.

Answering other critics, who in their memoirs claimed that the General Staff had no mobilization and deployment plans, Zhukov asserts that the plans were under constant revision, were reported to the country's leadership, and upon approval were immediately transmitted to the military districts. He admits that there was a strategic error in the plans, caused by Stalin's judgment that the Ukraine was the most threatening axis of potential German advance. As it turned out, the weight of the German blow against the Western Military District was such that it was necessary to shift the 19th Army and part of the 16th to the western axis from the Ukraine where they had concentrated in accordance with the deployment plans.[7]

Construction of new fortified areas on the western borders and disposition of the equipment in the old strong points were subjects of sharp disagreement in the Main Military Council during the spring of 1941. Zhukov and Timoshenko favored leaving the artillery and machine guns in the old fortified areas. Kulik, Shaposhnikov, and A. A. Zhdanov wanted to move these weapons to the new areas. Stalin resolved the issue in favor of transferring them to the new fortifications. Later, after a second report to Stalin, some weapons were allowed to remain in some of the old areas.[8] At the time of the German attack the new fortifications had not been completed and the old had not been completely dismantled. The Red Army had the worst of both worlds, despite considerable expenditure of labor and construction materials.

The plan for the wartime mobilization of industry was completed by the General Staff in May. Zhukov took it to Voroshilov, chairman of the Defense Committee, and "literally forced" him to take it and consider it. Despite Zhukov's telephone calls, Voroshilov took no action. After having the plan he then asked Zhukov for input on how and with whom the plan should be reviewed. At this Zhukov called Stalin, who convened a Politburo meeting, which appointed a commission. The basic elements of the plan had not been approved when the war began, due to what Zhukov describes as "many arguments and squabbles" in the commission.[9]

NOTES

1. Evgenii Tsvetaev, "Poslednii podvig G. K. Zhukova" (The last exploit of G. K. Zhukov) in Smirnov, *Marshal Zhukov*, pp. 330, 331.
2. Zhukov, *Memoirs* 1: p. 298.
3. V. Danilov, "General'nyi shtab RKKA v predvoennye gody (1936–iiun 1941)" (The general staff RKKA in the prewar years 1936–June 1941) in *VIZh*, no. 3 (1980), p. 70. "G. K. Zhukov: Iz neopublikovannykh vospominanii," (G. K. Zhukov: from unpublished recollections), *Kommunist*, no. 14 (1988): p. 97.
4. A. A. Grechko, et al., eds. *Istoriia Vtoroi Mirovoi Voiny, 1939–1945* (History of the Second World War, 1939–1945) (hereinafter *IVMV*), vol. 3 (Moscow: Voenizdat, 1974), p. 417.
5. Zhukov, *Memoirs* 1: pp. 308, 309.
6. Ibid., pp. 321, 322.
7. Ibid., p. 332.
8. Ibid., pp. 333–336.
9. For a complete discussion of the fortification question see Robert E. Tarleton, "The Life and Fate of the Stalin Line, 1926–1941," an unpublished seminar paper submitted to Professor Donald W. Threadgold, University of Washington, June 1991. Simonov, "Zametki," *VIZh*, no. 9: p. 51.

VIII

STALIN AND THE CHIEF OF THE GENERAL STAFF

As Zhukov recalled his hectic service as chief of the General Staff in the months before the war, he did not conceal or attempt to rationalize the overwhelming authority of Stalin in all questions. It was Stalin who was convinced that the Germans, in the event of war, would attempt to seize the Ukraine as their first objective and "no one then even thought of doubting his judgments and appreciation of the situation."[1] Bagramian reflects the same attitude on a lower level; on hearing Zhukov report on a change in doctrine in January 1941, he remembered that "this statement surprised everyone greatly. There was no one except Stalin who could be brave enough at that time to express such a 'seditious' although very sensible thought."[2] In his memoirs, Zhukov claims that he was convinced that all of Stalin's thoughts and actions were permeated with the desire to avoid war and with the conviction that he would be successful in doing so.[3] In his conversations with Konstantin Simonov, Zhukov opined that Stalin thought he had Hitler wrapped around his finger and therefore trusted him to an extent that he did not trust anyone else. As an example of this trust, Zhukov cited an exchange of letters between the two dictators in early 1941. Stalin wrote to Hitler expressing concern over information he had received that German troops were concentrating in Poland. Hitler replied that the troops were there for rearming and reforming beyond the reach of English bomber and reconnaissance aircraft. Hitler assured Stalin that he intended to observe strictly the existing treaty which he guaranteed on his honor as chief of state. Zhukov thought that Stalin believed Hitler's assurances.[4] Aleksandr Solzhenitsyn noted sardonically that Stalin's distrust of people was so great that it amounted to his world view. He distrusted his mother, God, fellow members of the Party, including those who had been exiled with him, peasants, workers, the intelligentsia, soldiers and generals, his closest associates, his wives, lovers, and his children and—he turned out to be right each time! The only person in the world he did trust was—Adolf Hitler![5]

The number of indicators of the imminence of hostilities continued to grow. In addition to the tactical intelligence flowing from the border military districts, Stalin was also receiving intelligence from such sources as Richard Sorge in Tokyo, directly from Beriia. Golikov, the head of the Main Intelligence Directorate, was also providing Stalin with reports, some of which, like those from Sorge, were not seen by Zhukov.[6] Timoshenko and Zhukov at last managed to convince Stalin that some precautionary measures were necessary. Permission was received to call up 500,000 reserves and to move four armies to the western military districts, but Stalin refused to sanction the placing of the border military districts on alert. According to Zhukov, Stalin feared that Hitler would consider that a provocation to war.[7]

This attitude of Stalin's was so clear to his close collaborators that it is difficult to credit those who have written that Stalin would have given serious attention to proposals for a preemptive attack on the German troop concentrations along the western borders of the Soviet Union. Viktor Suvorov, for example, argues in his book *Ledokol* (Icebreaker) that Stalin was preparing to attack the Germans in 1941. According to Dmitrii A. Volkogonov and Vladimir Karpov, a document exists in the archives of the Soviet General Staff, dated 15 May 1941, which is a plan to destroy the main German forces by a preemptive attack. In one version the document was signed by Zhukov and the minister of defense, Timoshenko. That the document was signed was denied in 1991 by Colonel General A. Kleimenov, then a deputy chief of the Soviet General Staff. He also denied that it had been considered by personages at a high level. If it had been, that fact would have been recorded. However, he did not deny that the question was discussed in some form or other.

In an article intended as a riposte to Suvorov, Anatolii Ivanov-Skuratov provides the text of a note written by Zhukov to Stalin on 15 May 1941, which may have accompanied the "plan" now in the archives. (It is not otherwise identified.) Zhukov proposed:

Considering that Germany at the present time holds its army mo-
bilized, with deployed rear services, it has the capability to pre-
cede us in deployment and to deliver a surprise attack. In order
to prevent that, I consider it necessary that in no case should we
give the initiative of acting to the German command, we should
preempt the enemy in deployment and attack the German army
at that moment when it is in a stage of deployment and has not
succeeded in organizing the front and the coordination of the arms
and services.[8]

Ivanov-Skuratov argues that Zhukov as chief of the General Staff
knew the state of readiness of the Soviet Army. If he was only proposing the launching of a preventive strike on 15 May, then prior to
that time there was no such plan. Suvorov's theories therefore fall apart
because they were based on preparations said to be in train long before that date. Ivanov-Skuratov judges that the plan was not adopted
by Stalin otherwise his conduct in the early days of the war would have
been very different. One can add that if there was such a plan, Soviet
Army artillery would have been with its infantry and tank units and
not collected in summer training camps where it was on 22 June 1941.

Contingency planning is a normal function of general staffs; in fact,
it is surprising that such a plan was not developed until May 1941,
considering the conditions that existed in Eastern Europe in 1941. The
General Staff also had to consider the bombastic statements of Voroshilov,
who when he was Commissar of Defense, proposed that if the Soviet
Union went to war it would fight on the enemy's territory and win with
little loss of blood.

The historian Aleksandr Nekrich wonders whether the plan might
have been related to the unexpected flight of Rudolph Hess to England
on 10 May 1941 and Stalin's conviction that Hess was sent to England
to reach an agreement on an Anglo-German attack on the Soviet Union.
From Stalin's perspective that would have been the worst of all possible outcomes of his policies.

Nekrich has no doubt that Stalin intended to participate in the European
war at an appropriate time but that 1941 was not that time. The military buildup that was under way in the Soviet Union was to reach its
fruition in 1942 or 1943. It was also significant that Stalin did not have

any European allies in May of 1941. There was every reason for attempting to hold off the German attack by shipping them more grain, oil, and ferrous metals. This reaction of Stalin and his responses to the actual attack during the early days of the war seem to make it highly doubtful that the Soviet leader would ever have chosen to start a war with Germany, and certainly not in 1941.[9]

On the night of 21 June, Zhukov observed Stalin as he struggled with the reality that war was indeed imminent. A German deserter had crossed the border in the area of the Kiev Military District and had reported that the Germans planned to attack the next morning. Learning this, Timoshenko, Zhukov, and N. F. Vatutin, Zhukov's deputy, went to see Stalin, having agreed among themselves that they would obtain a decision to put the forces on combat alert "no matter what it cost."[10] Stalin was inclined to disbelieve the deserter's story, saying that the incident was a provocation. Timoshenko gave the military opinion that the deserter was telling the truth. By this time other members of the Politburo had entered Stalin's office and he asked them what should be done. There was no answer. Finally, Timoshenko recommended that an immediate directive be sent to the troops, ordering a full combat alert.[11] In the drafting of the order, Zhukov and Timoshenko managed only with difficulty to have stricken from the text a sentence Stalin tried to insert stating that in the case of a German invasion the Soviet commanders of forward units should seek to meet with German commanders and attempt to settle the conflict.[12]

Early the next morning, after the alert order had been dispatched, reports began arriving from the Black Sea Fleet and the border military districts of the onset of the German attack. When Stalin was informed of this he could not respond for some time. Finally he arranged a meeting of the Politburo with Timoshenko and Zhukov in attendance. After hearing from Molotov that the German government had declared war, Stalin "sank in his chair and was locked in deep thought. There was a long, powerful pause." But even after he knew that the war had started, he modified the initial combat directive to ensure that Soviet troops, with the exception of the Air Force, did not violate the German border.[13]

During the Khrushchev regime the General Staff was blamed along with Stalin for failing to bring the border military districts to combat readiness in time to meet the German attack. The Soviet forces were assessed as adequate to meet the Germans and to give them a "crushing rebuff."

> A large share of the responsibility for the Red Army's unpreparedness lies on the leaders of the People's Commissariat of Defense and the General Staff—Marshal of the Soviet Union Timoshenko and General of the Army Zhukov. They badly misread the military-strategic situation that had developed and were not able to reach correct conclusions on the necessity of urgent measures to bring the armed forces to combat readiness.[14]

Marshal Rokossovskii also took the General Staff to task for the Soviet defense plan, saying that the line of existing fortified areas should have been defended instead of attempting to construct new fortifications "under the gaze of the Germans." Rokossovskii considered it the "sacred duty" of the General Staff to prove the obvious futility of this to the government and to defend the staff's proposals.[15]

The retrospective views of historians writing under Khrushchev, who had a score to settle with Zhukov and the General Staff, and of Rokossovskii, who was highly critical of Zhukov's command style and personally offended by it, conveniently overlook the authority and fear of Stalin which pervaded all echelons of the Red Army and Navy during the dictator's lifetime. Although Khrushchev found the political courage after Stalin's demise to expose some of his crimes, while the dictator was alive Khrushchev was merely another sycophant. And Rokossovskii, after spending almost three years in Beriia's prisons, was understandably wary of the tyrant. These criticisms are probably best ascribed to Soviet politics of the time, which after 1957 were intent on tarnishing the image of the country's greatest war hero. Speaking in 1966, Zhukov, possibly in response to these and other similar comments about his performance on the eve of the war, recalled Stalin's conviction that the war could be avoided. He also cited, as an example, Stalin's reaction to some unauthorized changes in Red Army dispositions in the Kiev Military District which Timoshenko had attempted to make. Beriia immediately reported them to Stalin, claiming that the military were being provocative. The result was that Zhukov was ordered to call the military district commander immediately, cancel the orders and punish the guilty ones. After episodes like that, commanders did not take risks. Zhukov concluded: "Let's say that I, Zhukov, feeling the danger hanging over the country, gave the order: 'Deploy.' They would report to Stalin. On what basis? On the basis of danger. Well, Beriia, take him to your basement."[16]

Notes

1. Zhukov, *Memoirs* 1: p. 332.
2. Bagramian, "Zapiski," *VIZh*, no. 1 (1967): p. 56.
3. Zhukov, *Memoirs* 1: p. 352.
4. Simonov, *"Zametki,"* *VIZh,* no. 9: pp. 50, 51.
5. Aleksandr Solzhenitsyn, *V kruge pervom* (In the first circle) (New York: Harper Colophon, 1969), p. 96.
6. Simonov, *"Zametki,"* *VIZh,* no. 9: p. 53. Zhukov, *Memoirs* 1: pp. 341, 345.
7. Simonov, *"Zametki,"* in *VIZh,* no. 9: p. 51.
8. Anatolii Ivanov-Skuratov, *Napadenie lzhe-Suvorov na Rossiiu* (The attack of the false Suvorov on Russia) in *Na Boevom Postu,* 8/9, 1992, pp. 30–32.
9. Aleksandr Nekrich, *"K istorii germano-sovetskoi voiny"* (To the history of the German-Soviet war) in *Russkaia Mysl',* 21 June 1991, p. 9. Anatolii Ivanov-Skuratov, "Napadenie lzhe-Suvorov na Rossiiu" (The attack of the false Suvorov on Russia) in *Na Boevom Postu,* 8/9, 1992, pp. 30–32.
10. Zhukov, *Memoirs* 1: p. 369.
11. Ibid., pp. 369–371.
12. Anfilov, *"U Zhukova."*
13. Zhukov, *Memoirs* 2: p. 10.
14. P. N. Pospelov, chmn. ed. comm., *Istoriia Velikoi Otechestvennoi Voiny Sovetskogo Soiuza 1941–1945* (The history of the Great Fatherland War 1941–1945) (Moscow: Voenizdat, 1961–1965) 2: p. 10. (Hereinafter *IVOVSS.*)
15. "Soldatskii dolg—K. K. Rokossovskii" (A soldier's duty—K. K. Rokossovskii) in *VIZh,* no. 5 (1989): p. 61. This article published in 1989 some portions of Rokossovskii's memoirs that were expurgated from his memoirs published in 1968.
16. N. G. Pavlenko, "G. K. Zhukov: iz neopublikovanny vospominanii" (G. K. Zhukov: from unpublished reminiscences) in *Kommunist,* no. 14, September 1988, p. 99.

IX

THE INITIAL OPERATIONS, 1941

Stalin appeared to recover quickly from his initial depression and by 1300 hours that same day, June 22, 1941, ordered Zhukov to Kiev (at Khrushchev's request) as representative of the staff of the commander in chief (the S*tavka*). He also told Zhukov that he had sent Marshals Shaposhnikov and Kulik to the Western Front with separate instructions. When asked who was going to direct the General Staff, Stalin replied, " 'Leave Vatutin here,' and then . . . somewhat irritatedly added: 'Don't lose time, we'll get along here somehow.' "[1]* Stalin's irritation may have stemmed from the recollection that he had lost control of himself that morning. For Zhukov, it should have served as a warning that Stalin considered his services to be dispensable.

Zhukov was met by Khrushchev in Kiev and soon received further indication that Stalin was in control. Vatutin told him by telephone that

---

*Cf. Khrushchev's version reported in his "secret" speech, that Stalin did not direct military operations for a "long time" after June 22—quoted in Strobe Talbott, *Khrushchev Remembers* (Boston: Little, Brown, 1970), p. 591. Zhukov addressed this point specifically in a paragraph deleted from the first nine editions of his memoirs: "They say that in the first week of the war I. V. Stalin seemed to become so lost that he could not even speak on the radio and had V. M. Molotov give his speech. This judgment does not correspond with reality. Of course in the first hours I. V. Stalin was confused. But, he soon returned to normal and worked with great energy. True he did display extra nervousness which sometimes upset the rhythm of our work." Zhukov, *Memoirs* 2: p. 10. V. Sokolov, "Slovo o Marshale Zhukove" (A word about Marshal Zhukov) in *Marshal Zhukov,* p. 217.

Stalin had ordered counterattacks designed to halt the enemy and drive him back into Poland. He had also directed that, in addition to his own, Zhukov's name be signed to the order. Zhukov, after objecting that neither the location nor the strength of the enemy was known, nevertheless agreed to allow his signature to be put on the order.[2] The counterattacks failed.

Late on the evening of the 26th, Stalin ordered Zhukov to return to Moscow to help restore the catastrophic situation of the Western Front. There, a combination of the unanticipated weight of the initial German thrusts, the systematic disruption of Front communications caused by air strikes, German diversionary operations, incompetent staff work, and the faulty forward dispositions of the Soviet defenders had completely overwhelmed the limited command capabilities of the Front's commander, D. G. Pavlov. In the memoirs, excerpts are provided from three conversations Zhukov had with the Front command on the 27th, 28th, and 30th of June. The excerpts demonstrate that neither Pavlov nor his chief of staff had a clear view of the situation. They also demonstrate that the Stavka had very little confidence in the ability of the Western Front command to make even the most elementary decisions regarding the reorganization of their shattered command, how and where to establish new defensive positions, and what to do about stocks of ammunition and gasoline that were in danger of being overrun by the enemy. Minsk fell on the evening of 28 June. On 30 June, Stalin ordered Pavlov relieved and recalled to Moscow. A. I. Eremenko replaced him initially and in early July Marshal Timoshenko took command of the Front.

When Pavlov returned to Moscow he was almost unrecognizable, his physical appearance had changed so much. He expected to be seen by Stalin and was worried about the consequences of his failures. Stalin refused to see him and told Zhukov to send him back from whence he had come. Zhukov later learned that he had been arrested at one of the intervening railroad stations and along with other members of the staff of the Western Front was tried and shot.[3]

Soviet military historians were prone to attribute the initial failures of the Western Front to the fact that the forward units were taken by surprise. Coupled with this rationale was the statement that if Soviet units had been alerted in time they could have given the invaders a deserved rebuff. Zhukov, in his memoirs, made no such claim. Instead,

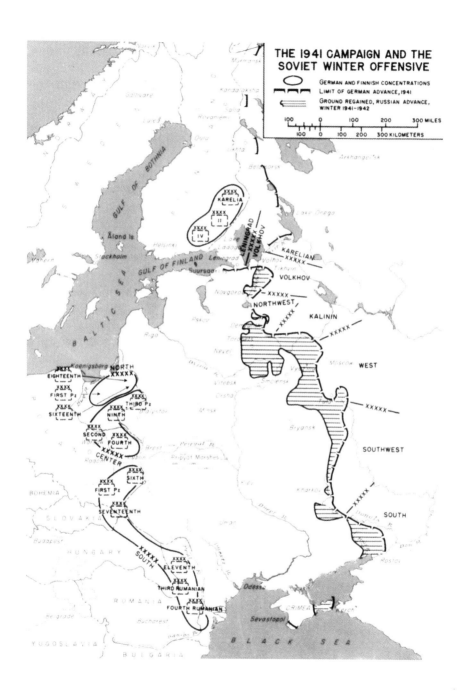

THE 1941 CAMPAIGN AND THE
SOVIET WINTER OFFENSIVE

in candid moments, he specifically questioned such assertions. It was his contention that in the postwar evaluation of the opposing armies as they were in the beginning of the war, Soviet military historians, perhaps because of the political regime they were laboring under and the requirements of postwar Soviet propaganda, did not give sufficient credit to the superiority of German equipment and the skill German tank units and their air support demonstrated as they cooperated on the battlefield. He also credited the mastery the German high command displayed in combining and directing the striking power of these forces on the decisive axes.

It was asserted frequently that the air units of the Odessa Military District were an exception to the chaos that enveloped the Baltic, Western, and Kiev Military Districts. That the Odessa Military District was singled out may have been due to the fact that Matvei V. Zakharov was chief of the General Staff during most of the 1960s, the period of "thaw" when some of the truth about the war was written in connection with the de-Stalinization campaign. In 1941 Zakharov was Chief of Staff of the Odessa Military District. It would have been expedient for historians to give his recollections great weight. Zhukov, however, labelled as *"vran'e"* (lies) the assertion that the air forces of the Odessa Military District were an exception to the rule.

Zhukov was similarly blunt in his characterization of the withdrawal of the units of the Western Front from the frontier, characterizing it as a rout (*begstvo*) rather than a retreat (*otkhod*). He dismissed with the word *drama* (drama) a description of the failed counterattack of the Western Front toward Senno and Lepel' which caused some damage to the invaders. A claim that despite the initial defeats the moral spirit of the Soviet soldier remained high and his belief in a final victory unshaken, Zhukov found to be exaggerated. He did, however, accept an account of the heroic defense of Peremyshl' by the 99th Rifle Division of the Southwestern Front, and it is so described in his memoirs. A. A. Vlasov, the division's commander in 1940, by that time was commanding the 4th Mechanized Corps.*

---

*In 1962, V. Anfilov published an essay *Nachalo Velikoi Otechestvennoi Voiny* (The beginning of the Great Fatherland War) (Moscow: Voenizdat, 1962). Zhukov apparently used this essay while he was working on his memoirs. In any event he under-

D. A. Volkogonov, in his biography of Stalin, has described the collapse of Stalin's morale in the next four or five days while he awaited news from the front that the invaders had been halted. On hearing that Minsk had fallen he suffered the "paralyzing shock" of realizing fully that the invasion carried a deadly threat not only to the Soviet state but also to the "wise and invincible leader" himself. He had exhausted all of his tested methods of leadership: he had sent his personal representatives, including a phalanx of four marshals (Kulik, Shaposhnikov, Timoshenko and Voroshilov), to the Western Front; he had issued orders to drive the invaders into German-occupied Poland; he had personally visited the Commissariat of Defense to threaten the military leadership; and he had instigated a legal process against the command of the Western Front that would end with their execution. But the *Wehrmacht* continued to advance. On 30 June, the other members of the Politburo, alarmed at the deteriorating situation at the front and the uncharacteristic lack of action by the "boss" (*khoziain*), called on him in his dacha. They brought with them a draft of a Party-state resolution forming the State Defense Committee (*Gosudarstvennyi komitet oborony:* GKO) to be chaired by Stalin. The frightened dictator, who may have thought the group was coming to arrest him, accepted the proposal.[4]

Following the creation of the State Defense Committee, Stalin's morale improved to the extent that he could give his "brothers and sisters" broadcast on 3 July. In the next two months all state, political, and military authority was concentrated in Stalin's hands. On the 19th of July he became the commissar of defense. On the 8th of August the Stavka became the *Stavka Verkhovnogo Glavnokomandovaniia* (The Headquarters of the Supreme High Command) with Stalin as the supreme high commander. This was the title he was to hold throughout the rest of the war. In conversation among themselves, Soviet marshals

---

lined many passages and wrote in it his comments on some of the author's statements. Sometime after Zhukov's death, his daughter Maria gave the marked copy to Anfilov, who described Zhukov's reactions to some portions of the essay in "*Rukoi Marshala Zhukova*" (By the hand of Marshal Zhukov) in *Krasnaia Zvezda* (*KZ*), 24 January 1992. Anfilov also deserves some notice for the fact that his 200-page book on the beginning of the war does not mention Georgii Konstantinovich Zhukov once! The mention of the heroic defense of Peremyshl' appears in Zhukov's *Memoirs* 2: p. 20.

and generals would often refer to him simply as *"verkhovnyi,"* as western military men would refer to their commander in chief as "the CINC."

At the end of July, after Zhukov had returned to Moscow from Kiev, he described a session of the Politburo as it discussed whether or not to replace Marshal Timoshenko, who had been given command of the Western Front after the arrest of D. G. Pavlov. Timoshenko, who was in Moscow, and Zhukov were summoned to Stalin's dacha. There they found almost all of the members of the Politburo. Without prior warning, Stalin announced that the Politburo had considered Timoshenko's performance as Front commander and had decided to replace him with Zhukov. He then asked Timoshenko and Zhukov for their opinions. Timoshenko remained silent but Zhukov spoke up, saying that Timoshenko had been in command less than four weeks and that frequent changes in Front command would have a negative effect on operations. Only M. I. Kalinin spoke in support of Zhukov's position. Stalin turned to the other members of the Politburo and said:

"Maybe we should agree with Zhukov?" "You are right Comrade Stalin," the voices resounded. "Timoshenko may still restore the situation."[5]

Timoshenko was seriously upset by this event. As they were returning to the Ministry of Defense, Timoshenko told Zhukov that he should not have intervened to save his position, saying that he was terribly tired of Stalin's constant carping and criticism (*dergan'e*).[6]* Timoshenko, who had been minister of defense and was senior in rank to Zhukov, had been saved by the latter's plea. But he held no resentment toward him. In 1969, Timoshenko recalled Zhukov and the way he dealt with Stalin:

---

*Timoshenko's daughter was married to Stalin's son, Vasilii. This relationship may have protected him from a harsher punishment than relief from command following the failure of the Khar'kov operation in 1942. See Chapter 12. S. P. Ivanov, *Shtab armeiskii, shtab frontovoi* (Army staff, Front staff) (Moscow: Voenizdat, 1990), p. 250. Zhukov considered Timoshenko to be persistent, strong-willed, and prepared in a tactical and operational sense. He felt that it was unfair to lump him with Voroshilov and Budennyi who were military failures in World War II after emerging from the Civil War as heroes. Anfilov, "U Zhukova."

You know Zhukov was the only person who feared no one. He was not afraid of Stalin. He protected me more than once from Stalin. Especially in the early period of the war. He was a brave man.[7]

In June and in mid-July, Stalin had demonstrated his readiness to have Zhukov serve outside of Moscow. In late July, Zhukov provided him with another opportunity, which Stalin did not hesitate to seize. The occasion was a classic conflict between military and political considerations, triggered by a military analysis and an estimate of the future plans of the German forces. Zhukov, after conferring with other General Staff officers, came to the conclusion that the enemy would in the near future attempt to crush the Central Front in order to cut off and isolate the Southwest Front.* They also concluded that the Wehrmacht's Army Group Center would not resume the offensive toward Moscow until the Central Front had been eliminated as a threat to the German right flank. Having thoroughly reviewed these conclusions, Zhukov sought an appointment with Stalin on July 29.

When Zhukov arrived he was told to await the arrival of Malenkov and Lev Z. Mekhlis, then Chief of the Main Directorate of Political Propaganda and a vindictive adherent of Stalin. (S. P. Ivanov referred to Mekhlis as "that gloomy demon.") When Mekhlis and Malenkov arrived (in his conversations with Konstantin Simonov in 1965–66, Zhukov added Beriia to those in attendance), Zhukov presented the basis for his conclusions to Stalin and recommended that the Central Front be reinforced and that Vatutin be given command of it. Some of the re-inforcement was to be at the expense of the troops defending the western approaches to Moscow and part would come from the Southwest Front. He also recommended withdrawing the Southwest Front behind the Dnieper River entirely—which meant giving up Kiev without a battle—and counterattacking and eliminating the German bridgehead at El'nia. Stalin reacted violently to the idea of giving up Kiev and used the word

---

*By the end of July 1941 seven Front commands were deployed against the invading German forces. From north to south they were: Northern; Northwestern; Western; Reserve; Central; Southwestern; and Southern.

"*chepukha*"—nonsense, rot, rubbish—in referring to Zhukov's proposal. The dictator also observed that Soviet troops didn't know how to attack. During this exchange Mekhlis contributed some questions hostile to Zhukov and his plan. Zhukov lost his temper and requested that he be relieved as chief of the General Staff and given a field command.

After a brief private conference, presumably with Malenkov and Mekhlis (and Beriia), Stalin told Zhukov that Shaposhnikov would again become the chief of staff, although his health was still not good.* Zhukov would be given command of the Reserve Front, but would remain a member of the Stavka. From 29 July 1941 until the successful conclusion of the war in Europe, Zhukov remained a member of the Stavka; he was appointed deputy supreme commander in 1942 and participated in the planning of most of the important operations on the Soviet-German front, but never again did he serve on the General Staff. From this time on, Zhukov was either the commander of a Front or was in the field as a representative of the Stavka, coordinating major operations.[8]

Zhukov was given command of the Reserve Front in part because his plan included the reduction of the German salient around El'nia, 82 kilometers southeast of Smolensk. That he wanted to take the offensive surprised Stalin, who commented, ironically, that Soviet troops up to that time had not managed one successful offensive.[9]

This operation was executed by the 24th Army and was successful in that the salient was reduced, but Zhukov's attempt to envelop the enemy's forces in the salient failed because, in Zhukov's (retrospective) opinion, there was a shortage of Soviet tanks. Nevertheless, even this partial success was important as a morale factor at this stage of the war.

Immediately after the battle, Zhukov visited El'nia and its modest museum. There he found original sheet music written by the composer

---

*Shaposhnikov had been relieved as chief of the General Staff, ostensibly for health reasons, in August 1940. He died of tuberculosis in 1945. He is usually treated with respect when he is mentioned in the memoir literature. S. P. Ivanov, commenting on his effectiveness as chief of the General Staff, says that he was severely traumatized by the purges and the fact that one of his closest relatives (his brother?) was in the "tenacious hands of Beriia." Ivanov, *Shtab armeiskii*, p. 250.

Mikhail Ivanovich Glinka, which had apparently been desecrated by the occupying troops. Glinka, who was born and raised nearby, was Zhukov's favorite Russian composer. He returned the muddied paper to the elderly caretaker, saying angrily that history would show that to our grandchildren.[10]

On the 8th of September Zhukov was back in Moscow, reporting to Stalin. The dictator admitted that Zhukov had been right on the 29th of July in regard to the Southwest Front and asked for his current thoughts on the situation. Zhukov again recommended that Soviet forces withdraw to the east of Kiev. Stalin then asked him for his recommendation on whom to send to command the Southwest Axis* (replacing Budennyi). Zhukov recommended that Timoshenko be given the post and, when asked, recommended that Ivan S. Konev replace Timoshenko as commander of the Western Front. Stalin accepted both of these recommendations but would not sanction a withdrawal from Kiev. Stalin then turned to the situation around Leningrad, describing the situation there as "catastrophic." He feared that the Germans would soon link up with the Finns, surround the city, and then be in position to envelop Moscow from the north. Stalin asked Zhukov to relieve Voroshilov and take command of the Leningrad Front, which had been activated on 23 August.[11]**

---

*On 10 July 1941, Stalin established three *napravleniia* (literally "directions," here translated as "axes") as intermediate headquarters commanding two or more Fronts. Stalin's professional military advisors opposed their formation. The axes were not successful and they were not used after mid-1942.

**By the 22nd of September, two weeks later, Kiev was surrounded, the Southwest Front had retreated 200 kilometers to the east and the Front commander had been killed. The Germans claimed to have taken 665,000 prisoners in the Kiev encirclement. Postwar, pre-glasnost' Soviet historians, citing the strength of the Front at the beginning of the operation, the losses suffered during the operation, and the number of troops who escaped through the encirclement, claim that the number of prisoners taken could not have been more than a third of that number. *IVOVSS*, vol. 2, pp. 110, 111.

NOTES

1. Zhukov, *Memoirs* 2: p. 13.
2. Zhukov, *Memoirs* 2: p. 14. Karpov, *"Soratniki"* in *Znamia*, no. 11, (1989): p. 134.
3. Zhukov, *Memoirs* 2: pp. 33–40. Anfilov, *"U Zhukova."*
4. D. A. Volkogonov, *Triumf i tragediia: politicheskii portret I. V. Stalina* (Triumph and tragedy: A political portrait of J. V. Stalin), Book 2, part 1 (Moscow: Novosti, 1989), pp. 163–175.
5. Zhukov, *Memoirs* 2: pp. 64–65.
6. Ibid.
7. S. Bystrov, *"V oktiabre 1957-ogo"* (In October 1957) in *KZ,* 21 May 1989, p. 4.
8. Zhukov, *Memoirs* 2: pp. 119–122. Simonov, "Zametki" in *VIZh,* no. 9: pp. 55, 56.
9. Simonov, "Zametki" in *VIZh* no. 9: p. 56.
10. Evgenii Vorob'ev, *"Kazhdaia piad' zemli"* (Each inch of land) in Smirnov, *Marshal Zhukov*, p. 160.
11. Simonov, "Zametki" in *VIZh,* no. 9: p. 56. Pospelov, *IVOVSS* 2: p. 89.

X

SAVIOR OF LENINGRAD AND MOSCOW, 1941–1942

Zhukov arrived at the headquarters of the Leningrad Front on the 10th of September where a meeting of the Front military council was in progress. The council had not been forewarned that he was coming. They were discussing the destruction of various installations within the city to prevent them from falling into the hands of the enemy. Specifically, the issue being discussed was the sequence in which the warships of the Baltic Fleet were to be scuttled. Zhukov immediately ordered that the ships be cleared of demolitions and moved to anchorages closer to the city from which they could support the city's defenders with their heavy guns and their 40 units of fire (*boekomplekty*). Zhukov told Konstantin Simonov in 1950 that he had rebuked those planning the destruction of the ships:

> How can you prepare those ships for destruction? Yes, it is possible that they will be destroyed. But, if they are, they must only be destroyed in battle, firing.[1]

Zhukov added that when the Germans did attack along the maritime sectors of the front, the naval gunfire was so effective that the enemy simply broke and ran.[2]

Other steps were also taken, including using a portion of the city's antiaircraft guns to reinforce the positions most vulnerable to tank attack. Construction was begun on deeply echeloned engineer defenses to include mines and electrified wire on all vulnerable approaches. Separate rifle brigades were formed from sailors of the Baltic Fleet, the local military schools, and the NKVD (the internal security troops). Soviet marines were used in small amphibious operations behind the German front lines. These measures frustrated all German attempts to take the city before the onset of the northern autumn. By the end of September, the Leningrad garrison was executing local counterattacks. Zhukov believed that these operations convinced the Germans to content themselves with siege operations, using aerial and artillery bombardment.

The Germans, who had been confident of capturing the city in early September, were also about to launch Operation *Taifun*—the assault on Moscow—in accordance with Hitler's directive of 6 September. That directive required Army Group North, which had had the mission of taking Leningrad, to return armored units to Army Group Center for *Taifun*, scheduled to begin in early October. On 21 September, Hitler ordered Army Group North to invest Leningrad and to conduct siege operations around it.

When his intelligence reported that the Germans were withdrawing some of their armored units from Army Group North, Zhukov was inclined to doubt it. When the reports were confirmed several days later he became convinced that the remaining German troops could not take the city,[3] and so assured Stalin when they met in Moscow a few days later. Had the Germans succeeded in occupying the "cradle of the Revolution," in addition to the boost in their morale and worldwide propaganda efforts, they would have been in a position to sweep down on Moscow from the north.

On the 5th of October, Stalin called Zhukov on the *bodo* (a secure telegraph system that linked the Stavka and the General Staff with the Front and field army commanders) and asked if he could return to Moscow immediately to discuss the situation on the left flank of the Reserve Front. Although Zhukov said he could return the next day, he actually did not leave until the 7th of October because of a problem with the 54th Army, then commanded by Marshal G. I. Kulik. After placing General Fediuninskii in command of the Front and the Front chief of staff, General Khozin, in command of the 54th Army, Zhukov left for Moscow. He arrived to find Stalin suffering from the grippe and irritated by the lack of information about the situation on the western front. Stalin was finishing a conversation with Beriia when Zhukov entered and overheard him tell Beriia to try to make approaches through his agents—in the case of a crisis—and to take soundings of

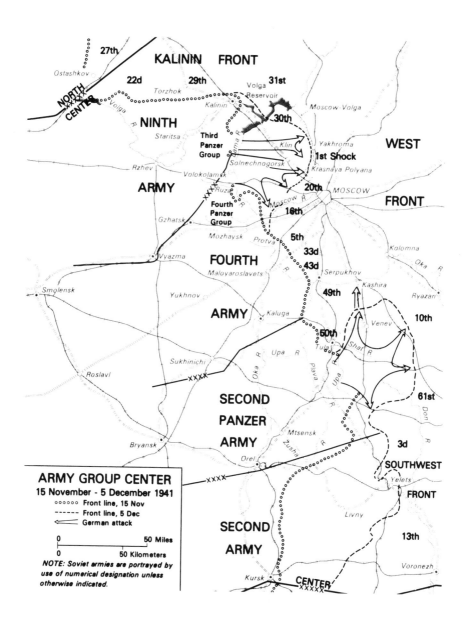

27th

KALININ FRONT

Ostashkov

22d   29th   31st
                    Volga
            Torzhok   Reservoir   Moscow-Volga

NORTH
CENTER   Volga   R   Kalinin
                                    30th

NINTH
        Staritsa   Third   Klin   Yakhroma   WEST
                    Panzer
                    Group   1st Shock
Rzhev   Solnechnogorsk   Krasnaya Polyana
            Volokolamsk
ARMY   Ruza   20th   MOSCOW   FRONT
                    Fourth   Moscow R
            Gzhatsk   Panzer   16th
                    Group
                    Mozhaysk   Protva   5th
        Vyazma   Kolomna
                    Malayaroslavets   33d   Oka   R
                FOURTH   43d   Serpukhov
Smolensk   Yukhnov   Ryazan
                                49th   Kashira
                ARMY   Kaluga   Venev   10th
                        50th   Tula   Shat   R
        Sukhinichi   Upa   R
    Roslavl   XXXX   Oka   R   Plava   R   Upa
                                            61st
                SECOND   Don   R
                PANZER   Mtsensk
    Bryansk   ARMY   Orel   Zusha   R   3d
                                        SOUTHWEST
        XXXX   Yelets   FRONT

ARMY GROUP CENTER
15 November - 5 December 1941   Livny
ooooooo Front line, 15 Nov   SECOND   13th
------- Front line, 5 Dec
⇐ German attack   ARMY   Voronezh

0   50 Miles
0   50 Kilometers   Kursk   CENTER
NOTE: Soviet armies are portrayed by   XXXXX
use of numerical designation unless
otherwise indicated.

the possibilities and conditions for concluding peace. Zhukov did not realize until later that Stalin was talking about making peace with the Germans! The man of steel was apparently losing his nerve again. After describing the difficult situation as he knew it, Stalin ordered Zhukov to go immediately to the headquarters of the Western Front, find out exactly what the situation was, and call him from there at any time of the day or night.[4]*

Zhukov stopped at the General Staff, picking up a map showing the current situation on the Western Axis and a cup of strong tea from its chief, Marshal Shaposhnikov, then proceeded by car to the headquarters of the Western Front. He and his security group used two vehicles for the trip: a Buick and an all-terrain vehicle. Arriving there after dark, he found the Front commander, General I. S. Konev, and his staff, huddled by candlelight over a situation map. On 30 September the German Army Group Center had launched an offensive aimed at Moscow by a series of attacks on A. I. Eremenko's Briansk Front. On the 2nd of October they had delivered what Zhukov called "mighty" blows on the Western (Konev) and Reserve (Budennyi) Fronts. The Briansk Front was in a very serious situation, with two of its armies in danger of being surrounded. The Western Front had attempted a counterattack which failed, and at the end of 6 October a significant number of its troops were surrounded west of Viaz'ma. Zhukov's impression was that the catastrophe at Viaz'ma could have been avoided. As early as the 27th of September the Stavka had warned of the possibility of an offensive in the near future by strong forces on the Moscow axis. The German offensive was not a surprise.

---

*Marshal G. I. Kulik was the same Kulik who had attempted to interfere with Zhukov's arrangements at Halhin Gol and is associated with various unfortunate decisions in the preparation of prewar Soviet defenses. As commander of the 54th Army which was located at Mga outside of the German forces investing Leningrad, he was given the mission of breaking through the blockade ring and relieving the besieged city. He proved to be incapable of organizing the attack. According to his biography in *SVE* he was reduced to the rank of *general maior* (one star) after this episode. He was retired in that rank in October 1946. He was tried with Col. Gen. V. N. Gordov and was executed in 1950. His rank of Marshal of the Soviet Union was restored posthumously in 1957. (See page 209.)

At 0230 Zhukov reported the situation to Stalin. In response to the dictator's questions he had to admit that four armies were in a German pocket west and northwest of Viaz'ma. He then set off to find Budennyi and the headquarters of the Reserve Front, reported to be somewhere in the vicinity of Maloiaroslavets. When Zhukov located the headquarters, at the former estate of the sugar baron Savva Morozov, near the Oblenskoe way station, he found that Budennyi was missing and Lev Mekhlis (representative of the Stavka) had taken charge. He was trying to collect and reorganize the retreating units of the Front.

Zhukov obtained little new information from Mekhlis. The officer in charge of Zhukov's security observed that relations between Mekhlis and Zhukov were strained. When Zhukov arrived at the Reserve Front Headquarters, Mekhlis asked him what he was doing there. Zhukov showed him a document signed by Shaposhnikov authorizing him to investigate the situation on the Reserve and Western Fronts. After reading it, Mekhlis returned it to Zhukov and said, "You should have said so." It was the only time in the entire war that Zhukov had to show a document.[5]

Zhukov left the Reserve Front Headquarters and headed toward Iukhnov, still searching for Budennyi. The surrounding countryside was familiar to him; his birthplace, Strelkovka, was within ten kilometers of Obninsk. His mother, sister, and his sister's four children were there and he was worried about how they would be treated by the invaders if it was discovered that they were related to Zhukov. He thought about going to them immediately, but decided he did not have time now when the entire western front was collapsing. He resolved to take them to Moscow at the first opportunity. (As it turned out, the region was occupied by the Germans within two weeks, but by that time he had moved his family to Moscow. When the Germans retreated in 1942, the village of Strelkovka was destroyed and his mother's house was burned to the ground.)[6]

Zhukov finally found Budennyi studying a map in a local government office in Maloiaroslavets. He had had no communication with Konev and the Western Front for 48 hours, nor did he know where his own headquarters was now located. Budennyi could only confirm what Zhukov already knew, that two of his armies were cut off. Zhukov directed Budennyi to return to his headquarters (which he located for him) and to report the situation to the Stavka; meanwhile Zhukov would continue to reconnoiter the situation in the direction of Iukhnov. Finding that Iukhnov was already in the hands of the enemy and that there was fighting in progress around Kaluga, Zhukov moved toward that city. He was found by a liaison officer who had a telegram from the chief of the General Staff conveying Stalin's order to return to the head-quarters of the Western Front.[7]

Stalin called soon after Zhukov's arrival there and told him that he was to be the new commander of the Western Front. The retreating units of the Reserve Front were also to be incorporated into his command. Konev was to be his deputy. At least that was the version published in Zhukov's memoirs.[8]

In one of his interviews with Konstantin Simonov, Zhukov related that in that same telephonic conversation, Stalin told him Konev was to be tried by a military court martial after a government commission, headed by Molotov, completed its investigation. Zhukov protested that another trial would only have a negative effect on the army. He re-called that the trial and execution of D. G. Pavlov had not helped the situation at the beginning of the war. Pavlov did not have the capability to command anything larger than a division and everyone knew it; therefore no one should have been surprised that he could not handle a Front. Konev, however, was more capable than Pavlov. Zhukov proposed Konev remain as his deputy. Stalin asked, suspiciously, if Konev was an old buddy of Zhukov's; receiving a negative reply, Stalin agreed. Zhukov sent Konev to command the far right wing of the Front.*

---

*On 19 October 1941, Konev's command became the Kalinin Front. As to Pavlov, Vladimir Karpov argues convincingly that he has not received fair treatment at Zhukov's hands. After Pavlov and the other officers of the staff of the Western Front were executed, Stalin, in order to rationalize this act, falsified and juggled facts in order to compromise his victims in the eyes of history. Karpov points out that the performance of the other Front commanders was equally bad in the first week of the war, citing specifically that of F. I. Kuznetsov, commander of the Northwest Front, from whom the General Staff did not receive a clear report on the situation during the first eighteen days of the war. During those eighteen days the Germans seized Lithuania, Latvia, and a portion of the Russian Republic and were well on their way to Leningrad. In 1965, Zhukov said that Kuznetsov, Pavlov, and Kirponos, the commander of the Southwest Front, were all poorly prepared for their posts and were lost in the difficult situation that developed at the start of the war. He said that Pavlov and Kuznetsov were especially unsuccessful. Karpov, "Soratniki" in *Znamia*, no. 11: pp. 161, 165; Anfilov, "U Zhukova."

In the interview with Simonov, Zhukov recalled an unpleasant encounter with Molotov two days later. Molotov called him and with a raised voice threatened to have him shot if he did not halt a localized retreat before a German attack that seemed to be threatening Moscow. Zhukov had not heard of the retreat, having only been in command two days and not being fully aware of the situation on the entire front. Molotov again raised his voice, asking why Zhukov had not been able to assess the situation in two full days. To which Zhukov replied that if Molotov could sort out matters faster then *he* should come and take command of the Front. Molotov hung up.[9] This episode is an illustration of what was known as the "Stalin style" of work. Soviet commanders were under continuous pressure to perform, if not from the dictator himself, then from his close associates. Using information furnished either through NKVD channels or those of the Main Political Administration, Stalin could and did query the field commanders directly on real or reported failures. It was not surprising that Zhukov's reaction to the failures of his subordinates was often almost as harsh.

Privately Zhukov was also blunt about the failures of his colleagues. Soon after taking command, Zhukov, perhaps exaggerating because he was asking for help, wrote to A. A. Zhdanov, member of the Military Council of the Leningrad Front, and told him that Konev and Budennyi had lost all the arms and equipment of their two Fronts and that he had received from them "only their reminiscences." From Budennyi, he had received the Reserve Front staff and 90 men; from Konev, the staff of the Western Front and two reserve regiments. He asked Zhdanov to send him some 50mm and 82mm mortars.[10]

Under enemy pressure from the front and political pressure from the rear, Zhukov organized the defense of Moscow. The Front headquarters was moved to Alabino, an army garrison 50 kilometers southwest of Moscow. Later, it was moved to Perkhushkovo, on the Smolensk highway, 30 kilometers from the Kremlin. A defensive line was begun, stretching in a broad arc from Volokolamsk to Kaluga through Mozhaisk and Maloiaroslavets. Shattered armies were re-formed. In the rear of the first-echelon defenders, engineers began the construction of antitank defenses on all likely tank approaches to Moscow. Those troops surrounded in the Viaz'ma and Briansk pockets continued to attempt to fight their way out of the encirclement, and when they succeeded they were collected and debriefed. Some were arrested, assigned to penal units, then reinserted into the line as riflemen. None were decorated, although Zhukov credits their continued resistance while cut off with contributing valuable time for the organization of the defenses.*

By the 13th of October, the Germans had resumed the offensive on all the approaches to Moscow. The State Defense Committee ordered the evacuation from Moscow to Kuibyshev of portions of the central government apparatus, the diplomatic corps, and the General Staff. Lenin's body was taken from its mausoleum and accompanied the fleeing bureaucrats.

Rumors of these moves reached Zhukov at the front, and he sent the head of his security detachment to find out what was really happening in the capital. N. Kh. Bedov, accompanied by another member of the detachment, borrowed Zhukov's sedan (because it still had Moscow city plates which would give it access to the Kremlin) and reconnoitered the city. Bedov could tell that Stalin was working in his Kremlin office; he also found out that a train was being loaded to evacuate portions of the General Staff, including its documents. He reported all that he had seen to Zhukov.[11]

David Ortenberg, the editor of *Krasnaia Zvezda* (the armed forces newspaper) during the war, had met Zhukov at Halhin Gol and visited him often at Perkhushkovo during the defense of Moscow. On 19 October, he received a copy of the order declaring martial law in the city of Moscow. One of its provisions included a ban on all night traffic without special permission. Violators were to be tried by a military court. Provocateurs, spies, and other enemy agents who incited violations of the order were to be shot on the spot. Alarmed by the tone of the order, Ortenberg sent one of his correspondents to interview the man who would be its chief executor—the commander of the Mos-

---

*Officers who escaped from encirclements, either singly or with troops, were interrogated and often listed as having "adapted themselves to the occupation regime." They were then given rifles and transferred to penal battalions where they had to serve for three months to become "clean." Because the penal battalions always were given dangerous missions, in one battalion, at least, they almost all perished. For more detail on these units see Chapter 16 (p. 147). Ivashov and Rubtsov, *"Vyzhit' shtrafniky bylo bol'shim schast'em"* (To survive in a penal unit was great [good] luck), in *KZ*, 19 March 1992.

cow Defense Zone, Lt. Gen. Pavel A. Artem'ev, an NKVD general. The correspondent returned with even more alarming information. The general called on the people of Moscow to be prepared for the streets to become the sites of hot combat, hand-to-hand encounters with the enemy. Each house should become a strong point, and German tanks should be met with Molotov cocktails and grenades thrown from doors and windows. Before publishing this alarming interview Ortenberg decided to discuss it with Zhukov.

When Zhukov read the interview he commented that it was better to be prepared for what would not happen than not to be prepared at all. Then Zhukov jokingly added that Artem'ev should prepare the Molotov cocktails and grenades for the front, where they were needed. Hearing this, Ortenberg deduced that Zhukov did not believe the situation was as critical as the Artem'ev interview indicated. Ortenberg rewrote the last paragraph in a more calming tone, closing with the thought that Moscow would be defended and that the battle was the beginning of the end of Hitler's campaigns.

Nevertheless, many of the residents of Moscow fled in panic toward the east. When Ortenberg discussed this with Zhukov, he was surprised to find that the Front commander was sympathetic toward those who were fleeing the capital. Here at the front we are certain, Zhukov stated, but are they, there, certain that we can defend the city? By "they, there" he meant Stalin.* Ortenberg provided two indicators suggesting that Stalin was not confident that Zhukov and the Western Front would hold

---

*Volkogonov also reports that on 7 October, according to Marshal K. S. Moskalenko, who was instrumental in the arrest and trial of Lavrentii Beriia in 1953, Stalin, Molotov, and Beriia sent to the Bulgarian ambassador in Moscow, Stamenev, a request for Bulgarian good offices in arranging a peace with Germany under which the Germans would receive the Baltic states, Moldavia, and parts of the territory of other republics. This would have been a second Brest-Litovsk, reprising the treaty the new Soviet state made with the Germans in 1918. The Bulgarian ambassador told the Soviet leaders that Hitler would never conquer the Russians and that Stalin should not be concerned. Volkogonov, *Triumf i tragediia,* Bk. 2, Part 1, pp. 172, 173. The details of Stalin's unannounced visit to the Ministry of Defense and the General Staff (see page 57) were provided, after Stalin's death, by Molotov in conversations with the authors Ivan Stadniuk and Vladimir Karpov.

the city. One was what seemed to be an unexplainable delay in an-
nouncing the creation of "guards" units in recognition of outstanding
combat performance. They had been created after the victory at El'nia,
but the fact had not been publicized. The dictator did not want to praise
the performance of army units in the context of the fall of the city.

The other was the unprecedented publication of Zhukov's picture
in *Krasnaia Zvezda* of 21 October 1941. It was the first time a Front
commander's picture had been published and it was done on Stalin's
order. Initially Ortenberg thought the picture was intended to instill
confidence in the population and the troops—to show them that an
experienced and successful commander was directing Moscow's defense. Also, he thought that Stalin might be trying to smooth over any
bitterness that might remain over Zhukov's relief as chief of the General
Staff. When Ortenberg discussed these rationales with Zhukov, however, Zhukov told him he was naive. Stalin did not believe that the
city would be held and if it wasn't, the photo would ensure that the
blame could be cast on Zhukov.[12]

This pessimistic perception of the military situation and the regime's
competence to deal with it had great impact on Moscow and its population. It may be best illustrated in such works of historical fiction as
Konstantin Simonov's *The Living and the Dead*. A leading character,
the military correspondent/political officer Sintsov, has the misfortune
of losing his documents (including his Party card) while escaping from
an encirclement.[13]* An officer acquaintance shuns him when he learns
that he is about to enter Moscow, a city under martial law, without
documents. Sintsov manages to do so, expecting to be arrested, but is
amazed when he walks to the center of the city without being stopped
and checked. The day he enters the city is 16 October, when fear that
the city is going to fall seems all-pervasive. In this state of panic, internal
security was forgotten. Later, whenever someone mentioned that day

---

*S. P. Ivanov reports that one commander who presented a list of those who had performed
well in fighting their way out of an encirclement was told, "We don't reward those
who were surrounded." Ivanov, *Shtab armeiskii,* p. 129. According to D. A. Volkogonov,
special camps were established behind the front lines by the NKVD to verify the stories
of those who had been encircled and had escaped. Volkogonov, *Triumf i tragediia,*
book 2, part 1, pp. 246, 247.

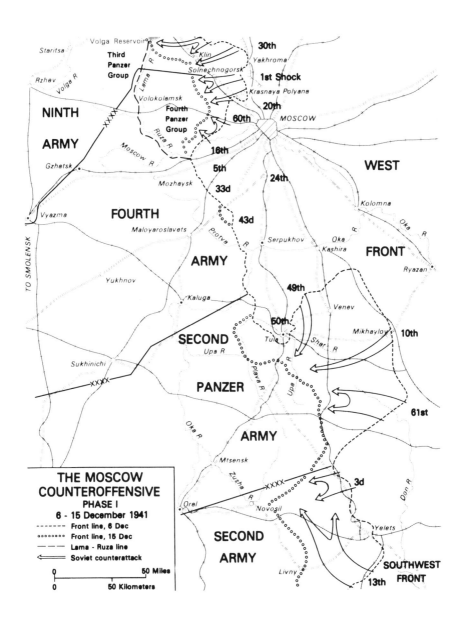

Staritsa

Volga Reservoir

Rzhev

Volga R

Third
Panzer
Group

Lama R

Klin

Solnechnogorsk

Yakhroma

30th

1st Shock

Krasnaya Polyana

NINTH

Volokolamsk

Fourth
Panzer
Group

Ruza R

Moscow R

60th

20th

MOSCOW

ARMY

Gzhatsk

16th

5th

24th

WEST

Vyazma

FOURTH

Mozhaysk

Maloyaroslavets

Protva R

33d

43d

Serpukhov

Oka R

Oka R

Kolomna

Ryazan

TO SMOLENSK

Yukhnov

ARMY

Kaluga

49th

50th

Kashira

Venev

FRONT

Mikhaylov

10th

SECOND

Upa R

Tula

Shat R

Sukhinichi

PANZER

Plava R

Upa R

61st

Oka R

ARMY

Mtsensk

Zusha R

Don R

THE MOSCOW
COUNTEROFFENSIVE
PHASE I
6 - 15 December 1941

Orel

Novosil

3d

Front line, 6 Dec
Front line, 15 Dec
Lama - Ruza line
Soviet counterattack

SECOND

Yelets

0   50 Miles

ARMY

Livny

SOUTHWEST

0   50 Kilometers

13th

FRONT

Sintsov would be stubbornly silent—it was as unbearable to remember the Moscow of that day, as it would be unbearable to
see a face that was dear to you warped by fear.[14]

As the Germans continued to advance, the composition of the Western
Front was modified to meet the changing situation. The Kalinin Front
was established on 19 October at the request of the Military Council
of the Western Front, to alleviate control problems caused by the great
breadth of the Western Front's zone of responsibility. Konev remained
in command. In mid-November, on the southern flank, as units of the
shattered Briansk Front reeled back on Tula, that unit was dissolved;
its 50th Army and some of its defensive responsibilities were given
to Zhukov and the Western Front. After this addition, the line of the
front with its various irregularities stretched some 600 kilometers. By
November, the front had stabilized to the extent that Zhukov could assure
Stalin it was safe to conduct the traditional military parade on Red Square
on the 7th, the anniversary of the October Revolution.

Perhaps encouraged by the lift in morale given by holding the annual parade while the city was under siege, Stalin ordered Zhukov to
conduct two preemptive attacks on the flanks of the Front, intended
to upset German preparations to renew the offensive. When Zhukov
demurred, citing the absence of reserves and the length of his front,
Stalin cut him off and ordered the attacks to proceed. Shortly after this
call from Stalin, Nikolai A. Bulganin, member of the Military Council, advised Zhukov that Stalin had called him to say that he and Zhukov
were getting "puffed up" and that reins would be found to control them.[15]

The attacks were undertaken by the 16th (Rokossovskii) and 49th
(Zakharkin) Armies, but they did not upset the offensive plans of the
Germans. On 15 November they threw 300 tanks against the 30th Army
of the Kalinin Front and continued on toward Klin the next day. There
were no Soviet reserves in that area because they had been used and
tied up by the enemy in the unsuccessful counterattack ordered by Stalin.
On the 16th, the Germans also launched a four-division attack in the
Volokolamsk area; by the 27th they had taken the city of Volokolamsk
but did not break through the deeply echeloned Soviet defenses beyond that point.

At about this time Stalin called Zhukov and asked, "Are you certain that we are going to hold Moscow? Speak honestly as befits a

Communist."[16] The dictator had lost some of his buoyancy. Zhukov replied that he was certain Moscow could be held but that he would need not less than two armies and at least 200 tanks. Stalin had the armies but not the tanks.

On the southern flank the German attacks resumed on 18 November. By the 26th, the Germans had enveloped Tula and cut the rail and highway links between that city and Moscow. By the 30th, heavy Soviet resistance and counterattacks had halted the German drive and in some areas had pushed it to the southeast.

At the same time the German advance on the northern flank continued. On the 23rd, the invaders entered Klin; on the 25th, the Soviet 16th Army retreated from Solnechnogorsk; and, on the 29th, a German tank unit crossed the Moscow-Volga Canal in the area of Iakhroma, where it was halted by forward elements of the 1st Shock Army.* The situation was in Zhukov's words "extraordinarily complicated."[17]

The situation and the tension it engendered in the high command are given by Zhukov as the reason for the dictator's explosive temper, which resulted in unreasonable orders and unnecessary casualties. Zhukov recalled Stalin's ire when he received a report that the city of Dedovsk had been lost to the enemy and then found that Zhukov was unaware of it. When Zhukov investigated, he discovered some confusion in the report—the village of Dedovo had been taken, not the city of Dedovsk. When Zhukov attempted to rectify the error, the dictator became even angrier; he ordered Zhukov to go to the area, taking with him the army commander, Rokossovskii, and also the commander of the adjacent army, L. A. Govorov, an experienced artilleryman, and help Rokossovskii organize the recapture of the village. Thus, two army commanders and the Front commander were ordered to plan an operation that was successfully executed by a company of infantry and two tanks.[18]

---

*"Shock" (*udarnaia*) armies were conceived as a force designed to break through the tactical zone of the enemy's defenses to clear the way for the introduction of armored units to exploit the gap. Those armies created in 1941 and early 1942 were weaker than prewar theory had proposed. Members of shock armies received extra pay.

Rokossovskii, who had commanded the 16th Army from September 1941, observed these episodes from the standpoint of a subordinate two echelons below the beleaguered dictator. According to Rokossovskii, Zhukov, who had complained about the activities of a state commission under Molotov, dispatched a special commission to investigate and punish those responsible for the loss of Volokolamsk. Rokossovskii recalled that this gesture of distrust by a senior commander "outraged me to the depths of my soul." Rokossovskii also blamed Zhukov for the unsuccessful preemptive counterattack undertaken shortly after the 7th of November parade which Rokossovskii had strongly opposed because of the limited number of troops available and the short time given to prepare the operation. He gave no indication that he was aware Zhukov was also opposed to it but was carrying out the direct orders of Stalin.[19]

In the uncensored version of his memoirs, portions of which have been published after his death, Rokossovskii did not mention that he attempted to go over Zhukov's head to obtain authority to withdraw his troops beyond the Istra River and the reservoir. Instead he gave the impression that the matter was all decided at the Front level. And, after quoting Zhukov's message reminding him that he, Zhukov, was the Front commander and ordering him not to move his troops, Rokossovskii commented:

But this was typical of Zhukov. In this order of his one could sense: I am Zhukov. His personal "I" very often took precedence over the common cause.[20]

Rokossovskii described the extraordinary episode of Zhukov's arrival at his headquarters with Govorov in terms that cause the reader to wonder if Zhukov had taken leave of his senses at this critical stage in the defense of Moscow. After reporting to Zhukov that the Germans had pushed his 18th Division back (at the village of Dedovo?), Rokossovskii was told by Zhukov that he had sufficient troops but that he did not know how to command; Zhukov announced that he had brought along Govorov, who was facing more enemy troops, to teach him how to command. All this in the presence of Rokossovskii's staff. While Zhukov went into the next room, Rokossovskii and Govorov discussed the situation. Suddenly, Zhukov returned, screaming at Govorov:

What are you doing? Whom have you come to teach? Rokossovskii?! He is repulsing all the German tank divisions and beating them. While a mangy motorized division has driven you back dozens of kilometers. Get back to your headquarters! And if you don't restore the situation . . .[21]

Rokossovskii explained that Zhukov's radical change in attitude came while in the other room, when he received the unpleasant news that the enemy had inserted a fresh motorized division into the line and had driven Govorov's army back fifteen kilometers. He left Rokossovskii's headquarters in a rage, muttering that he was going to restore order in Govorov's headquarters.[22]

Rokossovskii's feelings about Zhukov and his style of command were so strong that almost twenty-four years later, while filming a memorial on the Battle of Moscow on the banks of the Moscow-Volga Canal, he departed from his script and launched into a description of the "unworthy" and "crude" methods to which Zhukov had resorted during the battle.[23]* It apparently never occurred to Rokossovskii that what he was being exposed to was the "Stalin style" of leadership.

---

*During this same filming session, presumably after Rokossovskii's outburst, Zhukov admitted to the writer Evgenii Vorob'ev that he had insulted Rokossovskii when he lost his temper during the defense of Moscow. Zhukov also learned for the first time that when Rokossovskii was released from prison in Leningrad in 1940, due to a clerical error, he had wandered around the city without the fare to return to his former unit which was stationed at Pskov. After being unable to find a place to sleep he returned to prison and spent another night there until he obtained the necessary travel documents. Zhukov also told Vorob'ev that when Rokossovskii was presented to Stalin in 1941 as the commander of the 16th Army, Stalin asked him a series of questions to test his knowledge of the latest developments in weapons and tactics. Rokossovskii, having been in prison for three years, in many instances answered that he did not know or was beginning to learn about them. The irritated dictator finally wanted to know why he was so poorly informed. Rokossovskii answered that he had been in prison and had missed those developments. Stalin sighed, rose from his chair, patted him on the shoulder, and said that he had chosen a fine time to sit in prison. That phrase, full of sinister humor, remained in Zhukov's memory. An episode based on the real life occurrence can be found in Simonov's *Zhivye i mertvye*, book 2, *Soldatami ne rozhdaetsia* (Soldiers are not born), p. 677. Vorob'ev, "*Kazhdaia piad' zemli*" in Smirnov, *Marshal Zhukov*, pp. 168–170.

The reverse that had so disturbed Zhukov was the culminating point of the German campaign to capture Moscow. A surprise attack on the 1st of December at the juncture of the 5th and the 33rd Armies along the road to Kubinka broke through the Soviet line. It was blunted by the 32d Rifle Division and by the 4th of December it had been defeated. According to Zhukov, the Germans left on the battlefield 10,000 dead, 50 burned-out tanks, and much other equipment. In the 20 days of the second phase of their offensive on Moscow they had 155,000 men killed and wounded, lost 800 tanks, over 300 guns, and around 1500 aircraft. These losses, Zhukov believed, caused many German troops to lose hope in final victory and the German leadership to lose its aura of invincibility in the eyes of world public opinion.[24] The invaders were also disheartened by the onset of the Russian winter, for which the German Army was poorly prepared. Neither the troops nor their equipment were capable of operating in the temperatures of minus 31 and minus 36 degrees Fahrenheit which the German General Guderian, commander of the 2d Panzer Army, reported on his front before Tula on the 4th and 5th of December. The troops suffered from frostbite, tanks would not start, and frozen recoil mechanisms prevented machine guns and artillery from firing.[25] To this, Zhukov responded that the cold affected both sides, and if the Germans were not properly equipped it was because they had planned on a quick, easy victory.[26]

NOTES

1. Simonov, "Zametki" in *VIZh,* no. 7: p. 48.
2. Ibid.
3. Pavlenko, "Razmyshleniia" in *VIZh,* no. 10: p. 18.
4. Zhukov, *Memoirs* 2: pp. 202, 203.
5. N. Kh. Bedov, "Riadom s marshalom" (Along with the marshal) in Mirkina and Iarovikov, *Marshal Zhukov: Polkovodets,* p. 152.
6. Zhukov, *Memoirs* 2: pp. 209, 210.
7. Ibid., pp. 205–214.
8. Ibid., p. 215.
9. Simonov, "Zametki" in *VIZh,* no. 10: pp. 56, 57.
10. "Bez grifa 'sekretno'" (Without the "secret" stamp) in *KZ,* 13 October 1990, p. 3. Zhukov's letter was dated 2 November 1941.
11. N. Kh. Bedov, *"Riadom s marshalom"* (Along with the marshal) in Mirkina and Iarovikov, *Marshal Zhukov: Polkovodets,* p. 155. Karpov, "Soratniki" in *Znamia,* no. 12: pp. 133, 134.
12. D. I. Ortenberg, *"U Zhukova v Perkhushkogo"* (With Zhukov at Perkhushkovo) in *Krasnaia Zvezda,* 30 November 1991, p. 5.
13. Konstantin Simonov, *Zhivye i mertvye* (The living and the dead) (Moscow: Sovetskii pisatel', 1972), Book 1, pp. 219 ff.
14. Ibid., p. 265.
15. Zhukov, *Memoirs* 2: pp. 230, 231.
16. Ibid., 2: p. 233.
17. *SVE* 8: p. 171. Zhukov, *Memoirs* 2: p. 236.
18. Ibid., 2: pp. 236–238.
19. Ibid.
20. K. K. Rokossovskii, "Soldatskii dolg" in *VIZh,* no. 6, 1989, p. 54.
21. Ibid., p. 55.
22. Ibid.
23. Pavlenko, "Razmyshleniia", in *VIZh,* no. 10: p. 18.
24. Zhukov, *Memoirs* 2: pp. 239–243.
25. Earl F. Ziemke and Magna E. Bauer, *Moscow to Stalingrad: Decision in the East* (Washington, D.C.: U.S. Government Printing Office, 1987), p. 65. Guderian, *Panzer Leader,* pp. 196, 197.
26. Zhukov, *Memoirs* 2: pp. 239–240.

XI

COUNTERATTACKS BECOME A COUNTEROFFENSIVE

During the defensive battles in the latter part of November, Zhukov observed that the German strike forces northwest and southwest of Moscow were too exhausted to accomplish their assigned missions. Hoeppner in the northwest and Guderian in the vicinity of Tula had the mission of breaking through the Soviet defenses and enveloping the city to the east. As early as 29 November Zhukov assessed the German situation as critical. He asked Stalin to subordinate two of the reserve armies to the Western Front for a counteroffensive. Stalin asked, "Are you certain that the enemy has reached a crisis condition and doesn't have the capability to call up some new large reinforcements?"[1] Zhukov assured him that the enemy was exhausted and that the Front could contain any dangerous penetrations without reinforcements, but that if the Germans were allowed to hold and reinforce their advanced positions, that could cause complications. Stalin said he would check with the General Staff. Zhukov also had his chief of staff, Vasilii D. Sokolovskii, call the General Staff to reinforce his request that the Front be given the two armies.[2]

The Western Front counterattacks, which began on the 6th of December, had the relatively modest objective of driving the invaders back 20 or 30 kilometers. But they began the very night that Guderian, the German 2d Panzer Army commander, issued an order to withdraw to defensive positions on the Upper Don, the Shat, and the Upa, approximately 80 kilometers southwest of Moscow.[3]* Hoeppner also began

---

*Guderian recommended withdrawing farther, to the positions his army had held in

to retreat. The other armies in the German Army Group Center were authorized to adjust their positions to the pullbacks of the panzer groups.[4]

Considering the condition of the invaders and the fact that the Red Army had been reinforced since the German thrust on Moscow began in October, the initial Soviet gains were modest. But by the 16th of December, the left wing of the Front had driven Guderian's 2d Panzer Army back almost 130 kilometers. The German armored strike forces had yielded Solnechnogorsk, Klin, and Kalinin. Zhukov later admitted that at the start of their offensive actions he and his staff did not expect the successes that these counterattacks achieved. The counterattacks of the 1st Shock Army and Liziukov's operational group contributed to the development of a broader counteroffensive. Zhukov at this juncture believed that the Western Front should have been reinforced with two more armies, and the offensive continued with the aim of forcing the Germans back to the positions they had held in October. The Supreme High Commander, however, under the influence of the victories before Moscow, had become very optimistic. Stalin decided on a general offensive along the entire front.

Zhukov was summoned to a meeting of the Stavka on the evening of the 5th of January and informed that the Red Army was going to continue the offensive west of Moscow, but would also attempt to defeat the enemy before Leningrad and liberate the Don basin and the Crimea. These operations were to be executed in what Zhukov described as a very limited time frame. When Zhukov had the opportunity to speak, he urged that the offensive be continued on the western axis only. He argued that on his front the Germans had not yet been able to recover from their December defeats. On the other axes, however, the invaders were in strong defendable positions and the Red Army did not have sufficient artillery strength to break through them. Among the civilian members of the Stavka, only the economist N. A. Voznesenskii supported Zhukov. He stated that the Soviet supply situation was not yet adequate to support a simultaneous offensive on all fronts. Stalin's response was that Timoshenko was in favor of an offensive and that

---

October, but Hitler refused to approve. Guderian was relieved of command on the 26th of December 1941. Guderian, *Panzer Leader*, 196–203, 210.

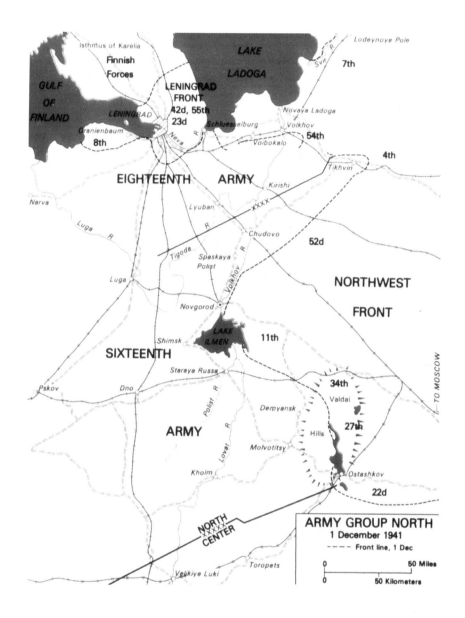

ARMY GROUP NORTH
1 December 1941
----- Front line, 1 Dec

0   50 Miles

0   50 Kilometers

it was necessary to grind the Germans down so that they would not be able to attack in the spring. With that he closed the meeting. As they were leaving, Shaposhnikov told Zhukov that he had wasted his time arguing with Stalin, that the entire question had already been decided. When Zhukov asked, "Then why did he ask for my opinion?" Shaposhnikov could only answer, "I don't know—I don't know, my friend" (*golubchik*—Shaposhnikov's favorite form of direct address).[5]

The Western Front, when the offensive resumed on 10 January, was given the mission of executing a double envelopment of the German Army Group Center—the reciprocal of the operation the Germans had tried and failed to complete in November and December. Viaz'ma was to be the meeting place of the northern and the southern wings of the Western Front. The reciprocal operation failed, as had its complement. By the end of April, what Zhukov and Voznesenskii had said in January had become painfully apparent at the front. Ammunition stocks had been reduced to the point where the daily expenditure of rounds per artillery piece was one or two.[6] As early as the 14th of February, the Western Front reported to the Supreme High Commander, in writing, that the shortage of ammunition was causing the attacking Red Army troops to suffer "very heavy losses" while not achieving corresponding successes.[7]

The second phase of the Moscow offensive was not fought without serious disagreements with the Supreme High Commander. Soon after the offensive started, on the 19th of January, Stalin ordered that the 1st Shock Army be placed in the reserve of the High Command. When Zhukov and his chief of staff, Sokolovskii, protested to the General Staff, they were told that this was a personal decision of Stalin. Zhukov called Stalin and was told to remove the army from his command "without any conversation." When Zhukov continued to protest, Stalin told him that he had many troops and that he should count the number of armies he had. Stalin then hung up. Shaposhnikov could only tell Zhukov what he already knew, "*Golubchik,* I can't do anything, this was a personal decision of the CINC."[8]

The official histories of the war attribute this decision to an underestimation by the High Command of the steps the Germans had taken to restore the morale and capabilities of their forces. Judging that the right flank of Zhukov's Western Front had adequate forces, the decision was made to transfer the 1st Shock Army to the Northwest Front.

There the Soviets had succeeded in almost surrounding a large body of German troops around Demiansk, and Stalin was anxious to complete their destruction. The result was that the Red Army did not succeed on either front. The northern wing of the Western Front was halted before Gzhatsk by 25 January, and the Northwest Front did not complete the liquidation of the Demiansk salient during the remainder of the year 1942.[9]

Underestimation of the restorative capability of the German Army also led to the encirclement and eventual destruction near Viaz'ma of a Soviet strike force. The recapture of Viaz'ma, an important rail and highway center, was the major Soviet objective of the counteroffensive. In late January, an operation utilizing parachute units, the cavalry, and three divisions of the 33d Army led by the army commander, M. G. Efremov, attempted to take the city by a *coup de main*.[10]* As the 33d Army units approached the city, the Germans closed what had been a gap in their defenses behind the attacking Soviet units and reestablished a strong defensive position through which the Soviets could neither return to the main forces nor be reinforced or resupplied (except by air). The encircled Soviet troops joined forces with partisan detachments in the area, managing to disrupt German rear area operations for two months. Some of the cavalry and parachute troops were able to fight their way out of the encirclement by taking an indirect route back to their own lines. Efremov felt that the rest of his troops were not physically capable of surviving a long march and therefore opted, against Zhukov's strong protest, to attempt to break out over a more direct route. He was cut off and eventually committed suicide to avoid capture. The 29th Army of the Kalinin Front had a similar experience during this phase of the offensive. It attacked early in February along with the 11th Cavalry Corps and the 39th Army and reached the approaches to Viaz'ma, only to be cut off and surrounded. The remnants of this army, 5,200 men of whom 800 were wounded, managed to rejoin the main forces in late February.[11]

---

*Zhukov refused to consider the 33d Army's action an "operation," saying that its commander, M. G. Efremov, had gone through an open gap in the German positions, had not protected his flanks, and had been cut off.

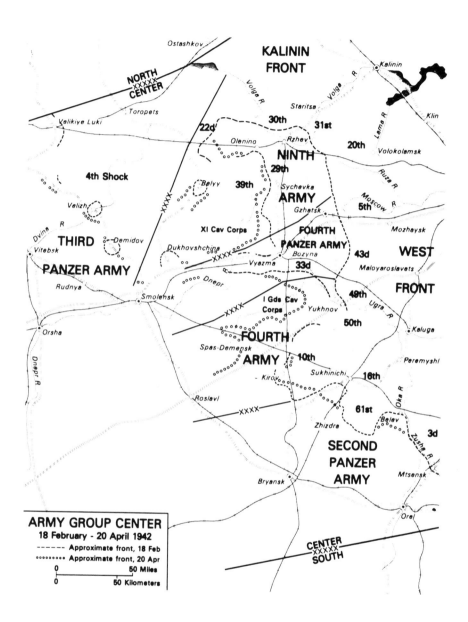

ARMY GROUP CENTER
18 February - 20 April 1942
----- Approximate front, 18 Feb
ooooooooo Approximate front, 20 Apr
0   50 Miles
0   50 Kilometers

Lieutenant General Efremov shot himself on either 17 or 18 April. His body was buried by the Germans in the yard of a badly damaged church and was recovered the next spring when the Soviet Army retook Viaz'ma. His son, then a lieutenant, helped find and identify the body.

Fifty years later, the general's son, now retired Colonel M. M. Efremov, published an article in the *Military Historical Journal*. He criticized Zhukov's "rash" decision to throw the 33d Army into a gap in the German position, offering a seemingly weakly defended route to Viaz'ma. Efremov points out that the 33d Army was at reduced strength due to the casualties it had suffered from being engaged in continuous offensive action since 18 December. The army was not reinforced with either personnel or equipment. The armies on its left and right, the 43d and the 5th, were attacking in diverging directions from the axis given the 33d Army. By the end of January, as the Germans were threatening to close the gap, Zhukov ordered General Efremov to move forward toward Viaz'ma and to leave his chief of staff to cope with keeping the gap open. On 2 February, the strike elements of the 33d Army were cut off from its support and supply elements.

On 10 March, General Efremov informed Zhukov that he was still engaging the Germans within the pocket, that he was running low on ammunition, and that he had 3,000 wounded troops with him. On 25 March, he reported that German tanks had appeared, disorganizing and penetrating his defenses. The death and illness rates among his troops had increased, due to exhaustion. Nevertheless, he appealed to Zhukov to organize an (airborne?) landing of reinforcements to open his communications to the rear and to advance on Viaz'ma. As we know, Zhukov had no reinforcements to send and ammunition was in short supply across the entire front.

Efremov then made the cardinal mistake from the point of view of his relationship with Zhukov. He appealed over Zhukov's head to Stalin, who directed Zhukov to take steps to break through the ring around the forward elements of the 33d Army. Zhukov's efforts were unsuccessful and Efremov was authorized to attempt to rejoin main elements of the Western Front. Here again he crossed Zhukov by choosing the shortest route to friendly lines instead of the roundabout route proposed by the Front commander.

Survivors and their relatives (who call themselves Efremovites—

Efremovtsy) over the years have combed the areas south of Viaz'ma for artifacts and the bodies of their colleagues, friends, and loved ones in efforts to reconstruct the epic of the 33d Army. Among relatives, a prime motivation is to remove the stigma of "missing in action" from their loved one's name and to prove somehow that he or she fell there in the spring of 1942. Under the Mekhlis rule, the worst disgrace was to be taken prisoner by the Germans. Those who were missing in action might have been among those former prisoners who chose never to return to the Soviet Union in 1945 and 1946.

The publication of Zhukov's unpublished recollections in 1988—in which he said that the Efremov attempt to take Viaz'ma was not an operation and cast the entire blame for its failure on Efremov—convinced those searching for the truth about the affair that Efremov would have been tried if he had survived. He probably would have been found guilty, despite an alleged analysis by the General Staff that Zhukov himself was responsible for the catastrophe. Unfortunately, the Efremovites do not provide a source citation for this assertion.[12]

From the 1st of February, the overall direction of these operations around Viaz'ma was the responsibility of Zhukov, who became commander of the reconstituted Western Axis on that date. Under this arrangement Zhukov retained command of the Western Front with F. I. Golikov as his deputy Front commander, while the Kalinin Front, under Konev, was also part of his command. This command assignment is not mentioned in Zhukov's memoirs, possibly because this part of the counteroffensive was not as successful as the December counterattacks. Zhukov, it will be recalled, had opposed Stalin's idea of a broad general offensive beginning early in January, in part because the Red Army did not as yet have the equipment (tanks in particular), ammunition, and supplies necessary for the undertaking. The successes achieved in December, impressive in themselves, had seemed to Stalin greater than they really were, since they were facilitated by coincidental planned German withdrawals. As the Germans withdrew to prepared positions and received reinforcements from the west, their supply situation became stronger and they took advantage of overenthusiastic Soviet commanders who thought they were pursuing a beaten enemy.

Zhukov devotes some attention to the fate of General M. G. Efremov, the commander of the 33d Army, and his unsuccessful efforts to take

Viaz'ma. One senses that there was more to this episode than Zhukov
cared to relate. For example, Zhukov notes that the chief of the Front
operations department, General V. S. Golushkevich, flew in to the encircled
troops on several occasions. But he does not mention that Golushkevich,
according to other Soviet sources, was "repressed" in 1942. Why? Was
he the scapegoat for the poorly conceived second part of the operation? Or was he one of the victims of Beriia's NKVD, who were already in 1942 trying to find grounds upon which to compromise Zhukov
and may have been looking for incriminating information?*

Soviet losses in the course of the German offensive and the Soviet
counteroffensive were on the order of 2,204,000 men—an appalling
figure, and more than three times that of the Wehrmacht's 615,000.
Russian researchers, who have been hampered by official reluctance
to permit access to the official records, presented these incredible figures
at a conference conducted by the Institute of Military History in connection with the 50th anniversary of the defense of Moscow. Almost half
of these losses, 959,000, occurred during the period when the Red Army
was being driven back toward Moscow. During the period of the counteroffensive ordered by Stalin (20 January–April 1942) an additional
948,000 casualties were sustained. The counterattacks during December
1941 cost 297,000 men. In the opinion of Russian military historians,
a fundamental reason for these losses was the conduct of infantry attacks
without artillery support. These attacks were ordered despite a Stavka
directive against the practice. That the attacks continued and the losses
mounted was not due to a lack of competence among the military
leadership or miscalculations by the military command. They were due

*Pavlenko speculates that Zhukov's popularity and fame among the Soviet people
had begun to irritate Stalin and that Beriia arrested Golushkevich after he had been
transferred to the Southwest Front, in order to coerce him into providing incriminating information against Zhukov. Golushkevich did not provide any such information
and was imprisoned until 1954 when he was rehabilitated and given an assignment
in the Military Scientific Directorate of the General Staff. The ostensible cause for
the arrest and sentence has not been publicized. Pavlenko, "Razmyshleniia" in *VIZh*,
no. 12: p. 29.

to the fact that in 1941 and early 1942 the military economy of the country could not meet the requirement of the forces for ammunition, artillery, tanks, trucks, and other equipment and was not able to until later in the year 1942.[13] This was precisely what Zhukov and Voznesenskii tried to tell Stalin before the counteroffensive started in early January.

Speaking of these losses and the reasons for them, one Soviet military historian was sharply critical of Zhukov and when asked what, under the circumstances, Zhukov should have done, said he should have resigned rather than attempted to execute orders that would lead to such casualties. Zhukov at that time was 46 years old. The reality of the situation in the Soviet Union did not allow Soviet generals the luxury of resignation and retirement which even Hitler afforded his recalcitrant generals. We can only speculate on Zhukov's fate if he had attempted such a course. It probably would have involved the intervention of Beriia.

Although the counteroffensive did not achieve the ambitious aims of Stalin's January plans, Hitler had been dealt the first check that he had experienced since coming to power in 1933. Zhukov in the popular imagination was given credit, along with Stalin, for saving Moscow. But the methods by which Zhukov demonstrated his "iron will" had made him numerous enemies in the military high command, among the political leadership, and in the person of the dictator, who did not look with favor on the emergence of a rival for popular esteem. David Ortenberg noted that in the 3 January 1942 list of decorations awarded for the Battle of Moscow the name Zhukov could not be found. Checking with an acquaintance on the General Staff, he was informed that Zhukov's name had been stricken from the list by Stalin. Much later, Ortenberg realized that if the services of Zhukov were too highly honored, Stalin's contribution would somehow be lessened.[14]

Vladimir Karpov has observed that during Stalin's lifetime some Soviet military historians, to the dictator's satisfaction, distorted the events leading to the battles before Moscow, comparing the Soviet retreats and the counteroffensive to those of Mikhail I. Kutuzov in 1812. In these versions Stalin lured Hitler and the Wehrmacht to the gates of Moscow in order to bring down on them the Red Army, reinforced with "fresh, well armed, trained troops." For F. I. Golikov, who had led the 10th Army into action in December 1941, "The defeat of the German fascist troops proved the superiority of the strategic plan of offensive operations, worked out by Comrade Stalin, over the strategy of the Hitlerites." Golikov's army consisted of 11 divisions, 9 of which had been formed in the space of three weeks from the reserves of the Moscow Military District and trained for 12 hours a day.[15]*

*According to Golikov the army finished its concentration in the area of Penza on 8 November; 15 days were devoted to combat training and 5 days were devoted to construction of facilities including *zemlianki* (mud huts) for living quarters. There were shortages of everything including warm clothing, and the weather was if anything colder than that experienced by the Germans as they approached Moscow. The majority of the troops were between 30 and 40 years of age. In some of the units up to 65 percent of the personnel had no military training. The army after moving to Riazan' attacked on the morning of 6 December.

NOTES

1. Zhukov, *Memoirs* 2: p. 244.
2. Ibid.
3. Simonov, "Zametki" in *VIZh*, no. 7, pp. 48, 49.
4. Ziemke and Bauer, *Moscow to Stalingrad*, p. 67.
5. Zhukov, *Memoirs* 2: pp. 254, 255. Zhukov's description of how the counterattacks grew into a counteroffensive is found in "G. K. Zhukov: Iz neopublikovannykh vospominanii" (G. K. Zhukov: From unpublished recollections) in *Kommunist*, no. 14 (1988): p. 93.
6. Zhukov, *Memoirs* 2: p. 265.
7. Ibid.
8. Ibid., p. 260.
9. Pospelov, *IVOVSS* 2: pp. 325, 337.
10. "G. K. Zhukov: Iz neopublikovannykh vospominanii" (see note 5), p. 96.
11. Pospelov, *IVOVSS* 2: pp. 326–332.
12. M. M. Efremov, *"Pod Viaz'moi vesnoi 1942 goda"* (Before Viaz'ma in the spring of 1942) in *VIZh*, no. 3, 1992. Iuliia Kapusto, *Poslednimi dorogami generala Efremova* (The last roads of General Efremov) Moscow: Politizdat, 1992, pp. 138–142. V. Okorokov, "Pravda o pokoinom marshale i pogibshem generale" (The truth about the deceased marshal and the fallen general), *Syn Otechestva*, 12 April 1991, p. 10.
13. V. Eliseev, *"Pobeda pod Moskvoy: Lozh' i pravda"* (The victory before Moscow: The lie and the truth), in *KZ*, 18 February 1992, p. 2.
14. Ortenberg, "U Zhukova," p. 4.
15. Karpov, "Soratniki" in *Znamia*, no. 12: pp. 145, 152, 153. Filip I. Golikov, *V Moskovskoi bitve* (In the Moscow battle) (Moscow: Nauka, 1967), pp. 8–51.

XII

THE STALINGRAD CAMPAIGN, 1942–1943

By mid-February the Soviet winter offensive began to sputter, and in March the spring rains and floods brought operations to a halt. At the end of March, Stalin convened a meeting attended by Voroshilov, Timoshenko, Shaposhnikov, Aleksandr M. Vasilevskii (Shaposhnikov's deputy), and Zhukov at which the plans for the summer campaign were discussed. Shaposhnikov, then chief of the General Staff—who was obviously suffering from his heart condition and asthma—presented the staff's appreciation of the situation which, according to Zhukov, was close to that of the dictator. The Germans were considered capable of two major offensive operations simultaneously: one in the direction of Moscow and one in the southern part of the country. Stalin believed that Hitler was more likely to resume the effort to capture Moscow.

Stalin accepted that the Red Army was still not strong enough to conduct a major offensive. He wanted to limit the army to an active strategic defense, to include limited offensives in the Crimea, in the vicinity of Khar'kov, and around Leningrad and Demiansk. He believed that these operations at the beginning of the summer would wear down and bloody the enemy while the Red Army built up its reserves in preparation for a broad counteroffensive. Zhukov, as commander of the Western Axis, continued to believe, as he had in January, that his forces should be reinforced and used to defeat the strong enemy forces still concentrated in the Rzhev-Viaz'ma area. While he agreed in general with Stalin's assessment of the situation, Zhukov was opposed to the number of limited offensives Stalin was proposing, on the grounds that they would consume reserves and complicate preparations for the eventual general offensive. He was again supported by Voznesenskii, who expressed doubt that the Soviet supply and equipment situation was as yet adequate to support broad offensive operations.

During this late March discussion, Zhukov felt that he had the support of Shaposhnikov and the General Staff, but Stalin reacted sharply to his proposal, saying that to attack solely on the Western Axis was a half measure. When Timoshenko, the commander of the Southwest Axis, was given the floor, he reported that the troops in his command were in a condition to make a preemptive strike against the Germans on his front to disrupt their summer attack plans. He supported Zhukov's recommendation for a strike against the enemy before the Western Front because it would hold the German forces there and because it would prevent their being used as reinforcements in other areas. Timoshenko was supported by Voroshilov, who remained a member of the Stavka despite his lackluster performance as its representative in the field. Zhukov again protested the idea of several limited attacks but received no second from Shaposhnikov. The meeting ended after Stalin gave instructions that limited offensives should be prepared in the Crimea, toward Khar'kov (the operation proposed by Timoshenko), and in the other areas.

Events of May and June demonstrated that Stalin had miscalculated badly. In the Crimea, the Germans launched a preemptive attack on 8 May which forced the Soviets to give up Kerch'. This victory enabled the invaders to concentrate all of their efforts on Sevastopol', which fell on 4 July after a nine-month siege. On 3 May, the Northwest Front began a month-long effort to capture Demiansk, which also failed.[1] At about this time Zhukov reports that Stalin, discussing the Crimean operation, remarked: "You see what defense leads to . . . Timoshenko will soon start his offensive. Have you changed your opinion about the method of operations in the south?" Zhukov replied that he had not.[2]

The offensive which Timoshenko launched had been scaled down considerably from the three-Front operation he had originally proposed in March. The previous versions had been rejected because they would have required the Stavka to commit too many reserves to the Southwest Axis. The forces to conduct the approved operation were to be those then available to the Southwest Axis, mainly those of the Southwest Front. The General Staff was directed to consider the operation an internal matter of Timoshenko's command.[3]

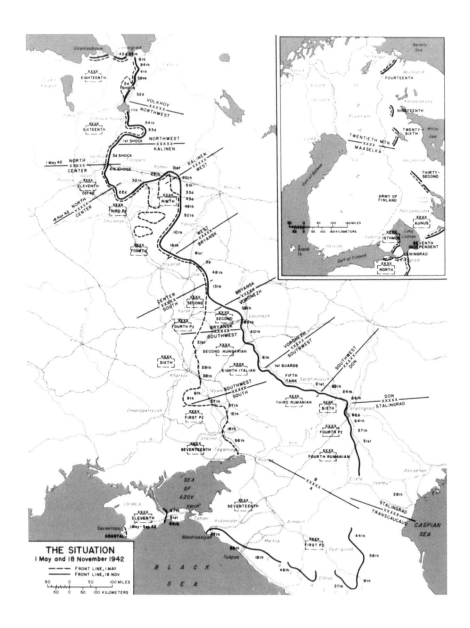

THE SITUATION
1 May and 18 November 1942

--- FRONT LINE, 1 MAY
—— FRONT LINE, 18 NOV

50   0   50   100 MILES
50   0   50   100 KILOMETERS

The Southwest Front began the offensive on 12 May, achieving some initial advances of 25 to 50 kilometers in the direction of Khar'kov. The main effort was made by the 6th Army, advancing to the northwest from its positions on the north face of the Barvenkovo salient. But five days later the Germans launched an attack through the 9th and 57th Armies of the neighboring Southern Front, advancing in two days to the flank and rear of the attacking 6th Army and the units of an operations group commanded by General Bobkin. By the 18th of May the acting chief of the General Staff, A. M. Vasilevskii, became so concerned with the situation that he recommended to Stalin that the Southwest Front offensive be called off and all forces turned to face the attacking Germans.

The Barvenkovo salient was key to the German plans. Hitler had decided that the 1942 summer campaign was to be fought in southern Russia, commencing with a blow toward Voronezh, a thrust down the Don River to Stalingrad (now called Volgograd), and a sweep across the Don basin to the Caucasus. The objective was to cut the lines of communication and supply between Moscow and important sources of food and raw materials, particularly oil. Prior to executing the operation, given the code name Blau (renamed *Braunschweig,* 30 June 1942), it was necessary to eliminate the Barvenkovo salient, a result of the winter operations of 1941–42. In early May, German forces were concentrated on both faces of the salient, intending to pinch it off. Timoshenko's offensive efforts, and the high command's estimate that the Germans were most likely to renew their effort to take Moscow, fitted nicely into the German plan. The Southern Front, commanded by R. Ia. Malinovskii, weakened by the preceding battles, was not equal to the task of securing the flanks and rear of the Southwest Front.[4]

That Nikita S. Khrushchev was a member of the Military Council of the Southwest Axis was an accident of history that received little notice in 1942. But in 1956, after he became the leader of the Soviet Communist Party and the Soviet state, he recalled these events in his famous "secret speech" as an example of Stalin's military incompetence. Khrushchev claimed that he had attempted to contact Stalin for permission to call off the Southwest Front offensive after it was clear that the Germans were threatening its flank and rear. Stalin refused to talk to him, and Malenkov told him that the offensive was to continue.

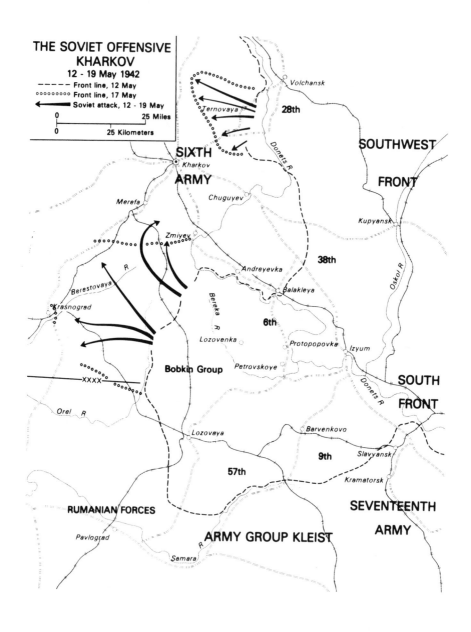

THE SOVIET OFFENSIVE
KHARKOV
12 - 19 May 1942
- - - - - - Front line, 12 May
ooooooooo Front line, 17 May
→ Soviet attack, 12 - 19 May
0   25 Miles
0   25 Kilometers

It was in this context that Khrushchev claimed that Stalin "planned operations on a globe."

In his memoirs, Zhukov flatly contradicted Khrushchev's version of these events. He claimed to have been present in Moscow when Stalin warned Timoshenko of the German concentration on his flank and rear. He also reported that on the evening Khrushchev called Stalin, Khrushchev had said the danger was exaggerated and there was no reason to call off the Southwest Front offensive. Thus Stalin, referring to reports of the Military Council of the Front, rejected Vasilevskii's (and Khrushchev's) recommendation to halt the attack. Zhukov commented:

> The existing version of alarming reports of the Military Council of the Southwest Front to the Supreme Commander does not correspond to reality. I assert that because I was present during the conversations with the Supreme [High Commander].[5]

One can surmise that Zhukov was so insistent in his denial of "the existing version" because it was Khrushchev's version. Those who controlled the Soviet media when Zhukov's memoirs were being cleared for publication were content to see Stalin's flamboyant successor given the lie. The party line was designed at that time to end the de-Stalinization campaign which Khrushchev had started with his secret speech in 1956.

By the 28th of May the Soviet offensive toward Khar'kov had failed completely. Soviet losses, according to German claims, were 240,000 troops and 1,500 tanks. The Germans clearly had the initiative and the question was where they would strike next. That they would attempt to exploit this success with a drive to the south was a logical possibility. But the Germans had put in motion an elaborate deception plan, Operation *Kreml,* along with a detailed concealment plan to mask the preparations to continue south with Operation Blau-Braunschweig. These plans, along with Stalin's conviction that the next German move would be toward Moscow, apparently influenced the Soviets not to reinforce the Southwestern Axis. Even the capture of some of the operations plans for Blau in mid-June did not change Stalin's mind as to the probable direction of the next German blow. He expected that the Germans would attack from the south, that their initial objective would be Tula, and that their final objective would be Moscow. Accordingly, when the Germans attacked on 28 June through the Briansk Front, commanded

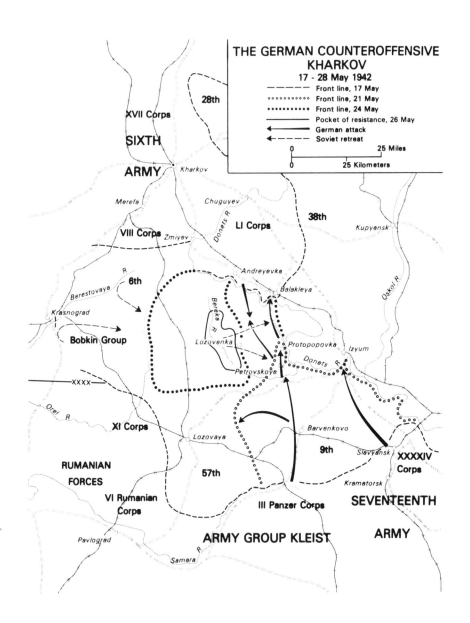

by Lieutenant General F. I. Golikov, Stalin and the General Staff focused Golikov's attention on the defense of the approaches to Tula, concentrating the major portion of a newly formed tank corps close to those approaches.[6]

The German attack moved due east toward Voronezh through the Briansk Front. Two days later, the German 6th Army launched an attack aimed at the Don south of Voronezh through Timoshenko's (and Khrushchev's) Southwestern Front.[7]* By 17 July, the Briansk and Southwestern Front defenses had been penetrated between 150 to 170 kilometers on a front of 300 kilometers. On 20 July, the Germans launched attacks against the Southern Front, commanded by Malinovskii, which resulted in the capture of Rostov on the Don. The way was open to Stalingrad and the Caucasus.[8]

During these events Zhukov remained in command of the Western Front, the Western Axis having been disbanded in early May 1942. According to Zhukov, the order to disband the Axis was issued as a punishment immediately following the conference at the end of March when he had disagreed with Stalin's spring offensive plans. He conducted two limited attacks, one on each wing of the Front, to prevent the Germans from shifting reserves to the south. They were successful according to Zhukov; they prevented the Germans from transferring three tank divisions and several infantry divisions to support Blau. Zhukov, however, felt that if he had had one or two more armies to support his attack on the right wing toward Rzhev, the entire enemy concentration in that area could have been defeated and the strategic situation significantly improved.[9] This, of course, had been his contention ever since the December 1941 counterattack before Moscow. But Stalin, who was receiving pleas for military help all the way from the besieged city of Leningrad to the Crimea, tried to satisfy all of them, with disastrous results.

The Stalingrad Front was established on 12 July in the expectation that the city on the Volga was the next German objective. Timoshenko

---

*The Southwestern Axis was deactivated 29 June 1942. Timoshenko remained in command of the Southwestern Front.

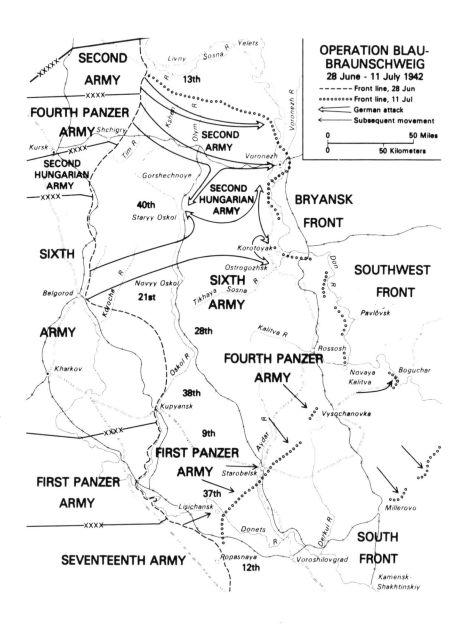

OPERATION BLAU-
BRAUNSCHWEIG
28 June - 11 July 1942

- - - - - Front line, 28 Jun
ooooooooo Front line, 11 Jul
⟵ German attack
⟵ Subsequent movement

0   50 Miles
0   50 Kilometers

was given command of the Front initially and Khrushchev designated a member of the Military Council. Timoshenko was relieved by V. N. Gordov on 22 July. By 1 August, it was decided to divide the Stalingrad Front in two and to designate A. I. Eremenko as commander of one of the Fronts. On 2 August, the Front boundary was drawn generally west to east through the city which stretches almost 20 kilometers along the Volga. The Front designated to defend the north half of the city and the area to the north of the city was named the Stalingrad Front; The other was called the Southeastern Front and Eremenko was given command of it. As the situation worsened, on 10 August the Stalingrad Front was subordinated to the Southeastern Front, and on 13 August Eremenko was named commander of both, while Khrushchev became the Military Council member for the joint command. Golikov became deputy commander for the Southeastern Front, with Gordov deputy commander for the Stalingrad Front.

Stalin recalled Zhukov to Moscow on 31 August. He told Zhukov that one of the reasons he had relieved Timoshenko was that Khrushchev had reported to him that at a critical juncture in the retreat to Stalingrad, Timoshenko had abandoned his headquarters in order to bathe in the Don River. Zhukov felt that Stalin did not deal more harshly with Timoshenko because the idea for the disastrous operation was his (Stalin's) in the first place. After describing the command changes to Zhukov (and telling him he did not consider Eremenko a "find"), he appointed Zhukov deputy commander in chief, telling him to fly to the area the next day.

On 30 September, the Fronts were again renamed: the Southeastern Front became the Stalingrad Front and the units north of the city became the Don Front. Eremenko and Khrushchev remained in command of the Stalingrad Front, while K. K. Rokossovskii was placed in command of the Don Front.[10]

When the Germans reached the Volga at Rynok on 23 August they broke the continuity of the Soviet defenses; however, Eremenko and Khrushchev remained nominally in command of both Fronts until 30 September. They were occupied almost totally with preventing the capture of the city. The headquarters of the Stalingrad Front was moved to Ivanovka, forty kilometers to the north, and two newly formed armies, the 24th and the 66th, began to concentrate there.

Zhukov was in the midst of directing a limited Western Front offensive when on 27 August he received a call from Stalin, directing
him to turn over command to his chief of staff and return to Moscow.
When he arrived at the Kremlin that night, Stalin told him that the situation
in the south was bad and it was possible the Germans would take
Stalingrad. The Germans had already reached the Volga at Rynok, thus
splitting the two Fronts, and Stalin wanted to restore the continuity
of the city's defense. He wanted Zhukov to fly to Stalingrad as soon
as possible and coordinate the attack of the 1st Guards Army, which
was being transferred hastily to the Stalingrad Front to cut through
the German corridor from the north and join with the 62d Army, which
was defending the city.

When Zhukov arrived at the headquarters of the Stalingrad Front
on the 29th of August, Vasilevskii, now chief of the General Staff, was
already there, and had been in the area since 12 August. Zhukov, after conferring with him, the deputy commander for the Stalingrad Front
V. N. Gordov, and the commander of the 1st Guards Army K. S. Moskalenko, determined that the 1st Guards Army could not attack until 3
September because its units had not closed into their attack positions,
nor had adequate ammunition been brought up to support the attack.
He so informed Stalin. When the attack was launched on the 3d it achieved
limited gains, but was halted far short of its objectives.

The failure of this attack plus Zhukov's report that the 24th and the
66th Armies, which were closing in the Stalingrad Front area, could
not attack until 5 or 6 September evoked a telegram from Stalin on 3
September. He stated that the enemy could take the city either tomorrow or the next day if the forces north of the city did not attack immediately. The telegram included an ominous remark that, "Delay now
is equivalent to a crime."[11]

Characteristically, Zhukov called Stalin immediately and reported
that he could order an offensive for the next morning, but the troops
of all three armies would have to begin the battle almost without
ammunition, which could only be brought forward by the evening of
the 4th of September. In addition, coordination of the infantry, artillery, tanks, and aviation could not be achieved earlier than that. Without
ammunition and coordination, nothing would be accomplished. This
provoked the following response from the dictator:

Do you think that the enemy is going to wait while you get yourself moving? . . . Eremenko says that the enemy can take Stalingrad with the first squeeze, if you don't strike him from the north.[12]

Zhukov told Stalin he did not share that view and eventually received permission to attack on the 5th. Stalin agreed reluctantly, telling Zhukov he would answer with his head if the attacks did not start then. On the 5th Stalin called Malenkov (who was with Zhukov) at three o'clock in the morning to verify that the offensive was about to begin.[13]

The attack began on schedule, but after an entire day of intensive combat the net advance was from two to four kilometers in some sectors. But the attack did have the effect of drawing German troops away from Stalingrad. This satisfied Stalin and he ordered the attacks continued. By 10 September, Zhukov came to the conclusion that the available forces of the Stalingrad Front were not capable of achieving the objectives they had been assigned and so reported to Stalin. The dictator ordered him back to Moscow for a face-to-face discussion of future courses of action.

The opportunity to describe the origins of the plan for the great Soviet counteroffensive at Stalingrad may have been one of Zhukov's principal motivations for writing his memoirs. During the Khrushchev years the fact of the presence of Zhukov and other representatives of the Stavka in and around Stalingrad during the battle was infrequently mentioned, and then it was usually in a critical vein. For example, Academician Samsonov, who became the official historian of the battle, mentioned Zhukov for the first time on page 456 of the first edition of his work, published in 1960. The work contains three references to Zhukov's role and four to that of Vasilevskii.[14] In Samsonov's fourth edition, published in 1989, there are 20 references to Zhukov, some of them multipage. Eremenko, the Stalingrad Front commander, was the principal military spokesman for the view that the victory at Stalingrad was largely due to efforts of those in the field—Eremenko, his political officer, Khrushchev, and the 62d Army commander, V. I. Chuikov.

Eremenko presented his first version of the battle in a pamphlet of 5,000 copies printed in Stalingrad in January 1958.[15] Eremenko's effort contained 131 pages and was sent to the typesetter on 10 October 1957, before Zhukov was relieved as minister of defense. When it appeared it had been edited to reflect some of the changes that had taken place in the meantime (e.g., Malinovskii is described on page 124 as "now minister of defense USSR"). Eremenko's *Stalingrad,* published in 1961 in an edition of 100,000 copies, complete with a pocket containing 22 maps, shows more clearly a heavy-handed effort to inflate Khrushchev's image, while deflating that of Zhukov, Vasilevskii, and Stalin. Eremenko was also permitted a considerable self-serving effort to enhance his role as the commander at Stalingrad.[16]

In his 1958 pamphlet, Eremenko made no claim to primacy in the planning of the counterattack that was to lead to the encirclement of the German 6th Army, writing:

> Somehow in September 1942, the question of the counterattack was touched on in a conversation with the Stavka. From that I understood that in the Stavka a plan for the counteroffensive was germinating.[17]

He went on to describe how he talked over his ideas with Khrushchev and that the result was a suggested plan for enveloping the German forces by coordinated attacks from north and south of the city. He wrote that early in October he was informed by Vasilevskii that these "projections" (*nametki*) of a plan had been approved by the Stavka.[18]

In his 1961 book, Eremenko claimed that he had the idea of a counteroffensive at Stalingrad almost before Stalin gave him the assignment to command there on the evening of 2 August, and suggested a counterattack to Stalin at that time. Stalin is also identified as the person Eremenko was talking to in the Stavka in September, and the matter of the counterattack was not "touched on" but was raised directly by Eremenko. Vasilevskii, in Eremenko's book version, reported the "plan of the offensive operation" (not "projections" of a plan) was adopted by the Stavka.[19]

Eremenko, in a summation, acknowledged that the plan was the result of the creative activity of the Party, the Military Councils of the other Fronts involved at Stalingrad, the Stavka, and the General Staff, but the reader is left with the distinct impression that this acknowledgement was for reasons of modesty and courtesy and that he and Khrushchev were the originators and the principal executors of the plan.

Four years later, in 1965, after Khrushchev had been deposed, Zhukov and Vasilevskii were permitted to publish their version of these events. According to their accounts, the basic plan for the counteroffensive was assembled by the General Staff on the 13th and 14th of September and approved by Stalin at the end of the month. The main considerations were that the concentration of Soviet reserves would be accomplished in October and that by that time new aircraft, tanks, and ammunition would also be available. Soviet intelligence indicated that the Germans did not have adequate forces and resources to accomplish their goals in the Caucasus *and* capture Stalingrad in the fall of 1942. The General Staff was also aware of the relative weakness of the Hungarian, Italian, and Romanian troops who were manning portions of the front north and south of Stalingrad. As Zhukov observed:

Who was capable of making the concrete calculations of the forces and means for an operation of such a scale? Of course, only that organ which had in its hands those material forces and means. In this case it could be only the Stavka of the Supreme Command and the General Staff.[20]

Years later Zhukov told Elena Rzhevskaia that he had confronted Eremenko and asked him why he had described the Stalingrad campaign the way he did. Eremenko replied that Khrushchev had asked him to do it.[21]

After presenting their plan to Stalin, Zhukov and Vasilevskii returned to Stalingrad to oversee the defense of the city. Stalin said he would think it over and calculate whether there were sufficient resources to implement the proposed plan. In the meantime, these initial discussions were not to be revealed to anyone.

Zhukov returned to the Stalingrad Front, north of the city, where the 1st Guards, the 24th and the 66th Armies, and Soviet air units had renewed their counterattacks on the German north flank to take pressure off the 62d Army in the city. He was there when Eremenko and Khrushchev, "in a quiet moment," paid a visit to the 1st Guards Army. Despite the fact that Eremenko was formally still in command of the Stalingrad Front, according to Zhukov he had to obtain permission from Stalin to make the visit. And, said Zhukov, the purpose of the visit

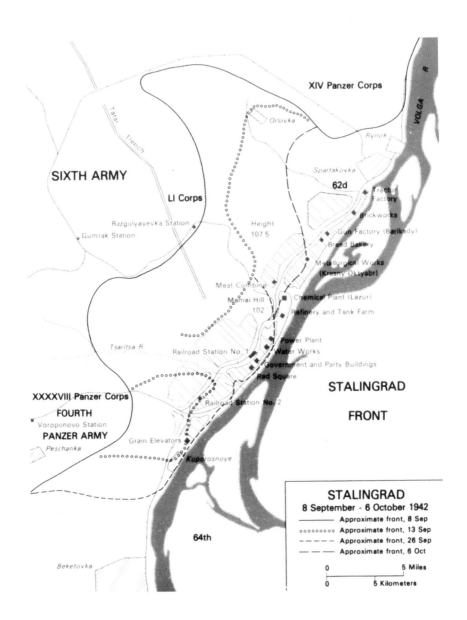

XIV Panzer Corps

Volga R.

Tatar Trench

Orlovka

Rynok

SIXTH ARMY

Spartakovka

LI Corps

62d

Tractor Factory

Brickworks

Razgulyayevka Station

Height
107.5

Gun Factory (Barikady)

Gumrak Station

Bread Bakery

Metallurgical Works
(Krasny Oktyabr)

Meat Combine

Mamai Hill
102

Chemical Plant (Lazur)

Refinery and Tank Farm

Tsaritsa R.

Power Plant

Railroad Station No. 1

Water Works

Government and Party Buildings

Red Square

STALINGRAD

XXXXVIII Panzer Corps

Railroad Station No. 2

FOURTH

FRONT

Voroponovo Station

PANZER ARMY

Peschanka

Grain Elevators

Kuporosnoye

STALINGRAD
8 September - 6 October 1942

———————— Approximate front, 8 Sep
ooooooooo Approximate front, 13 Sep
– – – – – Approximate front, 26 Sep
— — — — Approximate front, 6 Oct

64th

0   5 Miles

0   5 Kilometers

Beketovka

was to familiarize the visitors with the situation and so they could discuss how things were going in Stalingrad.[22] Eremenko stated in his book that the reason for the visit was that the Stalingrad Front was not putting enough pressure on the Germans. Perhaps in direct answer to this assertion Zhukov wrote:

> With all responsibility I declare that if it were not for the persistent counterattacks of the troops of the Stalingrad Front [and] the systematic air attacks it is possible that it would have been much the worse for Stalingrad.[23]

At the end of September, Zhukov and Vasilevskii went to Moscow to discuss the counteroffensive. At that time the Fronts and commands were again changed: the Stalingrad Front was renamed the Don Front and K. K. Rokossovskii replaced V. N. Gordov, who, according to Zhukov, could not get along with his staff or his subordinate commanders. The Southeast Front now became the Stalingrad Front, and the Southwest Front was to be reestablished north of the Don Front. After discussing these and other details, Stalin sent Zhukov to the newly named Don Front to select reserve concentration areas and reconnoiter attack positions. Vasilevskii returned to the new Stalingrad Front with a similar mission. On their return to Moscow, and after further discussions, they both signed the operations map depicting the offensive and Stalin signed under the word "Approved."[24]

Zhukov made two more visits to the Don Front in November. From the 1st to the 9th, accompanied by senior aviation, tank, and artillery officers, he reviewed the plans of the 21st, 65th, and the 5th Tank Armies. On the 10th, he joined Vasilevskii to review the plans and readiness of the Stalingrad Front. During these visits Zhukov often went to the forward areas of contact with the enemy in order to verify the readiness of the frontline troops. On this occasion, one of Zhukov's concerns was coordinating the linkup of the leading elements of the two jaws of the enveloping pincers to prevent an accidental fire fight when they closed. On the 13th, Zhukov and Vasilevskii were again in Moscow reporting to Stalin. After hearing their reports, Stalin again dispatched them to the front, telling them to check once more on the readiness of the troops and their commanders for the beginning of the offensive. On the 15th of November, Stalin authorized Zhukov to set the date

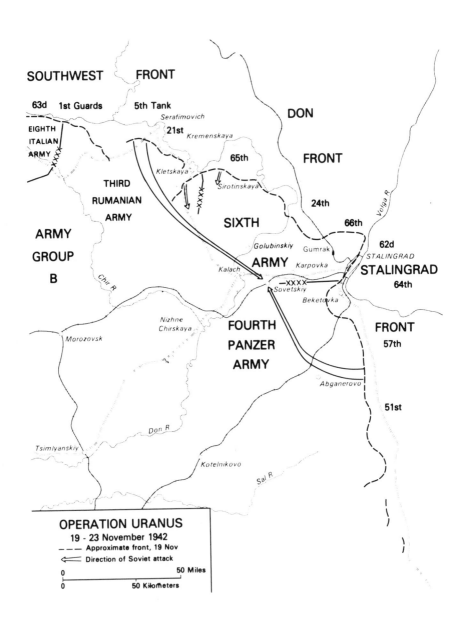

SOUTHWEST FRONT

DON

63d 1st Guards 5th Tank

Serafimovich

EIGHTH
ITALIAN
ARMY
XXXX

21st *Kremenskaya*

Kletskaya

65th

FRONT

THIRD
RUMANIAN
ARMY

Sirotinskaya

XXXX

SIXTH

24th

66th

ARMY
GROUP
B

Chir R

Golubinskiy *Gumrak*

ARMY *Karpovka*

Kalach

62d
STALINGRAD

STALINGRAD

XXXX
Sovetskiy

64th

Beketovka

*Nizhne
Chirskaya*

FOURTH
PANZER
ARMY

FRONT

57th

Morozovsk

Abganerovo

51st

Volga R

Don R

Tsimlyanskiy

Kotelnikovo

Sal R

OPERATION URANUS
19 - 23 November 1942
— — — Approximate front, 19 Nov
⇐ Direction of Soviet attack

0   50 Miles

0   50 Kilometers

for the start of the offensive. After conferring with Vasilevskii, he set the date of 19 November for the Southwest Front and 20 November for the Stalingrad Front.

While Zhukov and Vasilevskii were in Moscow on 13 November, it was decided that Zhukov would coordinate operations of the Kalinin and Western Fronts, timed to begin at about the same time as the one at Stalingrad to prevent the Germans from sending reinforcements from there to shore up the 6th Army. As a result, he was not in the area of the Stalingrad counteroffensive when it was launched on 19 November. Vasilevskii and the General Staff kept him informed about the success of the counteroffensive and about the closing of the inner ring around Stalingrad, the German 6th Army, and elements of the 4th Panzer Army on 23 November. That Zhukov was well informed is evidenced by his response to Stalin's request that he send his considerations on the liquidation of the German troops in the Stalingrad bag. In a message sent from the headquarters of the Kalinin Front on 29 November, Zhukov warned that the enemy would probably attempt to drive a corridor through to the surrounded 6th Army from the vicinity of Kotel'nikovo. He recommended that efforts be made to push the outer ring of the encirclement farther to the west to prevent the Germans from concentrating and driving a corridor into Stalingrad. He suggested that those forces within the encirclement be cut into two groups and the groups be defeated in detail.[25]

The offensive of the Kalinin and Western Fronts began on the 10th of December. The operation was also conceived as a double envelopment, this time of the German forces before Rzhev. The Kalinin Front was successful in breaking through the German positions on its front, but the Western Front, now commanded by I. S. Konev, could not penetrate those on its front. The ring could not be closed, and on Stalin's order Zhukov went to Konev's headquarters to determine why the Western Front had failed to execute its part of the operation. After assessing the situation, Zhukov came to the conclusion that it would be useless to repeat the attack because the enemy had divined the Soviet intention and had brought reserves in from other areas. He also determined that the Western Front command had made an error by underestimating the difficulty of the terrain in the area selected for their main effort. Also, in Zhukov's opinion, the Front had insufficient tanks, artillery, mortars, and aircraft to achieve a breakthrough. During the operation the Germans had managed to cut off and surround a mechanized corps of the Kalinin Front, and it was necessary to bring in a corps from Stalin's reserves to extricate it. Although the operation did not achieve all of its objectives, the Germans were prevented from transferring forces to the Stalingrad front.

Zhukov does not describe his encounters with Konev on this occasion, but considering the personalities involved (Konev reportedly had a bad temper), one can assume that there were some harsh words exchanged, particularly if Zhukov attempted to give Konev a lesson in terrain analysis. Konev had been humiliated when Zhukov intervened with Stalin to prevent his being tried in 1941, and now he was subjected to tutoring, which he unquestionably resented. Konev would not be a Zhukov supporter in the difficulties that lay ahead.

In the meantime, the Germans within the encirclement at Stalingrad offered stubborn resistance to the efforts of the Don and Stalingrad Fronts to liquidate them. And, as Zhukov had predicted, the newly formed German Army Group Don, commanded by Field Marshal Erich von Manstein, began assembling a relief force to break through the Soviet ring and free the entrapped 6th Army. Army Group Don also had the mission of protecting the rear and the prospective escape routes of the German troops engaged in the Caucasus.

The relief force, scraped together from various sectors of the Soviet front, occupied France, and Germany, attacked on 12 December from the vicinity of Kotel'nikovo and managed to reach a point about 30 miles from the southern face of the besieged 6th German Army by the 19th of December. Then and there, according to the Army Group Don commander, Marshal von Manstein, the 6th Army had its best chance of breaking out of the encirclement. It did not take it because the army commander, the future Field Marshal von Paulus, did not believe he had enough fuel for his tanks and, perhaps more importantly, Hitler could not countenance giving up the German position at Stalingrad. As the relief force tried to hold its exposed position to give the 6th Army time to organize a breakout attempt, Soviet pressure on the Army Group's left became so intense that on 23 December it was necessary to divert an armored division from the relief force. The relief force, itself under heavy Soviet pressure, was driven back to its starting positions at Kotel'nikovo by the 8th of January, and the attempt to relieve the 6th Army was, to all intents and purposes, over.[26]

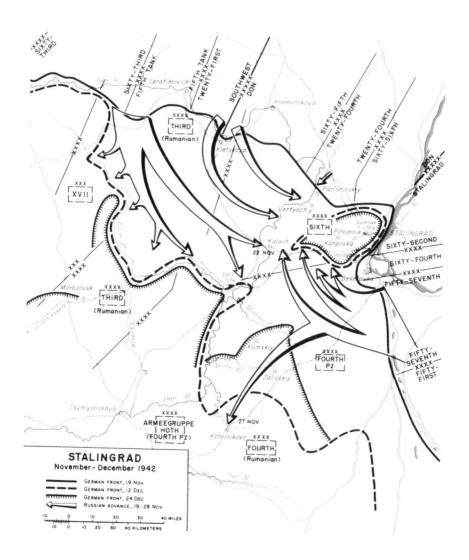

STALINGRAD
November–December 1942

————	GERMAN FRONT, 19 Nov
– – – –	GERMAN FRONT, 12 DEC
⊥⊥⊥⊥⊥⊥	GERMAN FRONT, 24 DEC
⟵	RUSSIAN ADVANCE, 19–28 Nov

10   0   10   20   30   40 MILES
10   0   10   20   30   40 KILOMETERS

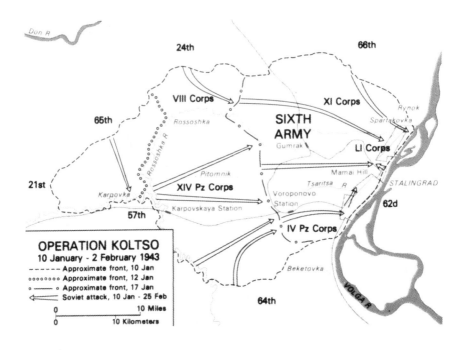

OPERATION KOLTSO
10 January - 2 February 1943
- - - - - Approximate front, 10 Jan
oooooooo Approximate front, 12 Jan
o ———— o Approximate front, 17 Jan
⇐⇐⇐⇐ Soviet attack, 10 Jan - 25 Feb
0   10 Miles
0   10 Kilometers

During these events Zhukov was in Moscow helping Stalin urge the
Soviet forces forward, as it appeared that there was a real possibility
of completing the rout of all the German forces in the south by driving to Rostov and cutting off the German troops in the Caucasus. At
the end of December, Stalin raised the question of combining all the
forces engaged in liquidating the German 6th Army under one commander, because dividing the responsibility between two commanders (of the Don and the Stalingrad Fronts) was interfering with the
completion of the mission. According to Zhukov, "someone" proposed
that the command be given to Rokossovskii. When Stalin asked his
opinion, Zhukov said that both commanders (Eremenko and Rokossovskii)
were worthy but that Eremenko, because he and the Stalingrad Front
had borne the brunt of the defense of the city, would be offended if
he were not given the command. Stalin dismissed this objection out
of hand and ordered the command to be given to Rokossovskii. Zhukov
was told to call both officers and inform them of the decision. When
Eremenko got the news he was so upset that Zhukov told him to call
back after he had composed himself. Fifteen minutes later he called
back and requested that Zhukov call Stalin and ask for reconsidera-

tion. When Zhukov proposed that Eremenko call Stalin himself, Eremenko said he had already tried to talk to Stalin; he had been told that Stalin refused to take the call, because Zhukov was handling all such questions. At Eremenko's request, Zhukov called Stalin, was cursed and ordered to issue an order immediately placing the armies in the Stalingrad Front under Rokossovskii's command. Eremenko would also be one of Zhukov's critics in the future.[27]

Under Rokossovskii's leadership the Don Front completed the destruction of the German 6th Army, whose commander surrendered on the 31st of January (Operation *Kol'tso*). As perhaps no one else could, Zhukov compared the ferocity of the battle to the counteroffensive at Moscow in 1941. He claimed that the German losses were so severe that they had a catastrophic effect on the strategic situation and shook the German war machine to its foundation. From a professional standpoint, he felt that organizing the Stalingrad counteroffensive had given him much more operational experience than the Moscow operation, because in 1941 the Soviets had only limited forces available, which did not permit the planning of the envelopment of large enemy units. For his performance in the great victory Zhukov was honored by being the first to be awarded the Order of Suvorov 1st Class.[28]

NOTES

1. Zhukov, *Memoirs* 2: pp. 276–279.
2. Ibid., p. 280. Shaposhnikov's physical condition and Voznesenskii's doubt are found in Sokolov, "Slovo o Marshale Zhukove," in Smirnov, *"Marshal Zhukov,"* pp. 228, 229.
3. P. N. Pospelov, *Velikaia Otechestvennaia Voina Sovetskogo Soiuza 1941–1945: Kratkaia istoriia* (The Great Fatherland War of the Soviet Union 1941–1945: Short history) (Moscow: Voenizdat, 1967), p. 159 (Hereinafter *Kratkaia istoriia.*) S. M. Shtemenko, *General'nyi shtab v gody voiny* (The General Staff in the war years) (Moscow: Voenizdat, 1968), p. 51.
4. Pospelov, *Kratkaia istoriia,* pp. 159–161.
5. Zhukov, *Memoirs* 2: p. 282.
6. Earl F. Ziemke, "Operation Kreml: Deception, Strategy, and the Fortunes of War," in *Parameters* Vol. 9, no. 1, 1979, pp. 72–83. M. I. Kazakov, *Nad kartoi bylykh srazhenii* (Over the map of bygone battles) (Moscow: Voenizdat, 1965), pp. 126–127. The second edition of this book, which appeared in 1971, provides an example of the different treatments Zhukov received during the Khrushchev and the Brezhnev regimes. In the 1965 edition Kazakov describes an episode (pp. 160, 161) in which Zhukov, as representative of the Stavka, demanded arbitrarily the punishment of an officer for a security violation. In the second edition published in 1971 the episode is not mentioned. During the Khrushchev regime, criticisms of Zhukov and the General Staff were encouraged and published.
7. Pospelov, *IVOVSS* 2: p. 478.
8. Ibid., pp. 419–422.
9. Zhukov, *Memoirs* 2: pp. 278, 293, 294.
10. A. M. Samsonov, *Stalingradskaia bitva* (The Stalingrad battle), 4th ed., (Moscow: Nauka, 1989), pp. 217, 218. Sokolov, "Slovo o Marshale Zhukove" in Smirnov, *Marshal Zhukov,* pp. 232, 233.
11. Zhukov, *Memoirs* 2: pp. 294–299.
12. Ibid., p. 298.
13. Ibid.

14. A. M. Samsonov, *Stalingradskaia bitva* (The Stalingrad battle), Moscow: Nauka, 1960.
15. A. I. Eremenko, *Stalingradskaia bitva* (The Stalingrad Battle) (Stalingrad: Knizhnoe Izdatel'stvo, 1958.)
16. A. I. Eremenko, *Stalingrad* (Stalingrad) (Moscow: Voenizdat, 1961).
17. Eremenko, *Stalingradskaia bitva*, p. 102.
18. Ibid.
19. Eremenko, *Stalingrad*, pp. 38, 326.
20. A. M. Vasilevskii, "Nezabyvaemye dni" (Unforgettable days) in *VIZh*, no. 10 (1965): p. 18. Zhukov, *Memoirs* 2: p. 325.
21. Elena Rzhevskaia, "B tot den', pozdnei osen'iu" (On that day in late autumn) in Smirnov, *Marshal Zhukov*, p. 312.
22. Zhukov, *Memoirs* 2: p. 307.
23. Ibid., p. 306.
24. Ibid., pp. 307, 308.
25. Ibid., pp. 341–342.
26. Erich von Manstein, *Lost Victories* (Chicago: Regnery, 1958), pp. 313–347.
27. Zhukov, *Memoirs* 2: pp. 352, 353.
28. Ibid., p. 358.

XIII

THE BATTLE OF THE KURSK SALIENT, 1943

While Rokossovskii was completing the Stalingrad operation, Zhukov spent the month of January on the Leningrad front. He, along with Voroshilov, was sent to coordinate an offensive of the Leningrad and the Volkhov Fronts, aimed at reopening overland communications between the city and the remainder of Soviet-held territory, which had been broken since the summer of 1941. The two Fronts attacked on 12 January, the Leningrad Front driving east and the Volkhov Front driving west. When the two forces met on the 18th, the Germans had been driven back from the shores of Lake Ladoga far enough to allow construction of a rail and road link to the city on the Neva. On that same day, Zhukov was promoted to the rank of Marshal of the Soviet Union. Two days later, Zhukov and Voroshilov visited the city and were touched that the survivors of the worst days of the blockade did not rebuke them for allowing the city to suffer so long.[1]

In mid-March, Zhukov was at the Northwest Front, which had been commanded by S. K. Timoshenko since shortly after his relief before Stalingrad the previous July. The Front was preparing to make a combat crossing of the Lovat' River, following the liquidation of the Demiansk salient, when Stalin called Zhukov for an update on the operation. Stalin also wanted to inform him of a command change he had made: V. D. Sokolovskii was to relieve Konev as commander of the Western Front. Zhukov provided no reason for this change, but says he took the opportunity to suggest to Stalin that Konev be given command of the Northwest Front and that Timoshenko be sent to the south as representative of the Stavka to "help" the commanders of the Southern and the Southwest Fronts. In effect, as a representative of the Stavka, Timoshenko would be performing functions similar to those he had performed as the axis commander the previous year.

As this conversation is described in the memoirs, Stalin said that he would have Konev call Zhukov for instructions and after that, Zhukov should return to Moscow to consider the situation of the Southwest and the Voronezh Fronts. When Konev called, Zhukov asked him what had happened. Konev knew only that he had been relieved as commander of the Western Front. As Zhukov related it, Konev was pleased with his new assignment to command the Northwest Front and thanked Zhukov for it. The morning of the next day, Zhukov returned to Moscow, apparently not waiting for Konev to arrive at his new headquarters.

This episode seems to be another instance when Zhukov intervened with Stalin to save Konev from demotion or worse. Stalin had been dissatisfied with Konev's performance in December 1942, probably remembering that he had considered having him tried in 1941, and now, in March 1943, had apparently relieved him without assignment. If this were the case, Zhukov may have chosen not to embarrass Konev by giving the details of the relief in his memoirs.[2]*

Zhukov arrived in Moscow late in the evening, after an all-day trip in an all-terrain vehicle over bad roads. He was told to report immediately to the Kremlin, where Stalin was conducting a meeting of those directly concerned with war production. Soviet industry was being strained to meet the demands of the forces and, to quote the memoirs, "The promised help from the USA under Lend-Lease was slow in arriving."[3] This meeting ended at three in the morning, after which Stalin invited Zhukov to dine with him alone, to talk about the situation around Khar'kov.

During the meal, the General Staff officer charged with keeping abreast of the situation on the Voronezh Front came in with a map and reported that enemy counterattacks now threatened the city of Khar'kov. The Germans, after their staggering defeat at Stalingrad, had managed

---

*Konev, in his memoirs, ascribed his "unjust" relief to clashes that he had with Bulganin, a member of the Front Military Council, who made biased reports to Stalin about Konev's performance as Front commander. According to Konev, Stalin later admitted that his relief was unjust. I. S. Konev, *Zapiski komanduiushchego frontom* (Notes of a Front commander) (Moscow: Voenizdat, 1991), pp. 582–585.

to extricate their troops from the Caucasus and stabilize the southern wing of the front along the Mius River. The Voronezh and the Southwest Fronts had seriously misjudged the German intentions, estimating that they were in the process of withdrawing behind the Dnieper. Both Front commanders had urged Stalin to allow them to attempt to crush the retreating enemy before they reached that important water barrier. Stalin and the General Staff had agreed with the conclusions of the field commanders, not realizing that the Germans were regrouping for a counterattack. These faulty assessments of German intentions also failed to consider the exhausted condition of the two Fronts, which had been advancing since late November of the previous year. The loss of Khar'kov was especially difficult for the Soviets to accept because the city had only been retaken from the enemy the previous month.[4]

Stalin ordered Zhukov to fly to the front immediately, telling him he thought that Golikov should be relieved. After Zhukov finished his supper, which he noted was really a breakfast since it was five in the morning, he left for the Ministry of Defense. By 0700, 17 March, he was on his way to the Voronezh Front, where he found that the enemy had already taken Khar'kov and was moving toward Belgorod. By the 18th of March, Belgorod had fallen, but Red Army reserves were blocking further German progress beyond that city. The southern face of what became known as the Kursk salient was delineated by these actions.

Kirill S. Moskalenko, who commanded the 40th Army of the Voronezh Front during these operations, reports that Zhukov, during a visit to Moskalenko's headquarters in late March, criticized the decision to try to defeat the retreating Germans east of the Dnieper. At that time, the Front's capabilities had been drained from its previous operations, and, after the capture of Khar'kov in mid-February, Zhukov felt it should have gone over to the defensive. It would then have been in a better position to defend the city against the German counterattack. Zhukov also criticized Moskalenko for pushing his army far ahead, based on a poorly substantiated decision. Moskalenko writes that Zhukov was not polite but, "I was not insulted: what he said was true."[5]

With the front stabilized, it was determined to "strengthen" the leadership of the Voronezh Front by replacing F. I. Golikov, who had been in command since the previous October, with N. F. Vatutin, the commander of the Southwestern Front. In the memoirs, Zhukov does not directly associate himself with this decision; the event is treated casually, with no discussion of any shortcomings in the Front leadership. But N. Kh. Bedov, the head of Zhukov's personal security detachment, recalled that while at the Voronezh Front, Zhukov, after hearing Golikov's report on the situation, listening to the interrogation of German prisoners of war and visiting troops in contact with the enemy, strongly urged the relief of Golikov. Bedov, who overheard only one side of the conversation, quoted Zhukov as saying, "Golikov is repeating his old errors. At Sukhinichi [during the counterattack at Moscow in 1942] he performed badly, commanding the 10th Army. And now he has committed a more serious miscalculation. We can't kill our troops." L. F. Miniuk, Zhukov's general for special assignments, also reported that Zhukov urged Golikov's relief to the General Staff.[6]

Whatever the truth of the matter, Golikov would never forget it. He blamed Zhukov for what he considered to be an unjust relief, and he would eventually get revenge.

The Kursk salient formed a large bulge on the eastern front stretching around 185 kilometers north to south and 175 kilometers west to east around the city of Kursk. It was reasonable to surmise at the time that the Germans were likely to attempt to reduce the salient. Reduction would enable the Germans, who were hard-pressed for manpower, to shorten their lines. More importantly, the shape of the salient perfectly matched the preferred German operational method—the double envelopment achieved by simultaneous breakthroughs at the base of the salient, to entrap the majority of defenders within the salient. By executing this operation, given the code name *Zitadelle,* the Germans could avenge the loss of the 6th Army at Stalingrad and throw the Soviet high command off balance.

Zhukov assessed German intentions, and on 8 April reported to Stalin that the main enemy effort would be made against three Fronts: the Central Front, which held the longest portion of the salient; the Voronezh Front, holding its southern shoulder; and the Southwestern Front on the southern flank of the Voronezh Front. He recommended reinforcement by antiaircraft and antitank units, particularly on the Central and the Voronezh Fronts, construction of passive defenses, and the assembly of reserves. He also recommended that no attempt be made to preempt the German attack—he wanted the enemy to exhaust itself on the Soviet defenses prior to launching a major counterattack.[7]

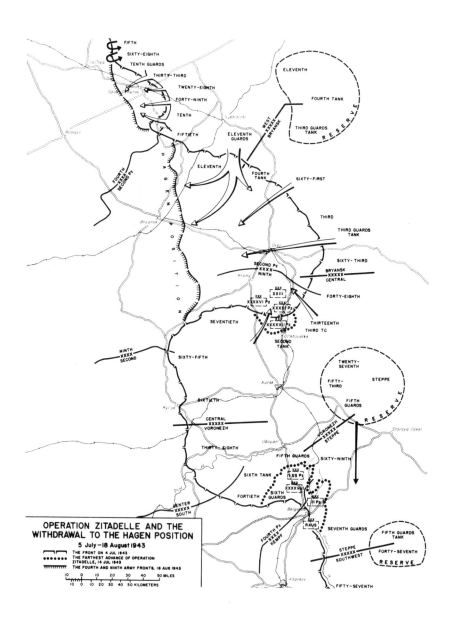

FIFTH
SIXTY-EIGHTH
TENTH GUARDS
THIRTY-THIRD
TWENTY-EIGHTH
FORTY-NINTH
TENTH
FIFTIETH
Spas Demensk
Sukhinichi
ELEVENTH GUARDS
ELEVENTH
Roslavl
FOURTH
XXXXX
SECOND Pz
ELEVENTH
WEST
XXXXX
BRYANSK
FOURTH TANK
SIXTY-FIRST

ELEVENTH
FOURTH TANK
THIRD GUARDS
TANK
R E S E R V E

Bryansk

H A G E N   P O S I T I O N

THIRD
THIRD GUARDS
TANK
Orel
SECOND Pz
XXXX
NINTH
SIXTY-THIRD
Kromy
BRYANSK
XXXXX
CENTRAL
FORTY-EIGHTH

XXX
XXXVI Pz
XXX
XXIII
XXX
XXXXI Pz
XXX
XXXXVII
THIRTEENTH
THIRD TC
Ol'khovatka
SECOND
TANK

SEVENTIETH

NINTH
XXXX
SECOND
SIXTY-FIFTH

TWENTY-
SEVENTH
STEPPE

FIFTY-
THIRD
FIFTH
GUARDS

R E S E R V E

SIXTIETH
Rylsk
CENTRAL
XXXXX
VORONEZH
Oboyan
Staraya Oskol

THIRTY-EIGHTH
Psel
VORONEZH
XXXX
STEPPE
FIFTH GUARDS
SIXTY-NINTH

Kursk

SIXTH TANK
SS Pz
XXXXVIII
SIXTH
GUARDS
FORTIETH
Belgorod
RAUS
SEVENTH GUARDS
FIFTH GUARDS
TANK
FORTY-SEVENTH
R E S E R V E

CENTER
XXXXX
SOUTH
FOURTH Pz
XXXX
KEMPF
STEPPE
XXXXX
SOUTHWEST
FIFTY-SEVENTH
Kharkov

OPERATION ZITADELLE AND THE
WITHDRAWAL TO THE HAGEN POSITION
5 July –18 August 1943

THE FRONT ON 4 JUL 1943
THE FARTHEST ADVANCE OF OPERATION
ZITADELLE, 14 JUL 1943
THE FOURTH AND NINTH ARMY FRONTS, 18 AUG 1943

10   0   10   20   30   40   50 MILES
10   0   10   20   30   40   50 KILOMETERS

In the memoirs, Zhukov's recommendations to Stalin are quoted in full. The recommendations of the Central and the Voronezh Fronts are also provided, the former dated 10 April, the latter dated 12 April. The Central Front recommended an attack by three reinforced Fronts; the Voronezh Front outlined its appreciation of the enemy's intentions and made no operational recommendations except that reserves be prepared and troops brought to a high level of readiness. These estimates, Zhukov takes pains to point out, were the only ones received by the General Staff and the Stavka on the situation around the Kursk salient.[8]

In a six-volume history of the war published during the Khrushchev regime, Zhukov's prescient appraisal of the German intentions was not mentioned. An excerpt from the Voronezh Front (Khrushchev became a member of the Front Military Council in February 1943) appraisal of the situation, dated 21 April, is provided which recommended an operation to destroy the enemy air capabilities and also preparations to meet "massed tank attacks." After the enemy had exhausted itself on the Soviet defenses, "choosing the favorable moment, the Red Army would go over to the counteroffensive and conclusively destroy him." A one-sentence paragraph provided the information that Marshals Vasilevskii and Zhukov were to coordinate the operations of the Fronts involved.[9]

By mid-April, a preliminary decision had been made to take up a deliberate defense and await the German offensive. However, it was not until early June that Stalin made the final decision to remain on the defensive, allow the enemy to exhaust himself on the deeply echeloned Red Army defenses, and then launch a counterattack. In the interim he wavered, wondering if the army was in condition to withstand the anticipated blow or whether it would allow the Germans to repeat their successes of 1941 and 1942. At least one of his Front commanders, Vatutin, supported by Khrushchev, recommended that a preemptive attack be launched in the Belgorod-Khar'kov area. This proposal was opposed by Zhukov and the General Staff.

In the meantime, vigorous preparations were under way to strengthen the field forces. Changes were made in their organizational structure and by the summer of 1943, five tank armies and eighteen heavy tank regiments had been created. The air force was also strengthened, both in numbers and in quality, with new planes. Each Front was now supported by an air army of 700–800 aircraft, making the Soviets numerically superior to the *Luftwaffe* on the Eastern front.[10] And, perhaps most importantly, the Steppe Front, commanded by I. S. Konev, was formed behind the salient to provide the defenders with a formidable reserve.

The losses suffered by the Red Army during the first two years of the war had also forced the Soviets to review the tables of organization for headquarters, rear services units, and enterprises. The resultant reductions freed 1.3 million men for combat service. The position of deputy commander for political affairs at the company level was abolished and the political staffs at higher levels were reduced. In the course of the year 1943, 122,000 political workers were transferred to line command positions.[11] In his memoirs, Zhukov commented on this reorganization of the political apparatus, saying only that it permitted Communists in the lower echelons more concrete leadership roles. He did not comment on the obvious increase in the available pool of junior combat leaders, but it may be that he remembered it when he faced a manpower problem as minister of defense in 1955.[12]

Hitler also wavered. Originally planned for mid-April, then postponed until sometime after the 28th, then the 12th of June, as Hitler waited for the delivery to the front of new tanks and pondered the effect of the German and Italian defeats in North Africa, *Zitadelle* finally was launched on the 5th of July. By that time the chances for exploiting the temporary Soviet weakness demonstrated at Khar'kov and Belgorod in the spring had long passed.[13]

While the two dictators were making up their minds, Zhukov was dispatched to the North Caucasus Front. Stalin was dissatisfied with the progress the Front was making toward accomplishing its mission. It had been established on 23 January under the command of General I. I. Maslennikov and given the mission of joining the Southern Front and encircling and destroying German Army Group "A" in the North Caucasus. German Army Group "A" was withdrawing under Soviet pressure from the positions it had reached in the summer and fall of 1942. The successful Soviet counterattack at Stalingrad had exposed the army group's lines of communication, and Stalin was impatient to cut them and gain another resounding victory. By mid-April, the German 17th Army (part of Army Group "A") had stiffened its position in the Novorossiisk area and was making local counterattacks on land, at sea, and in the air. The Germans were holding the Taman' Peninsula, almost a land bridge to the Crimea. In the Soviet General Staff, planners were concerned that the Germans were considering a counterattack, and Soviet failures were blamed, in part, on the Front leadership.

Zhukov's party, which included the commander in chief of the Air Force A. A. Novikov, the People's Commissar of the Navy N. G. Kuznetsov, and S. M. Shtemenko, representing the General Staff, arrived at the Front headquarters at Krasnodar on 18 April. There Zhukov met with the Front commander and three of his army commanders whose troops were mired in the inundated fields of the Kuban'-Azov lowland. The narrow paths through the fields were easily covered by enemy small arms, and only small, specially equipped detachments could operate over this terrain under such conditions.

Zhukov, after hearing the commanders, decided that the military decision would be sought south of the Kuban'. The next day, Zhukov met with the commander of the 56th Army, which was operating in that area. That army, commanded by Andrei Antonovich Grechko, the future minister of defense (1967–1976), was preparing to launch an attack to seize Krymskoi. Zhukov postponed the attack for five days, allowing additional ammunition, fuel, heavy artillery, and "a special division of the NKVD" to arrive. During those five days the Soviets achieved local air superiority, and Zhukov visited the corps and divisions and looked at everything "with his own eyes."[14] He ordered the construction of dugouts near the headquarters of the 56th Army, so that the visitors from Moscow could be closer to the action and not have to commute from Krasnodar; he also proposed that he and the Front commander have their observation post with the 56th Army.

The plight of the bridgehead that had been seized in February and was being held by assault troops of the 18th Army on Myskhako, a cape south of Novorossiisk, was not overlooked. On Zhukov's orders, the navy devoted additional assets to transferring supplies and ammunition to the bridgehead, which was separated by water from the main body of the Front. In Soviet parlance such a bridgehead is referred to as *malaia zemlia* (literally "small land or small earth"). During the Brezhnev era, this phase of the operation was given increased emphasis by Soviet military historians because Leonid Brezhnev, then a political officer with the 18th Army, was often in the bridgehead and "knew the thoughts and hopes of the troops. He knew how to support them, to instill confidence, courage, and optimism."[15]

On one occasion the small craft transporting Brezhnev struck a mine and he was thrown into the sea. He was saved by the "bravery and resourcefulness" of Soviet sailors.[16] While Zhukov was struggling with his editors and the censors to get his memoirs published, he was pressured to allow the insertion of a sentence stating that during his time with the North Caucasus Front he had wanted to confer with Brezhnev about the critical situation of the troops in the bridgehead but that Brezhnev could not be reached because he happened to be in the bridgehead at that time.[17] Zhukov accepted the insertion with a bitter laugh saying, "The wise will understand" [why the reference to Brezhnev had to be included].[18]

The attack that Zhukov organized was not launched until 29 April, and it encountered stiff German resistance. The strongly defended town of Krymskoi was taken on 4 May, but other strong points along the Kuban' River remained in enemy hands. The Soviet attackers eventually determined that they had moved up to what the Germans called "the Blue Line," a fortified belt protecting the Taman' Peninsula. Another five months and further reinforcements would be required to clear it.

The representatives of the Stavka returned to Moscow on 15 May, expecting to encounter the wrath and rebukes of Stalin, but Shtemenko reports that the dictator's reaction was relatively mild. He was content to replace the Front commander.[19] Zhukov did not comment on his own feelings in respect to the operation, but he could not count it as one of his notable successes.

After returning to Moscow in mid-May, Zhukov spent most of his time with the troops of the Voronezh and the Central Fronts. On 30 June, Stalin ordered him to remain on the Orel' axis, where the German main effort was expected, to coordinate the operations of the Central, Briansk, and Western Fronts. Vasilevskii was ordered to coordinate the operations on the southern face of the salient, the Voronezh Front. As it turned out, the German main effort was made against the Voronezh Front.

On the evening of 4 July, Zhukov was in the headquarters of the Central Front with its commander, K. K. Rokossovskii, when he received word from Vasilevskii that a captured German soldier had revealed under interrogation that the German offensive would start at dawn on 5 July. A prisoner taken by the Central Front around 0200 that morning confirmed that information, adding that the attack was scheduled to begin around 0300. Rokossovskii asked Zhukov whether this should be reported to the Stavka or whether an order should be issued to start the counter-artillery preparation. Zhukov ordered the preparation to begin and telephoned Stalin to inform him of his decision.

The Soviet counter-artillery preparation began at 0220 and caught the attackers as they were forming for the attack, which did not begin until 0530. Some units were taken by surprise and the initial attacks seemed disorganized and uncoordinated. But Zhukov admitted that despite the months of planning and intelligence collection available to the defenders, much of the Soviet fire was ineffective because it was area fire and not aimed at definite targets. Zhukov also concluded that the counter-preparation had been launched perhaps thirty to forty minutes early.[20] The captured German soldier may have confused reveille with the attack time.

The German attacks on the first day gained three to six kilometers in some places against the Central Front. The next day some of these gains were enlarged to ten kilometers at the cost of heavy losses in tanks and personnel. By 9 July, Zhukov could inform Stalin that the enemy did not have the strength to break through the defenses of the Central Front. Stalin inquired if it were not time to bring the Briansk Front and the left wing of the Western Front into action. Zhukov agreed, saying that an attack by these forces would prevent the Germans from accomplishing a badly needed reorganization. Those troops attacked on 12 July in the general direction of Orel', forcing the Germans to transfer units attacking the Central Front to reinforce their left flank. On 15 July, the Central Front joined the counterattack and, from Zhukov's viewpoint, the long-planned German general offensive had collapsed.[21]

While directing the operations on the northern face of the salient, Zhukov maintained continuous direct contact with Vasilevskii on the southern face. It soon became evident that in the area of Belgorod the German offensive was being led by generals with greater initiative and experience. Here Zhukov allowed himself a rare compliment for his enemy, "This was really the case. General–Field Marshal Manstein headed these forces."[22]

Manstein's appraisal of the battle on the southern face was that the Soviets by 13 July had suffered heavy losses—24,000 prisoners of war, 1,800 tanks, 267 artillery pieces, and 1,080 antitank guns—and that the battle was at its climax. At just this point Hitler ordered that Zitadelle be discontinued. He told his generals that the Western Allies had landed in Sicily, and since the Italians were not even attempting to fight, the next step might well be a landing in the Balkans or in southern Italy. Two new armies had to be formed, and these forces would be drawn from the Eastern Front. Manstein protested that breaking off the battle at that point was throwing away a victory. Hitler ruled against him, and he was soon ordered to hand over several armored divisions to the Central Army Group.[23]

Zhukov was at the command post of the Briansk Front on 12 July, where he was reached by Stalin and ordered to fly to the vicinity of Prokhorovka to undertake coordination of the operations of the Voronezh and the Steppe Fronts. The latter Front, commanded by General I. S. Konev, was in reserve behind the salient and, as Zhukov reiterates, had long been part of the long-planned, seven-Front counteroffensive that was to start when the Germans had been shattered on the Soviet defenses. Zhukov does not explain why his presence was necessary to coordinate what should have already been coordinated.[24] A possible explanation is that the crisis in the battle on the 12th had been felt in Moscow, and Stalin wanted his most experienced and reliable troubleshooter on the scene.

Reviewing this phase of the battle, Zhukov defended the initial dispositions that N. F. Vatutin, assisted by Vasilevskii, had made on the southern face of the salient. A history of Soviet participation in the war, published by the Ministry of Defense in 1965, attributed the early success of the German offensive in this area to a miscalculation of the direction of the German main effort by the command of the Voronezh Front. Zhukov provides his own list of the various factors involved: length of defended front; density of artillery and tanks per kilometer of front; and the location of reserves, to show that the calculations given in the short history were not correct. Vatutin, according to Zhukov, was a highly erudite and courageous commander.[25]

Zhukov also applied a corrective to the claims put forth by P. A. Rotmistrov that his 5th Guards Tank Army played the deciding role in destroying the armored forces of German Army Group South. According to Zhukov the claim was "immodest and it was not quite that way." The attackers had been worn down by the other armies of the Front and delayed by Soviet artillery and air forces in the previous battles. Hence Rotmistrov's army dealt with a very weakened German force, which had lost faith in the possibility of a successful conclusion of the battle. Zhukov also makes no mention of the claim that the battle was the largest armored engagement in history. He was probably referring to Rotmistrov's 106-page soft-cover brochure describing the battle, published in 1960. It provides a popularized account of what was probably the largest armored engagement of the war, in which over 1200 armored vehicles participated. Rotmistrov claimed that in the period 12–16 July his army destroyed or damaged 459 enemy tanks. The brochure may have also annoyed Zhukov because of the senior officers mentioned in the brochure; Nikita Khrushchev, member of the Military Council of the Voronezh Front at the time, is mentioned several times and is pictured in three of the brochure's eleven illustrations.[26]

As it became clear that Zitadelle had failed, Stalin became impatient to launch the full-scale counteroffensive, but was persuaded by Vasilevskii and Zhukov to delay its start for eight days while preparations were made: the troops of the Voronezh and Steppe Fronts refueled and resupplied, coordination established within the arms and services, intelligence collected and analyzed, and certain changes made in the organization for combat. Zhukov comments that Stalin was like a temperamental boxer who would get excited and want to give battle without regard to the time required to prepare. The Steppe Front required time to work out the specifics of its role in the counteroffensive. The Front had been in reserve and had to plan for its commitment wherever the battle in the Kursk salient dictated. Now the Front was given the mission of retaking Belgorod and then moving on to Khar'kov in coordination with the Voronezh Front. The attack of the two Fronts began on 3 August; Khar'kov was recaptured by units of the Steppe Front on the 22d.

The recapture of Khar'kov marked the end of one of the largest battles of the Second World War. Zhukov considered that the losses inflicted on the German forces in the battle—500,000 men, 1,500 tanks, 3,000 guns, and 3,700 aircraft—could not be replaced by an exhausted Germany. The end of the war was now only a matter of time. The Germans could conduct only defensive operations, although they might at times attempt counterattacks. Zhukov expected the Germans to defend stubbornly the Don Basin and what the Russians call the "left bank" Ukraine, that is, the part of the Ukraine that lies east of the Dnieper River.[27]

NOTES

1. Zhukov, *Memoirs,* 1st ed., pp. 461, 462. For some reason, possibly an editorial error, this episode is not mentioned in the 10th edition.
2. Zhukov, *Memoirs,* 10th ed., 3: pp. 8, 9.
3. *Memoirs* 3: p. 9.
4. A. M. Vasilevskii, *Delo vsei zhizni* (The business of an entire lifetime) (Moscow: Voenizdat, 5th edition, 1984), pp. 262–264.
5. K. S. Moskalenko, *Na Iugo-zapadnom napravlenii* (On the Southwestern Axis) (Moscow: Nauka, 1969), p. 450.
6. *Memoirs* 3: p. 10. N. Kh. Bedov, "Riadom s marshalom" (Along with the marshal) in Mirkina and Iarovikov, *Marshal Zhukov: Polkovodets,* p. 168. Sokolov, "Slovo o Marshale Zhukove" in Smirnov, *Marshal Zhukov,* p. 252.
7. Zhukov, *Memoirs* 3: pp. 13, 14, 15.
8. Ibid., pp. 13–21.
9. Pospelov, *IVOVSS* 3: pp. 246–250.
10. Zhukov, *Memoirs* 3: pp. 23–31.
11. M. V. Zakharov, chmn. ed. comm. *50 let Vooruzhennykh Sil SSSR* (50 years of the Armed Forces of the USSR) (Moscow: Voenizdat, 1968), pp. 333–338.
12. Zhukov, *Memoirs* 3: p. 28.
13. Earl F. Ziemke, *Stalingrad to Berlin: The German Defeat in the East* (Washington, D.C.: U.S. Government Printing Office, 1968), pp. 118–135.
14. Shtemenko, *General'nyi shtab,* pp. 67–85.
15. Grechko, *IVMV* 6: pp. 101, 102.
16. A. A. Grechko, *Bitva za Kavkaz* (The battle for the Caucasus) Moscow: Voenizdat, 2d ed., 1969, p. 323.
17. Zhukov, *Memoirs,* 1st ed., p. 477.
18. Pavlenko, "Razmyshleniia" *VIZh,* no. 11: p. 20. According to A. D. Mirkina, the Brezhnev insertion was removed from Zhukov's seventh and subsequent editions. Mirkina and Iarovikov, *Marshal Zhukov: Polkovodets,* p. 72.
19. Shtemenko, *General'nyi shtab,* pp. 88, 89.
20. Zhukov, *Memoirs* 3: pp. 43–46.

21. Ibid., pp. 48–51.
22. Ibid., p. 49.
23. Manstein, *Lost Victories,* pp. 448, 449.
24. Zhukov, *Memoirs* 3: pp. 53, 54.
25. Ibid., pp. 55, 56. The criticism is found in Pospelov, *Kratkaia istoriia,* p. 244.
26. Zhukov, *Memoirs* 3: p. 57. P. A. Rotmistrov, *Tankovoye srazhenie pod Prokhorovkoi* (The tank battle near Prokhorovka) (Moscow: Voenizdat, 1960).
27. Zhukov, *Memoirs* 3: pp. 58–75.

XIV

THE BATTLES FOR THE UKRAINE, 1943

The Voronezh and Steppe Fronts had not completed the recapture of Khar'kov when Stalin and the General Staff began planning the objectives of the campaigns for the fall and winter of 1943. For Stalin the objectives were clear. He wanted the two Fronts to continue the offensive immediately by means of frontal attacks to prevent the Germans from organizing defenses on the approaches to the Dnieper. Aleksei I. Antonov, then first deputy chief of the General Staff, during visits to the front told Zhukov of the Supreme High Commander's intention. Zhukov proposed instead an operation designed to cut off and envelop the German forces in the Don Basin. Antonov admitted that he personally agreed with Zhukov, but that Stalin believed that type of operation required more time than a series of frontal attacks. Nevertheless, Zhukov asked Antonov to pass his considerations to Stalin and to advise the dictator that the two Fronts were in need of personnel replacements and equipment replenishment.

Several days later Stalin called Zhukov to let him know that he had given instructions that reinforcements and tanks be furnished the two Fronts. However, he did not share Zhukov's view of how the next campaign should be conducted because Zhukov's plan would take too much time. Zhukov tried to argue with him, sensing that Stalin's mind was not yet set on a frontal offensive. But Stalin closed the conversation, stressing the need to reach the Dnieper speedily.

When Zhukov reported to Moscow on 25 August, the decision had been made. His proposals had been rejected, and the directives ordering the continuation of the offensive according to Stalin's conception had already been distributed to the field forces. After a discussion, led by Antonov, of the objectives that were to be assigned the various Fronts, the only issue to be resolved was the degree to which they were to be replenished and reinforced for the operation. In making these decisions, Stalin was in effect deciding where the main effort would be made.

Zhukov initially discussed the needs of the Voronezh and the Steppe Fronts with Marshal of Armored Troops Fedorenko, Marshal of Artillery Iakovlev, and General Smorodinov, representing the directorate responsible for providing unit replacements (*Glavupravform*). Then Zhukov reported his requirements directly to Stalin.

> The Supreme High Commander looked at his table of available armaments and that which I had earmarked for the Fronts. Then, taking, as usual, a blue pencil, he reduced all almost 30 to 40 per cent. "The remainder," he said, "the Stavka will give when the Fronts approach the Dnieper."[1]

The detailed directives for the two Fronts that Zhukov was coordinating were issued on 6 September. They were to continue the offensive with the objective of reaching the middle reaches of the Dnieper and establishing bridgeheads on the west bank of the river. There was no time for a detailed preparation in the field for the offensive. Zhukov believed the troops were very weary from the continuous previous battles, and there had been interruptions in the flow of supplies to the front. But, according to Zhukov, the troops (from private to marshal) "burned" with the desire to eject the enemy from their land.[2]

The offensive developed very slowly, but driven by incentives—a promise to the commanders of units making combat crossings of the Desna of the award of an Order of Suvorov, and for crossings of the Dnieper the granting of the title of Hero of the Soviet Union—the Fronts by the end of September had forced the Dnieper in a number of places and had secured bridgeheads from which further advances to the west could be launched.[3]

In the dash to the Dnieper, the city of Kiev, standing high on the west bank of the river, was an objective of significance for both sides. The Voronezh Front attempted to take the city with a blow from the Bukrinsk bridgehead south of the city and a secondary effort from the Liutezh bridgehead north of the city. German opposition around the

Bukrinsk bridgehead, however, was too strong, so the main effort was made from the Liutezh bridgehead, which involved transferring forces from the southern bridgehead to the one north of the city. The 3d Guards Tank Army, for example, in order to get in position for the assault made a 200-kilometer march parallel to the enemy's front, crossed the Dnieper twice, from west to east and then back, and also crossed the Desna. Zhukov notes that bad weather prevented enemy air surveillance, but it also hindered the movement of tanks and other heavy equipment. The assault began slowly on 3 and 4 November but by 6 November Kiev was considered to be in Soviet hands. At 0900 on the sixth, Zhukov, together with the Military Council of the 1st Ukrainian Front (including Khrushchev, whom Zhukov does not name), rode through the cheering crowds in the city.[4]*

The Steppe Front in the meantime had seized a bridgehead over the Dnieper on 30 September, which had been enlarged and joined with other bridgeheads including those of the 3rd Ukrainian Front south of Cherkassy. By the end of December the bridgehead stretched 400 kilometers along the front and was 100 kilometers in depth. The German situation in the Ukraine was in a crisis, and the emptiness of the claim that the Dnieper would provide the foundation of a defensive bastion— the "East Wall"—had been exposed for the propaganda that it was.

To rectify the situation the Germans attempted two serious counterattacks: one in mid-November against the 1st Ukrainian Front, in which they succeeded in recapturing Zhitomir and moving 30 to 40 kilometers east of the city; and another later in the month, which drove the 2d Ukrainian Front back 25 kilometers in some areas. In both instances the counterattacks were halted by the commitment of reserves, artillery reinforcements, and air support. By the end of December both sides had assumed defensive postures.

During this lull in operations, Zhukov was recalled to Moscow, where a broad review of the overall situation on the eastern front and in the world was conducted by what Zhukov described as an expanded ses-

*The Voronezh and Steppe Fronts were renamed the 1st and 2d Ukrainian Fronts on 20 October 1943.

sion of the State Defense Committee "with the participation of certain members of the Stavka of the Supreme High Command."[5] N. A. Voznesenskii briefed the group on the state of the Soviet war economy on behalf of the State Defense Committee, Vasilevskii and Antonov of the General Staff discussed the military situation, and Stalin himself addressed the international situation and the prospects for a second front. By the end of 1943, the Soviets had reclaimed more than half of the territory the Germans had overrun in 1941 and 1942. In so doing, the Soviet Army had inflicted losses on the Wehrmacht to the point where it could no longer conduct serious offensive operations. The German strategic posture had been reduced to conducting an active defense. The Soviet armed forces had been strengthened by the improved production and delivery to the troops of tanks and self-propelled and conventional artillery. The 1943 victories had been achieved with a vastly improved command and control system. Complex operations were now planned and executed with a confidence and a competence that were absent in the early phases of the war.[6]

The intensity of the military operations of the first two and a half years of war had taken its toll on those most directly involved in their execution. Zhukov thought that Vasilevskii looked tired. He and Zhukov had been operating under similar conditions since April, moving behind the front over roads torn up by massive movements of troops, heavy equipment, and supplies, or flying at low altitudes from headquarters to headquarters in liaison-type aircraft and landing at temporary landing fields. Added to the physical discomfort and the danger were the effect of numerous sleepless nights and the tension of the rapid and violent changes in the military situation. The cumulative effect of these stresses was particularly noticeable to Zhukov in the quiet of a Moscow office, where the noise of aircraft, artillery, and alarming reports from the front was absent. He does not admit directly that he evidenced the same combat fatigue, although this diversion from his account of events suggests that he was indeed experiencing the same symptoms.[7]

After the war Zhukov's chauffeur estimated that he had driven 175,000 kilometers behind the front with Zhukov. Zhukov added that he had worn out three aircraft. He did not mention that he had been almost hit by a mortar round during the battle of Kursk. The round had exploded so close to him that his hearing was permanently impaired. Being a representative of the Stavka or a Front commander was not a risks free occupation. Kirponos, the Southwest Front commander in 1941, Vatutin, the 1st Ukrainian Front commander in 1944, and Cherniakhovskii, the 3d Belorussian Front commander, were all killed. Rokossovskii was wounded, and Vasilevskii was hurt when his vehicle ran over a land mine.

Notes

1. Zhukov, *Memoirs* 3: pp. 79, 80.
2. Ibid.
3. Ibid., p. 83.
4. Ibid., pp. 83–85.
5. Ibid., p. 89.
6. Ibid., pp. 89–92.
7. Ibid., p. 89.

XV

THE 1944 CAMPAIGNS

During their sojourn in Moscow, Zhukov and Vasilevskii had dinner with Stalin several times in his quarters in the Kremlin. On one occasion Zhukov had the opportunity to raise again the question of the double envelopment, knowing full well that the dictator had been opposed to the employment of such tactics during the operations that cleared the east bank of the Ukraine. To his surprise, Stalin responded that, with the Soviet Army now more experienced and stronger, "We not only can but we must conduct encirclement operations." Zhukov stated in his memoirs that he and Vasilevskii were happy that at last the CINC understood the significance of offensive operations designed to encircle the enemy. This comment was excised from the first nine editions.[1]

When Zhukov returned to the front in late December he continued to coordinate the operations of the 1st and 2d Ukrainian Fronts. On the 24th of December, a reinforced 1st Ukrainian Front attacked in the direction of Zhitomir and Berdichev. The initial artillery and air preparation was so successful that two tank armies could be committed to the battle during the second half of the first day. By 30 December the 1st Ukrainian Front had torn a hole in the German lines 300 kilometers wide and 100 kilometers deep. Zhitomir and Berdichev were taken on the next day. A German counterattack drove the Soviets back some 30 kilometers, and the front stabilized briefly by mid-January along the line Sarny-Slavuta-Kazatin-Il'intsy.

On 7 January Zhukov visited the 2d Ukrainian Front, the left flank of which was attacking Kirovograd, which was taken the next day. On the Front's right flank, however, German resistance blocked further progress. Zhukov decided to halt operations and prepare the two Fronts to encircle the enemy formations, which formed a salient that was blocking the further forward movement of both Fronts. The salient was given the name of a town at its approximate center, Korsun'-Shevchenkovskii. Zhukov reckoned there were adequate Soviet forces available in the two fronts to achieve an encirclement aimed at the base of the salient. His recommendations for the operation were approved by the Stavka and the necessary directives were issued on 12 January.

An unseasonal thaw hindered preparations for the attack which finally was launched on 24 January. By 28 January the encirclement had been completed in spite of several fierce German counterattacks. The surrounded German forces in the pocket, unlike those at Stalingrad, continued to attempt to break out, while organizing attacks against the Soviets defending the outer face of the encirclement. On 9 February they refused Zhukov's ultimatum to surrender.

Zhukov was awakened from a sound sleep (he had been attempting to recover from an attack of grippe accompanied by a high fever) on 12 February to answer a call from Stalin. Konev, the 2d Ukrainian Front commander, had reported to him that the Germans had achieved a breakthrough on the 1st Ukrainian Front. Zhukov was not aware of the situation, but when he called Vatutin he was told that the Germans had penetrated only one or two kilometers and had then been halted. When he reported the facts to Stalin, the latter cursed him and Vatutin, saying that Konev had proposed taking command of all the forces on the internal front of the encirclement and completing the final liquidation of the Germans in the pocket. Zhukov attempted to point out to Stalin that the operation would be completed in three or four days without taking the complex step of resubordinating to Konev an army of Vatutin's Front; in spite of this a directive giving Konev command of the entire internal front was received within a couple of hours.[2]

As soon as Vatutin received the directive he called Zhukov, assuming that the new command arrangements had been ordered on his recommendation. Zhukov did not tell him that the idea had originated with Konev, nor did he mention his conversation with Stalin. Vatutin was particularly upset because he knew the 2d Ukrainian Front would receive credit for the operation and be saluted in Moscow when the victory was announced. And this was indeed the case. On 18 February, when the salute was fired in Moscow, it was fired in honor of the

2d Ukrainian Front. The 1st Ukrainian Front was not mentioned. Zhukov was at a loss to explain Stalin's motivation for committing what he considered to be "an unforgivable error."[3]

Stalin's anger and desire to punish Vatutin, and through him Zhukov, may have derived from his impatience with the length of time it was taking to liquidate the encircled Germans. Although the dictator had given Zhukov to believe that he was more favorably inclined toward encirclements, Zhukov told Konstantin Simonov that Stalin never forgot that the military had told him at Stalingrad that the operation would take one month after the pocket was closed, but that instead it took two or three months to complete. Zhukov also recalled that later in 1944, when Soviet troops were moving toward Chernovtsy and Proskurov, Stalin said that he sensed an encirclement was being planned. When he asked how long the operation would take he was told about a month. Recalling Stalingrad, he immediately told Zhukov to drive the enemy off Soviet territory without taking the time to encircle them, so that the spring planting could begin.

The last desperate efforts of the trapped Wehrmacht to escape were beaten back on 17 February. According to Zhukov, only a few tanks and personnel carriers loaded with generals, officers, and SS troops managed to avoid capture or death. According to Manstein, between 30 and 32 thousand troops came out of the pocket, the better part of six and one half divisions. However, after the ordeal of coming through the Soviet cordon under abominable weather conditions, the morale of the troops was so bad that they had to be pulled out of the line temporarily.[4]

When Zhukov returned to Moscow to report on the operation, he found that Stalin was impatient to resume the offensive and drive the invaders from Soviet soil. Zhukov was ordered to return to the 1st and 2d Ukrainian Fronts. He arrived at Vatutin's headquarters on 21 February, after staying in Moscow two days, and began preparations for an offensive in the general direction of Chernovtsy. The 2d Ukrainian Front was to attack toward Iassy. A complete spring thaw was in progress, rendering the task of resupplying the forward elements extremely difficult. The Russian word for the situation, *rasputitsa*, literally, the time of the year when the roads are impassable, probably gives a better understanding of the conditions than the impression left by the English word "thaw."

Zhukov was still at Vatutin's headquarters on the 28th of February when, after a two-hour conference with Zhukov, Vatutin decided to visit the headquarters of two of his frontline armies. Zhukov advised him to send his deputies to the armies, but Vatutin, saying that he had not visited those armies in some time, insisted on going himself. The next day he and his security detachment were ambushed by a band of Ukrainian separatists while en route from one army headquarters to another. Vatutin received a wound that was to be fatal even though he managed to survive evacuation to Kiev. He died there on 15 April, despite the ministrations of N. N. Burdenko, one of the Soviet Union's most eminent surgeons. Zhukov assumed command of the Front.[5]

The next phase of the offensive began on 4 March. According to Zhukov, the Germans were taken by surprise, since they assumed the Soviets could not resume the offensive in such weather conditions. According to Manstein, however, this was not the case. The Germans expected the Soviets would resume the attack because, for one reason, the mud affected the Soviet Army to a lesser extent than it did the German Army. Soviet tank tracks were wider than those of German tanks and "enormous numbers of American trucks had made their appearance on the enemy side. As they were still able to drive over open country . . . the enemy was also able to move the infantry of his tank and mechanized corps quickly."[6]

The German front was penetrated, and by 7 March two Soviet armies had pushed through the breach. To restore the situation, the Germans counterattacked, resulting in a battle the fierceness of which Zhukov claimed had not been seen since the battle of the Kursk salient. This battle lasted for eight days, until the Soviets, reinforced by a tank army, broke the German resistance. By 21 March the Soviets were moving rapidly to the south. On 29 March the city of Chernovtsy had been cleared of the invaders, and by the end of the month, twenty-three German divisions were surrounded by four Soviet armies, which were themselves in a weakened condition from their losses in the preceding battles. This encirclement was a result of developments on the battlefield and was not a planned Cannae. Some Germans managed to break out of the encirclement on 4 April, but Zhukov admits that he had no accurate count of the numbers of troops and equipment evacuated. By 12 April another pocket of German troops surrounded in Ternopol' was liquidated and the campaign was considered completed. The right bank of the Dnieper had been cleared of the invaders and the offensive had carried the Red Army to the Soviet border with Romania. On 2 April Manstein, one of the Wehrmacht's most capable field commanders, was relieved by Hitler.

For his leadership in the campaign Zhukov was awarded the first medal struck of the Order of Victory.[7]

NOTES

1. Zhukov, *Memoirs* 3: pp. 95, 96.
2. Ibid., pp. 102–112.
3. Ibid., pp. 113–115.
4. Manstein, *Lost Victories,* pp. 516, 517. Zhukov, *Memoirs* 3: p. 114.
5. Zhukov, *Memoirs* 3: pp. 115–118.
6. Manstein, *Lost Victories,* p. 524.
7. Zhukov, *Memoirs* 3: pp. 118–121. Manstein, *Lost Victories,* p. 546.

XVI

THE BELORUSSIAN AND UKRAINIAN CAMPAIGNS OF 1944

Zhukov returned to Moscow in early May. I. S. Konev took command of the 1st Ukrainian Front, but Zhukov, who claimed to be anxious to commence planning for the next major operation—driving the Germans out of Belorussia—did not await his arrival at Front headquarters. Instead he passed his good wishes and considerations on future operations of the Front to Konev through V. D. Sokolovskii, the Front's chief of staff. Stalin, when he approved the change of command, had told Zhukov that the Front remained his charge as representative of the Stavka. Zhukov does not explain why he was in such haste to return to Moscow. The start of the next operation, which would have the code name "Bagration," was over a month away, and common courtesy would seem to have required that Zhukov be present to hand over his command to his successor.[1] His haste may have been due to his feeling that he had proprietary rights to the conception and planning of operations in Belorussia because of his almost six years of prewar service there.

The decision to make the defeat and removal of the German occupiers from Belorussia the next major Soviet operation had been made by the Stavka on 12 April. Later that same month Zhukov had outlined his views on the campaign to Stalin and the chief of the General Staff, A. I. Antonov. Prior to that meeting, Antonov had told Zhukov, confidentially, what troop and equipment reserves were being established prior to the Belorussian campaign. This confidence was in violation of the dictator's strict prohibition against giving out this information lest anyone be overzealous in asking for reinforcements.[2] Zhukov was one of the more avid petitioners for help and may have been the prime influence behind the dictator's policy.

By May of 1944, the Wehrmacht position in Belorussia bulged toward the east, as they clung to Vitebsk, Mogilev, Zhlobin, and Pinsk. The center of their position was Minsk, on the direct route to Brest, War- saw, and Berlin. The bulge was not so pronounced that it could be called a salient and it differed also in that the Pripiat' Marshes paralleled the southern face of the bulge, a geographical circumstance that discour- aged any thought of a Soviet attempt to execute a double envelopment in the manner the Germans had attempted unsuccessfully at Kursk.

German intelligence became convinced that the Soviet summer offensive would be aimed somewhere south of the Pripiat' Marshes—probably against the front of Army Group North Ukraine, commanded by Walter Model. The Soviet buildup for the attack on Army Group Center, the German defenders in Belorussia, began early in May. The buildup was conducted with great secrecy and the Germans did not detect it until 30 May, but as the indications of Soviet intentions multiplied they were dismissed as a deception. The 1st, 2d, and 3d Belorussian Fronts and their neighbor to the north, the 1st Baltic Front, were heavily reinforced to the point where they had almost a two to one advantage in troops over Army Group Center and an even larger advantage in tanks, artil- lery, and aircraft.[3]

Zhukov was given the task of coordinating the operations of the 1st and 2d Belorussian Fronts, while Vasilevskii had the same task with the 3d Belorussian and the 1st Baltic Fronts. Because the 2d Belorussian Front would be under a new commander, Georgii F. Zakharov, S. M. Shtemenko, chief of the Operations Directorate of the General Staff, was detailed as an assistant to Zhukov with the specific task of coor- dinating the activities of the 2d Belorussian Front. Shtemenko found his situation to be unique: on the one hand he was subordinate to Zhukov, but he also had the authority to communicate directly with the chief of the General Staff. As Shtemenko describes Zakharov's awkward conduct as he took command of the Front, it was fortunate that Shtemenko was around to give assistance with the transition.[4]*

---

*According to Shtemenko, Georgii F. Zakharov had a strong temper and a unique way of viewing things. On his first inspection he informed his subordinate commanders that things had been unsatisfactory before his arrival and that he intended to correct them. He also attempted to change the organization and location of the main effort in the forthcoming offensive which had already been approved by the Stavka. He almost

Konstantin Konstantinovich Rokossovskii, Zhukov's old acquaintance from the Cavalry Command Course in the 1920s, his commander in the 7th Cavalry Division in the early 1930s, and his subordinate during the defense of Moscow in 1941, was commanding the 1st Belorussian Front when Zhukov arrived at its headquarters on the 5th of June. There is no hint in the memoirs of either man that there was any residue of the tension that had developed between them before Moscow in 1941. Zhukov reports that after a preliminary meeting with the Front command he proceeded in the next several days to inspect its armies, accompanied by Rokossovskii. In his memoirs, Rokossovskii reports that Zhukov played an active part in preparing the Front for the forthcoming operation. He does disclose that there had been a friendly disagreement between Zhukov and the Front command on which of the army sectors of operations promised the better chances of success. As they departed for their respective observation posts on the eve of the start of the operation, 24 June, Zhukov jokingly told Rokossovskii that he was going to General Gorbatov's 3d Army and that they would give the other armies of the Front a hand in crossing the Berezina. According to Rokossovskii, as things turned out, it was the 3d Army that needed a hand to cross the river.[5]

Pavel I. Batov, who commanded the 65th Army under Rokossovskii, in his memoirs published in 1962 provided a harsher and perhaps truer picture of Zhukov's methods prior to the start of an operation. Batov reports that Rokossovskii's subordinate commanders "sighed in distress" when they learned that Zhukov was to replace Vasilevskii as representative of the Stavka and coordinator of the 1st Belorussian Front. "He [Vasilevskii] contributed erudition, a broad range of thought and knew

---

made a fiasco of his initial meeting with his subordinates by examining them on such elementary matters as field manuals and tactics. Shtemenko was forced to intervene; he declared a break and tried to reason with Zakharov. After the break, the discussion seemed to be proceeding more normally when Zakharov produced a training aid on breaking through defenses, based on his experience in the Crimea, which was not appropriate for Belorussia. Sensing the unfavorable reaction of his audience, Zakharov decided not to pass out his training aid and the meeting was ended without further damage to his command authority.

how to deal humanely with subordinate commanders."[6]* The clear implication was that these were qualities that Zhukov did not contribute. Batov soon experienced the Zhukov command style firsthand. The 65th Army, attacking along with the 28th Army on the left wing of the Front, was given the mission of attacking toward Osipovichi, penetrating the German position and providing a gap through which the Soviet tanks would move to cut off the Wehrmacht's retreat. The 65th Army zone of action was a swampy area in which the Germans were strongly defending high, drier ground. To avoid these defenses, Batov's subordinates conceived the idea of laying corduroy routes through the swamps which tanks could use to bypass and surround the enemy strong points. Extensive field engineer support was required to cut and move the corduroy and put it in place, while maintaining strict security to avoid German detection.

These preparations were under way in early June when Zhukov and Rokossovskii unexpectedly made a dawn visit to the army command post with a large group of generals. Batov gives some idea of the size of Zhukov's entourage by recording that his army had to turn over twenty-nine dugouts to house the visitors. Zhukov immediately demanded to inspect the units in contact with the enemy and proceeded to do so, even though warned that it was safer to do so under cover of darkness. Zhukov and his party were wearing leather coats, which would have clearly identified them as senior staff officers if they were seen from German observation posts. Batov did succeed in reducing the size of the inspecting party, but he was sharply rebuffed when he suggested to Zhukov that he remove his uniform hat while he was assessing the German forward positions through binoculars. While attempting to climb to an auxiliary observation post apparently not too well installed in a tree, Zhukov lost his footing, could only reach halfway up the tree trunk, and tumbled down "beside himself with rage."[7] While returning to the army command post, Zhukov directed that the corps com-

*Zhukov's attitude toward Batov was colored by Batov's role in acquisition of the remnants of the 4th Tank Army in October 1942. The 4th Tank Army was practically destroyed trying to halt the Germans as they approached Stalingrad. What was left was given to Batov's 65th Army. Zhukov knew and highly esteemed V. D. Kriuchenkin, the former commander of the 4th Tank Army, and thought that Kriuchenkin should have been given the command. S. P. Ivanov, *Shtab armeiskii*, p. 457.

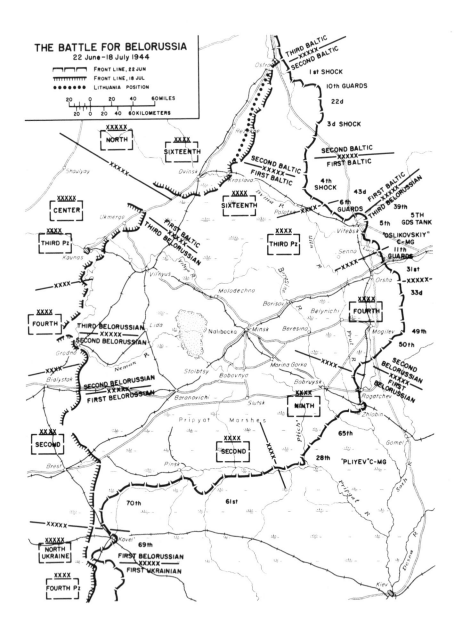

THE BATTLE FOR BELORUSSIA
22 June–18 July 1944

Front Line, 22 JUN
Front Line, 18 JUL
Lithuania Position

20   0   20   40   60 MILES
20   0   20   40   60 KILOMETERS

mander be relieved and the commander of the division that had constructed the unfortunate observation post in a tree be sent to a penal company.

Penal companies and battalions, according to the *Soviet Military Encyclopedia,* were:

> special military formations in which servicemen served punishment for civil and military crimes committed in war time. . . . During World War II military rank and decorations were removed and they [the servicemen] were used in the most difficult and dangerous sectors of combat operations.[8]*

Through the intervention of Batov and Rokossovskii the punishment in this case was mitigated to a reprimand for the corps commander and the relief and transfer of the division commander.[9]

Despite the possibility that the Germans would discover the Soviet intent, the corduroy routes were successfully laid before the advancing Soviet tanks and heavy equipment. The 65th Army attack on 24 June was so successful that Zhukov refused to believe Batov's noon report of his army's position and came forward in person to confirm it. When he arrived at 1500, he was satisfied with a brief report and immediately ordered lunch.[10]

---

*The regulations governing the penal units were approved on 26 September 1942 by G. K. Zhukov in his capacity as deputy minister of defense. Each Front was authorized to form up to three penal battalions of up to 800 men each. Each army was authorized to form from five to ten penal companies. Middle and senior officers were sent to the penal battalions, junior officers and lower ranks were sent to the penal companies. All who were sent to the penal units had their rank insignia and decorations removed in front of their unit, to be returned if they were rehabilitated. They were given the rank of "penal private." These units were to be placed in the most dangerous areas of the front or given the most dangerous assignments, and if they distinguished themselves their crime or misdemeanor, whatever it was, would be forgiven. These units usually suffered heavy casualties and any of the penalized who were killed in action were posthumously rehabilitated. Their families received the same pensions awarded others killed in action. Those who were wounded were restored to their former rank and status after they were fit to return to duty. Lt. Gen. L. Ivashov and Lt. Col. Iu. Rubtsov, "V proryv idut shtrafnye batal'ony" (Into the breakthrough go the penal battalions), in *KZ,* 25 December 1991, pp. 3, 4.

Later in the operation, Batov had another encounter with Zhukov. On 7 July his army was in the throes of capturing Baranovichi, an important rail junction. Taking the opportunity to freshen up after several days of continuous close-up direction of his troops, Batov had just finished shaving when Zhukov arrived at the 65th Army headquarters.

> "You are shaving? Using eau de cologne? Why haven't you taken Baranovichi?" In the hut, Zhukov continued to scold. In my long service in the army I have never experienced such humiliation. Radetskii [member of the 65th Army Military Council and head of its political directorate] kept a stone face.[11]

When Radetskii tried to support Batov, Zhukov turned on him and ordered him to go to Baranovichi and not return until the city was taken. Zhukov kicked over a stool and left, slamming the door.

After Zhukov's departure, Batov and Radetskii tried to understand the reason for Zhukov's anger and impatience. Radetskii attributed it to Zhukov's desire to be able to report to the Stavka that his Front had reached its objective before Vasilevskii's Front reached Vilnius. The next morning this conclusion seemed to be confirmed. When Radetskii reported that Baranovichi was in Soviet hands, Batov roused the sleeping Zhukov to tell him that the town was taken. Zhukov asked if Vilnius had been captured yet. When told that it hadn't, he said that he was going to sleep a little longer.[12]

The third edition of Batov's memoirs, published in 1974 during the Brezhnev regime, provides a strikingly different version of these events. Rokossovskii's announcement that Zhukov would be the representative of the Stavka is reported without any negative comment. The episode with the observation post in a tree is omitted. There is no mention of a penal company nor of the possible competition between Zhukov and Vasilevskii. A paragraph has been added testifying to the comradely relations between Rokossovskii and Zhukov:

> I observed the joint work of G. K. Zhukov and K. K. Rokossovskii more than once. . . . We always saw the exceptionally friendly, purposeful, and coordinated activity of these the greatest of our military leaders. . . . Their relations were distinguished by a deep mutual esteem, [and by] sincere comradely feelings.[13]

The fact that the negative version of Zhukov's conduct as representative of the Stavka was published in 1962, while Zhukov was in disgrace during the Khrushchev regime, and the more positive description of the same events was demanded during his partial rehabilitation during the Brezhnev era demonstrates the hurdles a Soviet author encountered in the pre-glasnost' era. A biographer is faced with the problem of choosing between the two versions. Zhukov, when reviewing his own career in the years after his second fall from power in 1957, admitted that perhaps he had been too harsh in dealing with the failings of his subordinates. In the last year of the war, when the defeat of Germany seemed certain, it was perhaps inevitable that a competition would develop among commanders to be the first to capture this or that objective and receive this or that accolade. And it seems clear that Stalin encouraged competition. The result was sour feelings between proud individuals who were the personification of proud units. There seems little doubt that Zhukov was a demanding, ruthless commander who often made snap judgments with little regard for the personal feelings of his subordinates. And, considering the character of his immediate superior, Stalin, it is doubtful that he would have survived otherwise. Batov's 1962 version of the events on the 1st Belorussian Front is probably the more accurate one.

The offensive that began on 24 June resulted in the capture of Minsk on 3 July. On 4 July, the 1st Belorussian Front was ordered to continue the offensive toward Baranovichi and Brest and to seize a bridgehead on the Western Bug. By 11 July, some 35,000 German prisoners had been taken, including twelve generals. On 7 July, Zhukov was called back to Moscow.

As was his practice, Zhukov visited the General Staff to obtain the latest information on the situation along the entire front. He was with its chief, A. I. Antonov, when Stalin called to inquire about his whereabouts. On learning that he was already in Moscow, the dictator invited both officers to join him for breakfast. It was then 1400 and, although they had long since breakfasted, they joined Stalin and Malenkov and Molotov, who came in later, for a discussion of the probable future course of the war and the Soviet role in it.

Stalin was in good form, encouraged by the latest reports from Vasilevskii on the progress of the two Fronts he was coordinating. From the manner in which Stalin presented his ideas, Zhukov gained the impression that he had thought long and hard about the future. All present were convinced that the final German defeat was only a matter of time. Stalin believed that the Soviets possessed sufficient strength to accomplish the task alone, but welcomed the opening of the second front by the Western Allies because it would shorten the war and provide relief to the Soviet people. Germany was exhausted in both human and material terms, while the Soviets were growing stronger as they reclaimed the Ukraine, Belorussia, and the Baltic states.

In response to a question about what hope the Nazi leaders had of escaping the current situation, Stalin likened them to a gambler risking his last money on the turn of a card. Hitler was counting on like-minded "imperialists" in Britain and the United States who had done everything to turn the Wehrmacht against the Soviet Union. Molotov added that Hitler would probably try to arrange a separate peace with American and English government circles. Stalin agreed, but thought that Roosevelt and Churchill would not enter into a deal with Hitler; instead, they would seek to form a German government they could control.

Stalin then turned to the immediate future, asking Zhukov if the Soviet forces moving up to the Bug were in condition to begin the liberation of Poland and continue, without a halt, to the Vistula. He also wanted to know where the 1st Polish Army could be employed. Zhukov assured him that the Soviet troops could not only continue on to the Vistula but they must also seize usable bridgeheads over the river. He recommended that the 1st Polish Army be aimed at Warsaw. Antonov agreed with Zhukov's recommendations.

The reason for Stalin's concern with the Polish force became clear later in the conversation. Zhukov was to meet the next day with Boleslaw Bierut, the Polish Communist head of the Committee on National Liberation, and others. Stalin intended to use these men to form the government of liberated Poland, and the committee was planning to issue a manifesto around 20 July claiming their right to do so. During the meeting with Zhukov it was decided that the committee would begin to organize the new government in Lublin after the Soviets took the city.[14] Stalin was determined to resolve the dispute with his British and American allies over which government was to rule in Poland after the Germans were driven out on his terms. It was to be the Lublin government and not the exiled prewar government of Poland in London.

It was perhaps his haste to consolidate the position of the Lublin Poles that caused Stalin to reject the recommendations of Zhukov and Vasilevskii to strengthen the 2d Belorussian Front and give it the mission of cutting off and destroying the German forces in East Prussia. For Zhukov the move was dictated by the military consideration that the Soviet right flank must be protected during the forthcoming operations in western Poland, Germany, and finally Berlin. The first time Zhukov raised the issue Stalin said that the Germans would fight to the last man to hold East Prussia and that it was of prime importance to liberate eastern Poland. When Zhukov approached him in private, Stalin put him off, saying that he would confer with Vasilevskii and the General Staff. There is no evidence that he ever did, and in 1945 East Prussia "hung over" the flank of the Soviet forces advancing toward Berlin and caused much concern.[15]

When Zhukov returned to the front he assumed coordination responsibility for the 1st Ukrainian Front and, in particular, its right flank, which in cooperation with the left flank of the 1st Belorussian Front was to ensure the capture of Lublin. Zhukov found the 1st Ukrainian Front to have more than adequate strength for the missions assigned it. Once again he attempted to have Stalin make an effort to eliminate the threat from East Prussia, but to no avail. The 1st Ukrainian Front launched its offensive on 13 July and the left flank of the 1st Belorussian Front resumed the attack on the 18th. Lublin was taken on 23 July, and by the end of the month the Red Army had retaken Brest, which had borne some of the heaviest German blows in the initial assaults on 22 June 1941. The German group of armies "Center" had been smashed. That the German Army was able to restore the situation Zhukov attributes, admiringly, to the effective use of short counterattacks, under the cover of which reinforcements from Germany and other areas of the eastern front were thrown into the breech.

Zhukov was lavish in his praise of the performance of Rokossovskii's 1st Belorussian Front in this operation. In contrast, he describes his disappointment in the serious shortcomings that were exposed in the operation by Konev's 1st Ukrainian Front to seize L'vov. Specifically, he singled out the failure of the Front's intelligence to define accurately the enemy's system of defensive fire, resulting in much Soviet firing and bombing with few results. He also accepted a share of the blame as representative of the Stavka, although he had not participated in the preparation of the Front's fire plan.

The success of the left flank of Rokossovskii's troops and Konev's right flank efforts created an opportunity to send P. S. Rybalko's 3d Guards Tank Army on a raid into the German rear area, cutting the communications of the German defenders of L'vov. Konev and Zhukov believed that this envelopment would ensure the early capture of L'vov. However, when Zhukov reported to Stalin, he was told that Khrushchev did not approve of the raid on the grounds that it would delay capture of the city. Stalin continued:

> You and Konev are trying to seize the Vistula. It is not going to go away from us. Finish the business with L'vov first.[16]

In addition to his desire to push the Germans out of eastern Poland, the dictator may have been impatient to at last capture the city that had eluded him during the Soviet-Polish War in 1920 under circumstances that had soured his relations with Lenin and raised questions about his strategic grasp ever since. Zhukov assured the dictator that L'vov would be taken before the 1st Ukrainian Front reached the Vistula. L'vov was captured on 27 July, and on the same day the Stavka ordered Konev to move up to the Vistula and seize a bridgehead over the river in the manner of the 1st Belorussian Front. The next day the 1st Ukrainian Front, led by the 3d Guards Tank and the 13th Army, closed on the Vistula and by 1 August had a sizeable bridgehead at Sandomierz.

On 29 July Stalin called to congratulate Zhukov on the award of his second Gold Star of a Hero of the Soviet Union. Later, M. I. Kalinin informed him that he received the award for his part in the Belorussian and Ukrainian campaigns. Zhukov's joy at receiving the medal was reinforced by the knowledge that both Fronts had strong bridgeheads over the Vistula. According to the archival record, Zhukov spent the first three weeks of August shuttling between the 1st and 2d Belorussian Fronts and the 1st Ukrainian Front as they consolidated their bridgeheads and reorganized for the next major operation, the move to the Oder.[17]

On 22 August Zhukov was recalled to Moscow, where the next day he was given a special mission by the State Defense Committee (GKO).

He was to proceed to the 3d Ukrainian Front, commanded by Marshal of the Soviet Union F. I. Tolbukhin, and coordinate the forthcoming operations in Bulgaria. Before leaving, Stalin had Zhukov spend some time with the Bulgarian Communist, Georgi Dimitrov, who predicted that the Bulgarian Army would not fight and that the Bulgarian people would welcome the Soviet Army.

On 5 September, the Soviet government, on the grounds that the Bulgarian government had continued to actively support Germany despite warnings from the Soviets, declared war on Bulgaria. On 8 September, as the 3d Ukrainian Front prepared to initiate hostilities, there were no detectable signs of opposition. Tolbukhin gave the order to dispatch forward detachments, and the men were welcomed everywhere. When Stalin received word from Zhukov that there was no opposition to the Soviet occupation, he ordered that the Bulgarian Army be allowed to retain their arms and equipment. In his original version, Zhukov noted that because of the "illegal" arrival of an Anglo-American military mission and the obvious intrigues of their governments, the Stavka ordered that a reinforced rifle corps be deployed in Sofia. In the 1969 edition, the stationing of the rifle corps was attributed to the fear of a German attack on the Bulgarian capital. Zhukov returned to Moscow at the end of September 1944.[18]

NOTES

1. Zhukov, *Memoirs* 3: p. 127.
2. Ibid, p. 124.
3. Ziemke, *Stalingrad to Berlin*, pp. 313–316.
4. Shtemenko, *General'nyi shtab*, pp. 245–249.
5. Zhukov, *Memoirs* 3: pp. 334–337. Rokossovskii, *Soldatskii dolg*, pp. 254–257.
6. P. I. Batov, *B pokhodakh i boiakh* (In campaigns and battles), 1st ed. (Moscow: Voenizdat, 1962), p. 268.
7. Ibid., p. 275.
8. *SVE* 8: p. 539.
9. Batov, *B pokhodakh*, p. 277.
10. Ibid., pp. 284, 285.
11. Ibid., p. 290.
12. Ibid., pp. 290, 291.
13. P. A. Batov, *B pokhodakh*, 3d ed., 1974, pp. 394, 400–403, 409–414. The quotation is found on page 410.
14. Zhukov, *Memoirs* 3: pp. 145–149.
15. Ibid.
16. Ibid., p. 159.
17. S. I. Isaev, "Vekhi frontovogo puti" (Markers of a frontal journey) in *VIZh*, no. 10 (1991), p. 31.
18. Zhukov, *Memoirs* 3: pp. 164–168.

XVII

RETURN TO FRONT COMMAND, 1944

Zhukov soon found himself in the midst of a major controversy. The uprising in Warsaw was in progress; Rokossovskii's 1st Belorussian Front was trying unsuccessfully to render direct military aid to the population of the city. Zhukov was sent in early October to clarify the situation.

By 1 August the 2d Tank Army had encountered fierce opposition on the approaches to Warsaw and under the pressure of counterattacks was forced to retreat from Praga, an eastern suburb of the city. The 2d Tank Army lost 500 tanks and self-propelled guns in these battles, a rare specific admission of loss by Soviet military historians. Troops of the 1st Polish Army, supported by Soviet Army engineers, artillery, and air forces, attempted a crossing of the Vistula at the Warsaw embankment and were forced back with heavy losses. North of Warsaw, the Soviet 47th and 70th Armies were engaged in an operation ordered by Stalin, suffering heavy casualties, the military purpose of which Zhukov could not understand. He called Stalin and requested permission to halt offensive operations to give the troops an opportunity to rest, reorganize, and receive reinforcements. Stalin ordered him and Rokossovskii to return to Moscow to discuss the matter.[1]

The meeting took place in Stalin's office in the presence of Molotov, Beriia, Malenkov, and Antonov, the chief of the General Staff. As Zhukov reported on the situation at the front he observed that Stalin was agitated. The dictator approached the map, paced back and forth, now directing his "penetrating look" at Zhukov and now at Rokossovskii. He even put his pipe aside "which always happened when he began to lose his cool (*khladnokrovie*) and control over himself."[2]

Molotov and Beriia, sensing that the dictator did not like what he was hearing, directed snide comments at Zhukov, as they were wont to do in such encounters. When Stalin asked if reinforcing the 47th Army would not help the situation, Zhukov replied that such a move would produce more casualties. Rokossovskii supported Zhukov half-heartedly. Finally, Stalin asked Zhukov for his recommendation. Zhukov gave him the same recommendation in person that he had given over the telephone: halt the offensive, gather reinforcements, and take Warsaw by enveloping it from the southwest and then continuing in the direction of Lodz and Poznan. Stalin broke off the briefing at this point, ordering Zhukov and Rokossovskii to rethink the matter while he conferred with his civilian colleagues.

Zhukov and Rokossovskii repaired to the library and spread out their situation map. Zhukov rebuked his colleague for not being more categorical in opposing Stalin's proposal that the 47th Army be reinforced and the offensive continued. Rokossovskii defended himself by asking Zhukov if he hadn't noticed that Beriia was inciting Stalin. He warned Zhukov that things could end badly. He knew, he said, because he had been in Beriia's torture chambers.

Fifteen or twenty minutes later Malenkov appeared and asked if the officers had thought of any other plan of action. Zhukov said they hadn't. Malenkov assured Zhukov that they would support him. When they rejoined Stalin, he announced that it had been agreed that the 1st and 2d Belorussian Fronts could go over to the defensive. Stalin delivered the decision in an unfriendly tone, hardly looking at the officers, then dismissed them abruptly. Zhukov took that as another bad sign.[3]

Stalin's irritation and impatience were a reflection of the pressure that was being put on him by Allied public opinion to do something to relieve the heroic Poles, who were being crushed inside the Polish capital while the Soviet armies were what seemed a short distance away. The Soviet defense for their apparent inability to mitigate the horror in Warsaw was that the uprising instigated by the London-based Polish government-in-exile had not been coordinated with them; its leaders had refused to accept Soviet liaison and coordination, and as a result the Soviet forces, particularly the 1st Belorussian Front, were scattered and depleted from their drive to the Vistula. Stalin was probably also still annoyed by the recent visit to Moscow of the head of the Polish government-in-exile, Stanislaw Mikolajczyk (which apparently was timed to coincide with the start of the uprising), during which he had demanded 80 percent of the seats in the postwar Polish parliament for his party.[4]

It is also possible that Zhukov and Rokossovskii were being treated to a performance by the dictator designed to convince them that he was allowing them to persuade him to halt the Soviet offensive for purely military reasons. Stalin was playing the part of a leader who sincerely wanted to help the Poles in Warsaw but on the advice of his generals was reluctantly ordering a pause to enable the 1st Belorussian Front to regroup. Malenkov's assurance to Zhukov that he had their "support" was a unique and suspicious occurrence. Stalin's henchmen rarely supported those who were proposing a course of action the dictator opposed. There was no doubt that Stalin did not want an organized group led by someone loyal to the London government-in-exile in Warsaw when the Soviet forces and the 1st Polish Army controlled by the Lublin government arrived in the Polish capital.

The next day Stalin called Zhukov and asked his opinion on whether the time had come to discontinue the practice of using representatives of the Stavka to coordinate future offensive operations of the Soviet forces. Zhukov felt that the unpleasant encounter of the previous day was not the only reason for the question. "The war was coming to an end, there remained only to conduct a few concluding operations, and I. V. Stalin surely wanted that he alone would be at the head of those operations."[5] Zhukov agreed with Stalin, commenting that the number of Fronts had been reduced, that the length of the front had shortened, and, he might have added, the quality of staff work and communications had improved so that direct control of the forces at the front from Moscow was much more feasible than it had been in 1941. After asking whether Zhukov would take the change in operating procedure personally and being assured that he would not, Stalin told Zhukov that he was to replace Rokossovskii as commander of the 1st Belorussian Front, now deployed on the main axis toward Berlin. When Zhukov demurred out of consideration for Rokossovskii's feelings, Stalin brushed that objection aside, saying, "We are not pretty maidens."[6] In Zhukov's presence he telephoned Rokossovskii and informed him that he was being shifted to command the 2d Belorussian Front. Zhukov was right. Rokossovskii was upset; after that the friendly relationship he had enjoyed with Rokossovskii for many years was never the same.

Zhukov believed that Rokossovskii suspected that he himself had arranged the transfer in order to have the glory of commanding the final assault on Berlin.[7]

In conversations with Konstantin Simonov, Zhukov gave a slightly different version of the events that preceded Stalin's decision to control the final campaigns of the war on the eastern front. Zhukov recalled that in the autumn of 1944, after the completion of the Belorussian campaign, Stalin claimed that his proposal for the sequence in which to launch the Fronts had turned out to be better than the sequence proposed by Zhukov. When Zhukov denied that he had proposed some other sequence for committing the Fronts, Stalin reached into a drawer in his desk, pulled out the directive for the offensive, and told Zhukov to read it aloud. When Zhukov read past the place where it became clear that Stalin was mistaken, Stalin asked Malenkov and then Beriia to read the directive. Neither could read the directive in a way that supported the dictator. Stalin took the directive and returned it to his drawer, saying nothing, but all felt his irritation. Subsequent conversation that day was strained. Soon after that incident he proposed that the practice of sending representatives of the Stavka to coordinate the multi-Front operations be discontinued.[8]

NOTES

1. Zhukov, *Memoirs* 3: pp. 169, 170. Pospelov, *IVOVSS* 4: pp. 244, 245, 246.
2. Zhukov, *Memoirs* 3: p. 171.
3. Ibid., p. 172.
4. Pospelov, *IVOVSS* 4: p. 242.
5. Zhukov, *Memoirs* 3: p. 173. This remark was deleted in earlier editions.
6. Ibid.
7. Ibid.
8. Simonov, "Zametki" in *VIZh,* no. 10: p. 59.

XVIII

From the Vistula to the Oder, 1945

Zhukov inherited Rokossovskii's complete and experienced staff when he assumed command of the 1st Belorussian Front on 16 November 1944. Stalin offered to transfer any key staff personnel Rokossovskii wished to accompany him to the 2d Belorussian Front, but Rokossovskii elected to leave the staff intact so that they could experience the eventual capture of Berlin. This gesture was so unusual in Stalin's experience that he expressed his gratitude to the disappointed Rokossovskii.[1]

The 1st Belorussian Front, consisting of 7 Soviet field armies (2 of which were "shock" armies), 2 tank armies, 2 tank corps, 2 cavalry corps, and the 1st Polish Army, was deployed along the Vistula from a point approximately 20 kilometers north of Warsaw to the city of Jozefow, 200 kilometers to the southeast. The 16th Air Army provided the Front with air support. The 5th Shock Army and the 69th Army held bridgeheads on the west bank of the Vistula. The 1st Polish Army was poised on the east bank of the river southeast of the city, awaiting the opportunity to march in and claim the honor of liberating the Polish capital.

Work began immediately on the plan for the forthcoming offensive, which was to take the Red Army to the Oder, followed by a final drive on Berlin. The plan for the move to the Oder was finished and approved in Moscow by the end of the month. The target date for beginning the operation was mid-January 1945. Preparations for this first major operation outside of Soviet territory were complicated by the absence of the partisan intelligence on the Wehrmacht which had been furnished while the Germans were operating in the Soviet Union. Hostile intelligence and

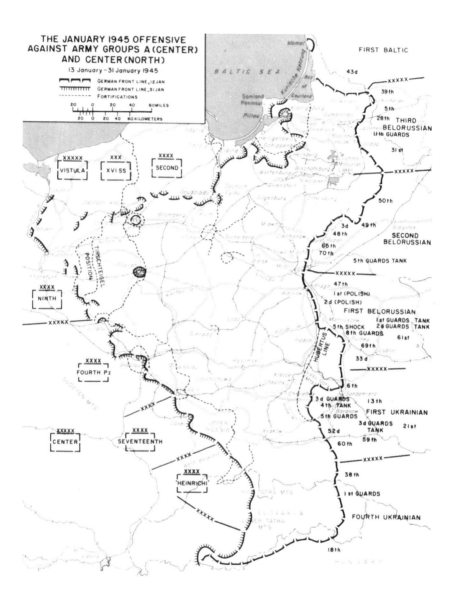

THE JANUARY 1945 OFFENSIVE
AGAINST ARMY GROUPS A (CENTER)
AND CENTER (NORTH)

13 January – 31 January 1945

GERMAN FRONT LINE, 12 JAN
GERMAN FRONT LINE, 31 JAN
FORTIFICATIONS

sabotage activities now threatened Soviet troop, supply, and maintenance movements to a much greater extent than they had while Soviet communications ran through friendly territory. The logistical problems
of transferring troop replacements, armaments, equipment, ammunition, and supplies also became more difficult as the Soviet forces moved
westward; after the rail bridges over the Vistula were rebuilt or replaced,
the narrower gauge of the surviving rail nets in Poland and Germany
required that transshipment points had to be established where the two
track systems met.[2]

I. S. Konev's 1st Ukrainian Front, Zhukov's neighbor to the south,
began the offensive on 12 January with a force that Zhukov considered to be almost as strong as his. It gained twenty kilometers on the
first day. The 2d (Rokossovskii) and 3d (Cherniakhovskii) Belorussian
Fronts launched their attacks to the north against East Prussia on
13 January and achieved more modest results against strong German
resistance. Zhukov's troops began their offensive on 14 January. Because of some uncertainty about the strength and determination of
the German defenders, it was decided to open the attack with a reconnaissance in force (*razvedka boiem*). After a thirty-minute artillery preparation, the forward divisions of the 1st Belorussian Front, attacking
out of the two bridgeheads, probed the enemy's forward positions with
one or two battalions of infantry, supported by tanks and self-propelled
guns. When the demoralized enemy interpreted the reconnaissance in
force as the main attack and started to withdraw, the main forces of
the Front, supported by all its artillery and the bulk of its aircraft, joined
the attack. By 1300 on the first day of the offensive, a breech in the
German positions was created large enough to allow the commitment
of the 11th Tank Corps. The next day the 1st and 2d Guards Tank Armies
entered the fray and, as Zhukov had predicted in September, the German occupiers of Warsaw, also pressured by the 47th Army which
threatened to envelop the city from the north, began to withdraw from
the city.[3]*

---

*The Soviets claim that the starting date was moved up several days to accommo-
date the Western Allies who were recovering from the German offensive in the Ardennes.

By 17 January, the 1st Belorussian Front was abreast of the 1st Ukrainian Front, even though it had started two days after Konev's troops. On 25 January, Zhukov could report to Stalin that the Front command had decided to continue the offensive with the aim of reaching the Oder and attempting to seize a bridgehead over the river in the vicinity of Kustrin. Stalin became alarmed, warning that when the Front reached the Oder it would be separated from the 2d Belorussian Front by 150 kilometers. Zhukov should wait while Rokossovskii completed the operation in East Prussia—about ten days. Zhukov urged the CINC to allow him to continue to the Oder. The Germans had a prepared defensive position, the Mezeritskii fortified area, portions of which had been built before the war as defense against Poland,[4]* which was not yet fully manned. Delay would give the Germans the opportunity to complete their occupation of this position; breaking through it would be more difficult and result in losses. Zhukov proposed that his Front be reinforced by one army to fill the gap with Rokossovskii's troops and that the offensive be continued. Stalin said he would think it over.

The 1st Belorussian Front continued to advance while Stalin and the Stavka considered Zhukov's proposal. The next day reconnaissance elements of the 1st Guards Tank Army reached the fortified area and captured a number of prisoners, who confirmed that many of the fortified area's strong points were not manned but that reinforcements were en route. After reorienting the axis of advance of the Front's right flank armies to the northwest to help close the gap separating it from the 2d Belorussian Front, and after further conversations with Stalin (but no reinforcements), Zhukov decided to continue the advance. The 1st Guards Tank Army overcame the remaining resistance in the fortified area, and the main elements of the Front reached the Oder and seized a bridgehead near Kustrin by 1–4 February.[5]

As the Front closed up on the Oder, portions of V. I. Chuikov's 8th Guards Army (the former 62d Army, the defenders of the city of Stalingrad),

---

*The Mezeritskii fortified area was constructed between the Warta and the Oder rivers before the war, 1932–1937, and modernized in 1944 and 1945. It was protected from the east by a system of lakes joined by canals. Dams were built so that the approaches to the area could be flooded.

the 69th, and the 1st Guards Tank Armies were left to reduce the German garrison holding Poznan. Chuikov commanded this operation, which was not completed until 23 February.[6]

From the Kustrin bridgehead the 1st Belorussian Front was seventy kilometers from Berlin, and Zhukov issued a warning order to his army commanders to collect their troops, replenish their fuel and ammunition supplies, and prepare to continue the advance and seize Berlin by 15 or 16 February. There was no enemy force on the front capable of mounting a serious counterattack, nor had the enemy formed a continuous defensive line, but there were indications that some ten or eleven divisions were being transferred to the east from the western front. Some of those divisions were to reinforce Army Group Vistula, which had been formed in eastern Pomerania on 26 January and placed by Hitler under the command of Heinrich Himmler, head of the SS in addition to other responsibilities.

As Soviet preparations were in train, the indicators from eastern Pomerania became more threatening. General Heinz Guderian, who had been acting chief of the German Army General Staff since the failed attempt on Hitler's life in July 1944, conceived the idea of a counterattack east of the Oder, initially aimed at cutting into the flanks of the 1st Belorussian Front. What resulted was Operation *Sonnenwende* (Solstice), which Earl F. Ziemke ranks as "one of the war's closest approaches to a planned fiasco."[7] Instead of a typical *Kiel und Kessel* (wedge and pocket) German offensive, in which two armored forces would drive deeply into the extended Soviet lines and meet to create a pocket, Hitler decided to relocate one portion of the forces intended for the operation. The Germans nevertheless attacked at Stargard on 14 February with only the northern pincer achieving limited initial success. The offensive, conducted by the inexperienced staff of the Eleventh SS Panzer Army and hampered by rain and mud, was discontinued 18 February after it had gained at most five kilometers (Zhukov thought it had gained twelve).[8]

The effect of this attack on the Soviets was far out of proportion to its limited success. The Stavka, considering the difficulty the 2d Belorussian Front was having in its offensive in eastern Pomerania and concerned by the potential the Germans had demonstrated at Stargard, decided to liquidate the German forces there. Zhukov was directed to turn four combined armies and two tank armies to cooperate with the 2d Belorussian Front in finally removing the German threat from that area. The action that Zhukov had been advocating since the previous fall was at last undertaken.

The remainder of the 1st Belorussian Front held its bridgehead over the Oder against German counterattacks, including more than 5,000 aerial sorties by the Luftwaffe against the 5th Shock Army in two days. The Germans were flying from concrete runways in and around Berlin while the Soviet Air Force could not take off from the soggy dirt airstrips in western Poland. Zhukov's northern wing and the 2d Belorussian Front spent the remainder of February and the entire month of March liquidating German resistance in eastern Pomerania.

Almost twenty years later, in March 1964, Chuikov, now a marshal, Commander in Chief of the Ground Forces, and chief of Civil Defense, in an article published in a Soviet journal argued that Berlin could have been taken in February and the war shortened by three months if Zhukov had not paused on the Oder. He admitted that there would have been some risk, but "in war one often has to take risks."[9] Zhukov was permitted to reply to Chuikov in June 1965. He was in the eighth year of his second disgrace at the time, but his principal accuser, Khrushchev, had been deposed in October 1964. Nevertheless, the process of achieving permission to publish Zhukov's refutation was long and complicated. The editors of the *Voenno-istoricheskii zhurnal* conferred with the Main Political Directorate and the chief of the General Staff, M. V. Zakharov, but could not move the page proofs forward. Finally, Zhukov, hearing of the difficulty, intervened and permission was received to publish his version of the events. Chuikov complained, and a high level commission consisting of Marshals Bagramian, Zakharov, Konev, Moskalenko, Rokossovskii, and Sokolovskii was convened. The commission rejected Chuikov's point of view.

Zhukov devoted the better part of eight pages in his *Memoirs* to his refutation of Chuikov, citing both the German Generals Wilhelm Keitel and Heinz Guderian that plans had been made to use the east Pomeranian bridgehead to strike down on the Soviet bridgehead at Kustrin. On the question of risk, Zhukov recalled the defeat of the Soviet Western Front before Warsaw in 1920, which he attributed to the careless and insecure forward movement of the Front toward the Polish capital. He did not name the "careless" Front commander (Tukhachevskii) nor did he mention Stalin's role in the defeat and the controversy that followed.[10]* He also stressed the material condition of the Front and the losses it had suffered after its 500-kilometer advance across Poland. His conclusion was that to have attempted to seize Berlin in February would have been a "purest adventure" (*chisteishaia avantiura*).[11] In Soviet usage the word "avantiura" in itself implies unfounded risk.

With the advantage of hindsight and the knowledge of what a fiasco the German attack at Stargard became, it is not clear that there was as much risk attached to continuing the offensive on Berlin from the Oder as Zhukov thought. Zhukov's warning order of early February suggests that at the time he believed that the logistics problems could be solved in a week or ten days. His intelligence indicated only disorganized resistance before him. But he had become convinced early in the fall of 1944 that action should be taken to eliminate the threat that the German forces in East Prussia posed to the right flank of any move toward Berlin. When word of the pending German effort from Stargard reached him, he accepted it at perhaps more than face value. What he did not know was the command arrangements that Hitler had installed there: Himmler commanding Army Group Vistula and an inexperienced and incompetent staff at the head of the Eleventh SS Panzer Army, a force assembled at great effort, could hardly have accomplished the mission contemplated by Guderian. The almost two months' delay allowed the Germans to concentrate what remained of their forces to protect Berlin. This was similar to the situation that Zhukov had avoided when he urged Stalin to permit him to seize the Mezeritskii Line before it could be fully garrisoned.

Early in March, during the course of the operation to remove the threat from eastern Pomerania, Zhukov was called to Moscow by the Supreme Commander. Meeting Stalin in his dacha, Zhukov was struck by his appearance; in his movements and conversation Zhukov sensed

---

*In 1920 Stalin was a member of the Military Council of the Southwest Front which was closing on L'vov when the Front was ordered to transfer Budennyi's 1st Cavalry Army to Tukhachevskii's Western Front as it approached Warsaw. Stalin refused to countersign the transfer order. When the transfer was eventually effected the Western Front had already been taken in the flank by the Poles and forced to retreat into Russia

great physical fatigue. During the four years of the war Stalin had become completely tired out. He worked under severe tension during the entire time, had never gotten sufficient sleep, and had suffered especially through the defeats of 1941–1942.

Zhukov also had an opportunity to ask the dictator about his oldest son Iakov, who had been captured by the Germans in 1941. After a long pause, Stalin said that, according to the information he had received, Iakov was being held in isolation while the Germans attempted to convince him to betray his country. Stalin was certain that Iakov would never return from captivity because he would choose death rather than cooperate with the enemy. Stalin may not have known that Iakov was already dead, having thrown himself on the barbed wire at Sachsenhausen and been shot by the guards on 14 April 1943.[12]*

Stalin also shared with Zhukov his impressions of the Yalta Conference, which had just been concluded. His appraisal of Franklin Roosevelt was favorable but he was suspicious of Winston Churchill. The latter, Stalin told Zhukov, was still trying to install Mikolajczyk as head of the Polish government, although the Poles had already made their choice and did not want Mikolajczyk.

The next evening Zhukov and General Staff Chief Antonov met with Stalin to review the Berlin operation. Malenkov, Molotov, and other members of the State Defense Committee were also present. Antonov reviewed the plans and preparations for the operation and they were approved by the CINC.[13]

The final meetings for the assault on Berlin took place in Moscow 29 March–2 April 1945.[14]

---

*Volkogonov believes that Stalin was more concerned that Iakov would eventually break and cooperate with the enemy than he was over the possibility of his son's death.

NOTES

1. Rokossovskii, *Soldatskii dolg,* 5th edition, p. 286.
2. Iu. V. Plotnikov and N. N. Chaban, "Tyl Sovetskikh Vooruzhenykh Sil v gody Velikoi otechestvennoi Voiny" (The Rear Services of the Soviet Armed Forces in the years of the Great Fatherland War) in *Istoriia SSSR,* no. 1 (1975), pp. 19, 20.
3. Zhukov, *Memoirs* 3: pp. 183–187.
4. *SVE* 5: p. 231.
5. Zhukov, *Memoirs* 3: p. 192.
6. Ibid.
7. Ziemke, *Stalingrad to Berlin,* p. 445.
8. Ibid., pp. 445–448.
9. Zhukov, *Memoirs* 3: p. 201. Chuikov's three-part article appeared in *Oktyabr,* in March, April, and May 1964. He repeated his charges one year later in *Novaia i noveishaia istoriia,* no. 2 (1965): p. 7.
10. Pavlenko, "Razmyshleniia" in *VIZh,* no. 12: p. 36.
11. Zhukov, *Memoirs* 3: p. 192.
12. Ibid., pp. 211, 212. Volkogonov, *Triumf i tragediia,* Book 1, part 1, pp. 269, 270.
13. Zhukov, *Memoirs* 3: pp. 213, 214.
14. Ibid., pp. 219–224.

XIX

THE CAPTURE OF BERLIN, 1945

In his history of World War II Winston Churchill observed that as a war waged by a coalition draws to an end, political aspects have a mounting importance.[1] He then related how he, as the British prime minister, urged the Western coalition's commander in chief, Dwight David Eisenhower, to make an effort to reach Berlin before the Soviets. Churchill believed that the Western Allies would benefit in postwar Europe from the prestige and influence of taking the German capital and receiving the final German surrender. At the time he made this proposal, the Western Allies had just crossed the Rhine and were some 500 kilometers from Berlin. The Soviet Army was about 70 kilometers away on the Oder.

Eisenhower had decided to complete the envelopment and reduction of the Ruhr, the industrial heart of Germany, then move in three main thrusts: to the Elbe across the center of Germany; toward Lübeck across northern Germany; and into southern Germany, Austria, and Czechoslovakia. Eisenhower reasoned that if he should plan to cross the Elbe for the purpose of investing Berlin, he would have to immobilize the other units along the remainder of his front. The Soviets in all probability would surround the city long before the Western Allies arrived. He was also advised that the cost in Allied casualties might be as high as 100,000 men. To accept Churchill's recommendation he felt "to be more than unwise; it was stupid."[2]

For purposes of coordinating the eventual junction of the two forces along the Elbe, Eisenhower communicated the latter part of his decision directly to Stalin—to Churchill's irritation.[3] On 7 April, in a message to General George C. Marshall, Eisenhower, in a gesture that seemed more accommodating to Churchill's proposal than it was in fact, said that he was ready to move toward Berlin if the combined chiefs of staff so decided but only after he had taken Leipzig and if it could be done without too many casualties. The Soviets were still poised on the Oder.

Aware that there were differences among the Western Allies over whether they should try to capture Berlin, knowing that most Germans preferred to surrender to them rather than to his troops, and suspicious that the Western Allies were engaged in negotiations for a separate peace with Germany, Stalin was anxious to take the city as soon as possible. When Stalin received Zhukov in his Kremlin office late at night on 29 March, he opened the conversation by observing that German resistance in the west had collapsed and that the Wehrmacht was not trying to stop the Western Allies. What remained of German capabilities to resist was being concentrated to defend Berlin against the Soviet Army. Zhukov confirmed this by showing Stalin the 1st Belorussian Front intelligence situation map. The Soviets calculated that the Germans had concentrated more than a million men, 10,000 artillery pieces and mortars, 1,500 tanks and assault guns, and 3,300 combat aircraft on the Berlin axis. Stalin wanted to know when the offensive could begin. Zhukov replied that he and Konev could start in two weeks, but that Rokossovskii was involved in taking Danzig and Gdynia and could not start at the same time as the other two Fronts. Stalin ruled, almost offhandedly, that the operation would have to start without Rokossovskii. At this point in the conversation he showed Zhukov a letter from an unidentified "well-wisher," informing him of the efforts of Hitler's agents to arrange a separate peace with the Western Allies. The Allies had rejected the German proposals, but Zhukov did not exclude the possibility that the way would be opened to the Allies to take Berlin. Later the chief of the General Staff, Aleksei Antonov, was summoned and shown the same letter. Antonov evaluated it as one more proof of the backstage machinations of Hitler's emissaries and "English government circles."[4]*

---

*Adam B. Ulam in *Stalin: The Man and His Era* (New York: Viking, 1973), pp. 611, 612, claims that the news of a possible deal between the defeated Germans and the Western Allies unhinged Stalin and cites as evidence the message he sent to Roosevelt accusing the Allies of chicanery. Stalin's message was answered by Roosevelt in "chilling" terms. Luckily for Stalin this episode, which would have contributed to Roosevelt's growing disillusionment with Stalin, occurred shortly before the President died.

The next day Antonov and Zhukov reviewed the draft plan for the Berlin operation, which incorporated fully the plan submitted by the 1st Belorussian Front for the offensive. On 31 March, Konev was called in and shown the plan. According to Shtemenko, Konev was disturbed that the boundary between the 1st Belorussian and his 1st Ukrainian Front was drawn to exclude any operations by his Front against Berlin, but he did not say anything. When Stalin looked at the boundary, without a word he took an eraser and corrected it so that it ended fifty kilometers southeast of the city, permitting units of Konev's Front to attack the city from the south if necessary. Recalling this event in 1966, Konev speculated that Stalin made this correction deliberately, with the idea of encouraging a competition between Zhukov and Konev for the honor of being the first unit to reach the German capital.[5] It seems more likely that Stalin was concerned that the forces of the 1st Belorussian Front might not be adequate to take the city without help.

When the 1st Belorussian Front reached the Oder in early February and established the Kustrin bridgehead, there was no organized resistance between it and Berlin. By 16 April when the attack on Berlin was launched, Hitler had collected and organized for the defense of the capital the best of what was left of the shattered Wehrmacht. Zhukov had no option other than a frontal attack out of the bridgehead against the first German defensive belt, which was dug in on the floor of the Oder valley. The attackers then faced the Seelow Heights, which overlooked the valley from steep escarpments of 40 to 50 meters. Twelve to 15 kilometers west of the river and stretching along it for about 20 kilometers, the heights were defended by the second belt of German defenses. Zhukov believed that the enemy planned to halt the Soviet offensive along this wall and it was here that the bulk of their forces were deployed.[6]

On 14 and 15 April the Front conducted a reconnaissance in force, similar to that employed at the start of the campaign from the Vistula, with the aim of finding out more about the enemy's system of defensive fire and luring the defenders into moving reserves into the forward area. Zhukov concluded that the effort was successful. German artillery responded, revealing some of its firing positions. Reserves were moved forward, and when the Soviet reconnaissance units did not continue the attack some of the German commanders believed that the Soviet attack had failed.[7]

That the 2d Belorussian Front would not be able to join the offensive over the Oder for several days meant that Zhukov would be moving toward Berlin with his right flank exposed. To be prepared for any contingencies on his right, Zhukov decided to move the 1st Guards Tank Army to an attack position directly behind that of the 8th Guards Army. In the original plan the two tank armies were to join the battle after the enemy's defenses were penetrated and would envelop Berlin from the north and northwest. From the new position, in Zhukov's opinion, the 1st Guards Tank Army could move more rapidly to reinforce the 8th Guards Army if the situation required. Stalin approved the change.[8]

To neutralize the enemy's positional advantages, Zhukov decided to initiate the main attack two hours before dawn on 16 April and illuminate the battlefield with 140 antiaircraft searchlights. These powerful lights, it was hoped, would also blind the defenders and facilitate the rapid collapse of the enemy forward positions. Long before the actual attack, troops of the 1st Belorussian Front rehearsed the use of the searchlights in tactical exercises in areas behind the front. Some of his generals did not think the lights would be effective. Zhukov queried his troops after the exercises. Those on the attacking side said that the defenders were visible as the attack moved forward; those acting as defenders said they were blinded by the light and had become confused. All the soldiers approved this new approach, but some generals were doubtful.[9]*

In the dark, early morning hours of 16 April 1945, after a thirty-minute air bombardment and artillery preparation, the searchlights were turned on and the infantry and tanks moved into the attack. For Zhukov,

---

*Aleksandr V. Gorbatov, who commanded the 3d Army under Zhukov, was one of the generals who voiced his doubts about the use of searchlights at the start of the operation. He was concerned that a night attack from the crowded bridgehead could cause a confused intermingling of attacking units. Why try to turn night into day—would it not be easier to await the dawn? He apparently was not convinced that the lights would effectively blind the defenders. He also thought, but did not voice his opinion, that the density of troops and equipment in the bridgehead would lead to excessive casualties. Gorbatov believed that it was not advisable to take the city by a frontal attack and doubted that the Germans could be deceived into expecting the attack would come from any place other than the Kustrin bridgehead. A. V. Gorbatov, *Gody i voiny* (Years and wars), Moscow: Voenizdat, 1969, pp. 351, 352.

observing from an observation post in the 8th Guards Army area, it was a picture of impressive force beyond anything he had experienced in his entire lifetime.[10]

The military effectiveness of this enormous sound and light show is debatable. Zhukov reported that during the morning of 16 April his troops moved forward on all sectors of the front. But as the defenders recovered from their initial shock, they began to direct artillery and mortar fire from the Seelow Heights. Groups of German bombers began to appear from their bases around Berlin. This opposition grew as the attacking troops approached the high ground. According to other accounts, the attackers became confused in the mud, smoke, and darkness, and the Soviets were fortunate that the defenders allowed them to reorganize and continue the attack.[11]

By 1300 on 16 April, Zhukov realized that the German defenses on the Seelow Heights were basically intact and that the attackers would have to change their organization for combat if they were to take the heights. He decided, after conferring with the army commanders, to commit both of his tank armies to the assault. Zhukov's decision to insert the tank armies at this phase of the battle is strong evidence of the pressure he felt to move forward at all costs. He knew that Konev was looking for the opportunity to enter Berlin before him. In the original plan the tank armies were to be committed after the German defenses in front of the bridgehead had been overcome, and it was obvious from his description of the defenses that scaling the Seelow Heights was hardly the ideal mission for a tank-heavy force. When he reported this decision to Stalin, Zhukov could tell from the tone of the dictator's voice that he was irritated. He told Zhukov sharply that the decision to move the 1st Guards Tank Army behind the 8th Guards Army had been a mistake, and he asked if Zhukov was certain that he could take the Seelow Heights the next day. Zhukov, trying to remain calm, said he thought he would take the heights by the end of the next day. Stalin then informed Zhukov that Konev had not encountered as much resistance on his front and therefore the Stavka was considering turning Konev's two tank armies to approach Berlin from the south and ordering Rokossovskii to accelerate his preparations to cross the Oder and envelop the city from the north. Zhukov agreed that Konev's two tank armies should be turned toward Berlin, but warned that Rokossovskii could not be ready to join the offensive west of the Oder before 23

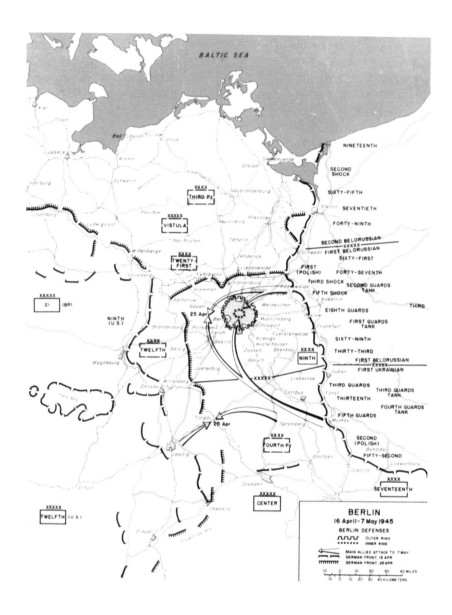

BERLIN
16 April – 7 May 1945
BERLIN DEFENSES
ꟿꟿꟿ OUTER RING
••••••• INNER RING
MAIN ALLIED ATTACK TO 7 MAY
GERMAN FRONT, 15 APR
GERMAN FRONT, 25 APR

April. Stalin, rather dryly, said goodbye and hung up. They did not converse for the next three days.

In a later recollection of these events, Zhukov pictured Stalin as reacting very calmly to the news of the problems that the 1st Belorussian Front was having in overcoming the German defenses. He quoted the dictator as saying that the more German reserves that were beaten on the Seelow Heights, the fewer would be left to defend Berlin.[12] One cannot explain this contradictory report of the dictator's behavior except to attribute it to a casual, faulty remembrance of events given in a conversation, as opposed to the more probable written and edited version of what really occurred.

The next day, the Front received a copy of the Stavka's order to Konev and Rokossovskii. Konev was directed to turn his two tank armies north through Zossen (the headquarters of the German Army and future locale of the headquarters of the Group of Soviet Forces in Germany) toward Berlin. Rokossovskii was ordered to accelerate his crossing of the Oder and to envelop Berlin from the north with a portion of his force. Two deletions from Zhukov's original manuscript provide some indication of the tension that had been caused by just a one-day delay in Zhukov's offensive. After his telephone conversation with the CINC, Zhukov admitted that he felt depressed. (*Nastroenie u menia bylo nevazhnym.*) He knew that Stalin became very irritated when even minor details (*melochi*) did not work out well. In Zhukov's mind his problems before the Seelow Heights were "details." What he may not have known or taken into account was that the U.S. forces had reached and crossed the Elbe, and in Stalin's mind there was a possibility that they would soon be approaching Berlin. The U.S. 2d Armored Division had reached the Elbe on 12 April, and established a bridgehead which was immediately counterattacked by the Germans and abandoned on 14 April. The U.S. 83d Infantry Division established a bridgehead to the south, which was maintained but not reinforced. There apparently was no serious attempt to reinforce these bridgeheads for a move toward Berlin. Nevertheless, given Stalin's concern over the possibility of Allied perfidy, even these probes must have increased his anxiety.

The other deletion in the original manuscript related to the decision to turn Konev's tank armies to the north. Zhukov related that when the word reached his staff, he lied to M. S. Malinin, Front chief of staff, saying that Stalin had told him about the move during his conversation the day before. Malinin was very sensitive about correct staff procedure, which required even the Stavka to confer with Front head-quarters before ordering such a change in plans. The Front staff probably felt that the change was unnecessary and that it implied criticism of the Front's performance.[13]

The 1st Belorussian Front carried the Seelow Heights on the morning of 18 April. There it was struck by a German counterattack mounted by available reserves and including troops drawn from within Berlin. Only on 19 April did the Germans begin to withdraw into the defenses of the capital.

In reviewing this phase of the battle, Zhukov did not admit that any mistakes had been made. He did say that the enemy on the Seelow Heights had been somewhat underestimated and that the prepared defenses there, including those on the reverse slopes, should have been given more attention, particularly by his artillery officer, V. I. Kazakov. With the benefit of hindsight, he thought that the task of taking Berlin should have been a two-Front operation, with the boundary for the Fronts drawn from Frankfort/Oder through the center of Berlin. He also would have employed Rokossovskii's Front differently, concentrating its strike elements along Zhukov's right flank and employing a light covering force on the lower Oder. These variations were not considered during the planning for the operation because of what Zhukov calls subjec-tive reasons. An advance on a broad front was easier for the Stavka to manage, and the High Command (Stalin) decided that this concept would be the basis for the final plan.

In one of his conversations with Konstantin Simonov, Zhukov added some details to his account of the battle for Berlin. He questioned whether, as Konev later reported, Stalin had asked Konev about the possibility of moving Zhukov's two tank armies through Konev's zone because they were being held up at the Seelow Heights. These two armies had already been committed by Zhukov, and the difficulty of having them disengage, reorganize, and move over to Konev's front should have been obvious to such a tactician as the dictator fancied himself. It is not clear from the published version of Konev's memoirs what the dictator had in mind. As Konev recalled the conversation, Stalin asked whether it would be feasible to move Zhukov's "mobile troops" through the breakthrough that had occurred on Konev's front. Zhukov assumed that Stalin had in mind his two tank armies. In any event, Konev explained the difficulty to Stalin and volunteered to send the two tank armies of his Front north to Berlin; Stalin had agreed on that course of action.[14]

Once the Seelow Heights were overcome, the Front advance to Berlin increased its velocity, although the tank armies continued to be constrained to operate in close coordination with the Front's other forces. They could not reach what the Soviets call operational freedom (*operativnyi prostor*), due to the nature of the terrain and the system of rivers, lakes, and canals around the city.

The first artillery rounds were fired into the German capital on 20 April, and the next day units of the Front broke into the outskirts of the city. On 25 April, units of the 1st Belorussian Front joined with those of the 1st Ukrainian Front to complete the encirclement of the city. Zhukov did not discuss the question of which units had reached the city first.

According to Konev, Zhukov did not want to hear that troops other than the 1st Belorussian Front had participated in the capture of Berlin. When units of the 1st Ukrainian Front entered the city on 22 April, he ordered General Chuikov to keep track of the movements of Konev's troops. This did not prevent numerous clashes over the operational boundaries between the two Fronts. When the troops of Rybalko's 3d Tank Army and P. F. Batitskii's 27th Army reached a position 300 meters from the Reichstag, Zhukov shouted at Rybalko, "Why have you appeared here?"

Several times Stalin himself had to intervene between the squabbling Front commanders, each time moving the boundary farther west, thereby expanding the zone of the 1st Belorussian Front, and sometimes requiring the Ukrainians to give up ground they had captured to Zhukov's troops.[15]

Berlin was the largest urban objective that the Soviet Army faced during the war. The defensive advantages of a well-constructed European city had been enhanced by fortifications, particularly in its central area, and there were underground communications that permitted concealed and protected troop movements. Some of the large buildings such as the Reichstag were defended on several floors.

While Konev's two tank armies attacked Berlin from the south and southwest, six armies of the 1st Belorussian Front, supported by the 16th Air Army, were used to capture the last stronghold of the Third Reich. Each army was given a zone of operations in which they proceeded to reduce the defenses street by street and building by building. From 21 April until 2 May, 1,800,000 artillery rounds were fired on the city and its defenders—equivalent to 36,000 tons of metal.

Zhukov hoped he would be able to complete the capture of the city by 1 May—May Day, the day of the annual Moscow parade. He realized on 30 April that this would not be possible and so informed Stalin. Expecting the dictator to be upset, he was surprised when Stalin calmly told him not to hurry but to save his people—that they did not need unnecessary losses! The defenders of the Reichstag began to surrender on 1 May, but small groups continued to fight until the morning of the 2d.

On 1 May, the chief of the General Staff of the German ground forces, General Krebs, appeared at General Chuikov's headquarters with the news that Hitler had committed suicide and with authority to negotiate an armistice. Zhukov immediately sent his chief of staff, V. D. Sokolovskii, to supervise the discussions with Krebs, telling him to accept only the unconditional surrender of Nazi Germany.

He then had Stalin awakened to tell him the news. Stalin regretted that Hitler had not been taken alive. He inquired about the whereabouts of Hitler's remains, and reiterated to Zhukov that only unconditional surrender would be acceptable. Stalin asked that Zhukov not disturb him again until morning (it was then about 0500 Moscow time) unless something extraordinary occurred because he was very tired and had to appear that day at the annual May Day parade.[16]

Sokolovskii then informed Zhukov that Krebs claimed he did not have the authority to agree to an unconditional surrender. Zhukov told him to advise Krebs that the Germans had until 1000 hours to agree or else suffer a devastating strike, after which Berlin would be in ruins. The Germans did not answer by 1000 and at 1040 received what Zhukov described as a hurricane of fire directed at the Reichschancellery where the remnants of the German high command were believed to be. That building was not taken until 2 May. By 1500 that day the battle was essentially over. The remainder of the Berlin garrison surrendered—around 134,000 troops.

According to statistics published in 1963, Soviet casualties for the period 16 April–8 May 1945 for the 1st Ukrainian, 1st Belorussian, and 2d Belorussian Fronts were 304,887 troops wounded, missing, and killed in action. The Western Allies in contrast suffered a total of 260,000 casualties on the western front from 1 January until 8 May 1945.[17]

It was soon to become apparent that the Soviet position in Eastern Europe was not based on the influence and prestige derived from the capture of Berlin. Rather it would be based on domination over the local Communist and left-leaning parties, the installation of a police and internal security system patterned after and controlled by the centralized Soviet police and internal security apparatus, and the physical presence or proximity of the Soviet armed forces. The latter were used in times of internal crisis, such as in East Germany in 1953, in Poland and Hungary in 1956, and in Czechoslovakia in 1968. The system was to last almost 45 years and those who lived under it have suffered, but it is difficult to argue that much would have changed if the British and Americans had taken Berlin first.

NOTES

1. Winston S. Churchill, *The Second World War—Triumph and Tragedy* (Boston: Houghton Mifflin, 1953), p. 455.
2. Dwight D. Eisenhower, *Crusade in Europe* (New York: Doubleday, 1948), p. 396.
3. Ibid., pp. 398–403, 410, 411.
4. Zhukov, *Memoirs* 3: pp. 220, 221.
5. Ibid., p. 222. Shtemenko, *General'nyi shtab*, pp. 329, 330. I. S. Konev, *Sorok piatyi* (Forty-five) (Moscow: Voenizdat, 1966), pp. 92, 93.
6. Zhukov, *Memoirs* 3: p. 241.
7. Ibid., p. 237.
8. Ibid., pp. 224, 228.
9. Ibid., pp. 227, 240. Mirkina and Iarovikov, *Marshal Zhukov: Polkovodets*, p. 305.
10. Zhukov, *Memoirs* 3: P. 240.
11. Ibid., pp. 240, 241. Ziemke, *Stalingrad to Berlin*, p. 474.
12. Zhukov, *Memoirs* 3: pp. 242–244. Simonov, "Zametki," in *VIZh*, no. 10: p. 60.
13. Zhukov, *Memoirs* 3: pp. 242–244.
14. Ibid., pp. 244, 246. Simonov, "Zametki," in *VIZh*, no. 10: p. 60. Konev, *Sorok piatyi*, pp. 116, 117.
15. I. S. Konev, *Zapiski komanduiushchego frontom* (Notes of a Front commander) (Moscow: Voenizdat, 1991), p. 599.
16. Zhukov, *Memoirs* 3: pp. 256–266.
17. Ibid., pp. 267–270. Pospelov, *IVOVSS* 5: p. 290.

XX

THE ALLIED CONTROL COUNCIL FOR GERMANY

One of Marshal Zhukov's immediate concerns following the surrender of the Berlin garrison was verification of the suicides of Hitler and Goebbels, Hitler's propaganda minister. He inspected the Reichschancellery as soon as it was cleared but could not find the burial sites, causing him to suspect, initially, that Hitler, Goebbels, and Bormann, Hitler's secretary, might have escaped. As he was leaving the chancellery, the bodies of Goebbels' six children were found, but Zhukov confessed that he did not have the heart to look at the bodies of the children, who were killed by their parents before they committed suicide.

He did not discover until some 20 years later that personnel from the 3d Army of the 1st Belorussian Front had found Hitler's remains shortly after the fall of Berlin and had positively identified them with the aid of Hitler's dentist. This information was communicated immediately to Stalin, probably through Beriia, and was verified by a general sent to Berlin by Stalin. Zhukov had difficulty accepting the account of the author of a book on the subject, someone who had served as an interpreter for the group that identified the remains—first, because the body had been found and reported to Stalin by personnel subordinate to Zhukov's command without his knowledge and, second, because long after the facts had been reported to him Stalin pretended that he did not know for certain what had happened to Hitler. Zhukov could not think of any reason why Stalin should have kept the information from him.[1] It may be that Stalin enjoyed knowing something about Zhukov's command that the commander himself did not know. It may also have been Stalin's design to hold the information to see what stories and myths would arise in the West about the demise of the Nazi dictator.

The next day, accompanied by General Berzarin, the newly appointed Soviet commandant of the city, and Artur Pieck, son of the German Communist leader, Zhukov toured the ruins of the Reichstag, marveling at the strength of its walls and the possibilities it provided its defenders. The walls of the building were so thick that medium artillery could not penetrate them. The cupola and other parts of the superstructure provided vantage points from which multilayered fire could be concentrated on all approaches.

On 7 May, Stalin called to inform Zhukov that a surrender ceremony was to be held in Reims that day, but that he had insisted the surrender be signed in Berlin the following day before the high commanders of all the countries of the coalition. The signing in Reims was to be considered preliminary. Representatives of the Allied high command would arrive the next day, as would the German representatives. Eisenhower, who conducted the signing at Reims, considered the signing in Berlin a formality performed to demonstrate Allied unity. He felt it inappropriate to attend the Berlin ceremony personally after he had already accepted a total German surrender. Eisenhower's deputy, British Air Chief Marshal Tedder, was sent to Berlin to represent him. The Soviets, however, considered it to be the official end of the war with Germany and have celebrated 9 May as a national holiday ever since.[2]*

Zhukov presided at the Berlin ceremony, which was conducted early in the morning of 9 May. Andrei Ia. Vyshinskii, then a deputy minister of foreign affairs and notorious as the prosecutor in the purge trials of 1937–38, was sent from Moscow with the instruments of surrender and with instructions to remain in Berlin and serve as Zhukov's political advisor. One witness, Maj. Gen. John R. Deane, the head of the wartime U.S. Military Mission to Moscow, observed that during the ceremony Vyshinskii, who was seated two places away from Zhukov,

---

*Those correspondents who witnessed the ceremony at Reims were enjoined not to publish the news of the signing until the Allies issued a joint statement. One news agency published the story before the release hour.

constantly bobbed up to whisper instructions in Zhukov's ear.[3] Zhukov recorded, without reference to Vyshinskii, that the ceremony ended in forty-three minutes, after which the German representatives were dismissed.

Following the ceremony, Zhukov hosted a banquet for the participants, which General Deane described as unforgettable. On Zhukov's instructions, all of the dishes served were Russian or from one of the Soviet republics. The first dish was *shchi,* Russian cabbage soup. Deane believed that the food was imported specially from Moscow. The toasts were endless; Zhukov was observed drinking his toasts with a light white wine, although many others drank the traditional vodka. The affair lasted until 0600 the next morning, and Zhukov proudly recalled dancing a Russian folk dance that he remembered from his youth. General Deane, unfortunately, did not record his impressions of the Russian marshal's dancing.[4]

Later that day, Zhukov was informed that all the documentation relating to the German surrender had been received by the Stavka. D. A. Volkogonov, in his biography of Stalin, depicts Stalin as considering Zhukov's speech closing the ceremony a humdrum ending to a long and terrible war. He also relates that the ceremony had been delayed two to three hours by the carelessness of a member of the Soviet Ministry of Foreign Affairs, who had dropped four lines from the text of a document on the German capitulation sent from Moscow.[5] The activities of the victorious Soviet troops and their advisors were under continuous surveillance and their peccadillos the subject of timely reports to Moscow.

Zhukov devoted several pages in his memoirs to the activities of his command in restoring communal services in Berlin, ensuring that there would not be famine in the city, and reorganizing the local government. On 9 May, Anastas I. Mikoyan, then deputy chairman on the Council of People's Commissars, arrived to assess the situation and determine local needs. One suspects he also came to investigate the possibilities for reparations. In these activities the political apparatus in the Soviet armed forces played a leading role, assisted by surviving German Communists and other antifascist organizations. Zhukov met with leaders of the Communist Party of Germany, Wilhelm Pieck and Walter Ulbricht, and with Otto Grotewohl, a German socialist, who together would eventually form the Socialist Unity Party of Germany and would provide the leadership for the German Democratic Republic when it was proclaimed in 1949.[6]

Later in May, Stalin informed Zhukov that he was to be the Soviet representative on the Allied Control Council for Germany. Eisenhower, Field Marshal Montgomery, and Gen. Lattre de Tassigny would represent the Western Allies. Each of the principals would have a political advisor, and Vyshinskii would perform that function for Zhukov. As Stalin gave this assignment to Zhukov, he briefly discussed some of the current problems of Soviet relations with the British and the Americans. The new American president, Harry Truman, seemed to be agreeing with Churchill that the Western Allies should take a firmer stand toward the Soviets. Stalin also complained that Montgomery had failed to disarm certain German formations in the British zone of occupation and that the Americans were continuing to occupy a large portion of the area that had been assigned at Yalta to the Soviets for occupation. For his part, Zhukov recommended that Allied troops not be permitted to take up their zones of occupation in Berlin until they withdrew to their predesignated zones. Stalin agreed. He also warned Zhukov that he would often find himself in the minority in the Council.[7]

Churchill had already used the expression "iron curtain" in a letter to Truman, dated 12 May, to describe the obstacles that the Soviets had placed between the Western Allies and their rights of access and influence in the Soviet-occupied areas of Eastern Europe. At that time he advocated a meeting with Stalin before the Allied armies moved to their agreed zones of occupation in Germany. He was concerned that the powerful armies of the Western Allies would soon be leaving Europe, either to the Far East to conclude the war with Japan or home to be demobilized, leaving Western Europe defenseless before Soviet power. This meeting eventually took place in Potsdam in mid-July. By that time, the U.S. forces had been withdrawn to their agreed zone, and whatever leverage that continued occupation of portions of the Soviet zone would have provided had disappeared.[8]

The day after Zhukov returned from Moscow with Vyshinskii at his side, he received a courtesy visit from Eisenhower. Eisenhower made a favorable impression on Zhukov by his simplicity, his relaxed approach, and his sense of humor. The meeting was brief, but Zhukov did not waste the opportunity to ask Eisenhower to remove his troops from the Soviet zone and to tell U.S. Gen. Carl Spaatz, who was also present, that in the Soviet zone of Germany the U.S. Air Force could fly only in established air corridors. Perhaps to Zhukov's surprise,

Eisenhower agreed with him, saying he would insist that the American troops be withdrawn. Zhukov speculated over who would make the decision to withdraw the troops and concluded that since this was a matter of high politics, it would be Churchill and Truman.[9] One wonders if it had been the other way around—if the Soviets had occupied portions of the U.S. and British zones—whether Zhukov would have felt free to tell a foreign official that he was going to insist Stalin give the order to withdraw. For one thing, although Eisenhower had a political advisor in Robert Murphy, he was just that—an advisor. Within the overall guidelines of U.S. policy, Eisenhower was a relatively independent operator. Zhukov, on the other hand, was severely limited by the presence and authority of Vyshinskii. Stalin had made it clear to Harry Hopkins in Moscow in 1945 that Zhukov would have little power concerning political affairs in Germany.[10]

Eisenhower and Zhukov were to have several occasions for direct contact during the next several months, until Eisenhower left Europe in November 1945. These included the sessions of the Allied Control Council, Zhukov's return visit to Eisenhower's headquarters in Frankfurt, and Eisenhower's visit to Moscow and Leningrad in August 1945.

In his contacts with Zhukov, Eisenhower found him to be "a firm believer in the Communist concept," who saw the Soviet system of government "based on idealism," as compared to the United States system which was based on "materialism." Zhukov, Eisenhower wrote, felt that the United States system appealed to all that was selfish in people. He asked Eisenhower to understand a system

> in which an attempt was made to substitute for such motivations the devotion of a man to the great national complex of which he formed a part. In spite of my complete repudiation of all systems that involved dictatorship, there was no doubt in my mind that Marshal Zhukov was sincere.[11]

Zhukov was disturbed by liberties the Western press had taken with the person of Stalin and with the details of his own life. Despite Eisenhower's attempts to convince Zhukov of the virtues of a free press and the "free or competitive enterprise" system, Eisenhower felt he had made no impression on Zhukov. To Eisenhower, Zhukov "always seemed to be profoundly convinced of the essential rectitude of the

Communist theory" and "his own adherence to the Communistic doctrine seemed to come from inner conviction and not from any outward compulsion."[12]

Considering the circumstances, it would have been remarkable if Eisenhower could have achieved some change in Zhukov's political views. Since Eisenhower could not speak Russian, nor could Zhukov speak English, all conversations were conducted through interpreters. As professional military officers, both men had only indirect contact with the economic and political systems they were representing, but of the two, it is probable that Zhukov's early experiences as the son of a poor peasant and as an apprentice furrier in capitalist Russia resulted in a depth of political conviction as great as or greater than that of Eisenhower. It may also be possible that, although Zhukov admits he had difficulty with certain aspects of Marxist-Leninist-Stalinist theory, the manifest political indoctrination he had received over the years had better prepared him to defend his beliefs against an opponent such as Eisenhower, who was relatively unschooled in political theory.

In his appraisal of Zhukov as a great captain, Eisenhower was especially generous. Zhukov, he wrote, "had had longer experience as a responsible leader in great battles than any other man of our time."[13] Noting that Zhukov usually had been sent to the decisive sector of the Soviet front, and judging from his description of some of the battles, their locale, and the reasoning behind his decisions, Eisenhower concluded that "it was clear that he was an accomplished soldier."[14]

These discussions between the two leaders also brought home to Eisenhower the differing views of the two sides when it came to assessing the human costs of military operations. As an example, Zhukov told Eisenhower about the Soviet Army's method of attacking through a minefield: send the infantry through first to provide protection for those removing the antitank mines, regardless of casualties from antipersonnel mines. Zhukov eschewed what the U.S. Army considered vital to the maintenance of morale—unit rotations in the forward areas, short leaves and furloughs, and development of techniques to reduce battlefield risks. Eisenhower, of course, was aware of the disadvantageous circumstances in which the Soviet Union entered the war. Nevertheless, he left the impression that the Soviets may have paid an inordinately high cost for their victories.[15]

Zhukov's account of his conversations with Eisenhower seems to have been written in a much more critical vein, designed to conform to Soviet propaganda themes on such topics as the opening of the Second Front, the difficulty of the cross-channel operation in 1944, the effectiveness of Lend-Lease, and the dispute between Eisenhower and Churchill over whether or not to attempt to take Berlin. When Eisenhower told him that the Allies were not prepared in 1943 to undertake such a large amphibious operation as the channel crossing, Zhukov wrote that this was far from the truth. They could have opened a second front, but consciously did not hurry, awaiting more significant damage to the Wehrmacht and greater exhaustion of the Soviet Army. He quoted Eisenhower as saying that the Allied invasion of the continent was begun in easy conditions and continued without special opposition from the German defenders of the coastline. Zhukov went on to express his wonder when he saw the American film "The Longest Day," based on the facts of the invasion, which he claimed showed the enemy as much stronger than he was in fact.

In a general appraisal of Allied operations on the continent, Zhukov wrote that, in the main, they were operations to overcome German mobile defenses, in contrast to the deeply echeloned defenses with which the Soviets were forced to contend. He cited Eisenhower as saying that his greatest problem was developing and maintaining the lines of communication, supply, and evacuation behind his forces. He found Eisenhower reluctant to talk about the German counterattack in the Ardennes at the end of 1944. From the meager responses of Eisenhower and those accompanying him, Zhukov concluded that the Germans had taken the Allied high command by surprise, and the Americans could not withstand the enemy attacks. The sense of alarm and concern that the German attack aroused in the Allied high command caused Churchill to send a message to Stalin on 6 January 1945, informing him of the difficult situation caused by heavy casualties and by Allied loss of the initiative. Zhukov cited the delivery to Moscow of Churchill's letter by Air Chief Marshal Tedder, Eisenhower's deputy, as proof of the sense of urgency behind the missive. The Soviets, faithful to their obligations, responded in exactly one week by launching an attack on the entire front, which forced the Germans back to the Oder-Neisse line. Eisenhower told Zhukov that for the Allies the Soviet offensive was

a long-awaited moment, because it meant the Germans could not reinforce their western front.[16]*

It is difficult to believe that Eisenhower portrayed the cross-
channel invasion in the terms used by Zhukov. Eisenhower may have
sketched it modestly, in a simplified form that was poorly conveyed
by interpreters, and Zhukov remembered what he wanted to remember about the operation.[17] It is also strange that Eisenhower did not
mention the massive deception operation which convinced the Germans
that the landings on 6 June were not the main effort but were to be
followed by landings at other points on the coast. (They therefore withheld
their attacks on the Normandy landing beaches.)

Zhukov was completely misinformed about the purpose of Air Marshal
Tedder's mission. Tedder may have carried the actual copy of Churchill's
letter, but because of weather and other transportation problems, he
did not arrive in Moscow until 14 January 1945, two days after the
Soviet offensive from the Vistula had already begun. Churchill had sent
his letter on 6 January and had an answer from Stalin the next day.
Presumably it was sent via British diplomatic communications. Tedder's
mission, according to Eisenhower, was to make arrangements for
coordination, such as establishing lines beyond which the air forces
could not drop bombs as the two forces came closer together in Germany in the late winter and spring of 1945. According to General Deane,
the principal objective of Tedder's visit was to find out what the Soviets
would be doing at the end of March, when Eisenhower expected to
be making combat crossings of the Rhine. Stalin assured Tedder that
the Soviet Army would keep the Germans fully occupied so they would
not be able to reinforce the western front with troops from the east.[18]

Zhukov, as have other Soviet memoirists and historians, accused
unnamed bourgeois writers of overestimating the contribution to the
Soviet victory of the supplies and equipment furnished the Soviet Union
under Lend-Lease. By his calculation, the aggregate amount of the aid
supplied came to 4 percent of the amount the Soviets supplied them-

---

*General Deane, who was in Moscow at the time of the invasion, arranged to have
motion pictures of the operation shown to Soviet military officers about a week later.
He reports that they were amazed at its magnitude.

selves. According to Zhukov, this was hardly enough to play a deciding role in the outcome of the war. He does provide some numbers which in themselves must have impressed the average reader: 400 thousand cars and trucks, 18 thousand aircraft, and 11 thousand tanks.[19] To fully appreciate these numbers, however, he should have noted that all this equipment was delivered over the ocean while the U.S. was fighting a full-scale war with Japan—a factor most Soviet historians tended to ignore.

From the beginning of his association with Zhukov, Eisenhower was guided by his belief that success in the joint government of Germany would be measured by the degree to which the Western Allies overcame Soviet suspicion and distrust. He felt that a great responsibility devolved on those in Berlin who were in daily contact with the concrete problems of restoring postwar Europe. In personal as well as official relationships, he strove to demonstrate good faith, respect, and friendly intent. It was this attitude that caused Eisenhower to urge that the Allies move back to their agreed occupation zones, while others were recommending that the situation be used to influence Soviet behavior in other areas. It was this approach that led some, including members of his own staff and command, to believe that he had come under Zhukov's influence. Ambassador W. Averell Harriman has said that Eisenhower assured him that his friend Zhukov would succeed Stalin and usher in a new era of friendly relations. Harriman later came to believe that military leaders were the last to discover that the era of wartime cooperation was over and that Soviet policy was being set by the leadership of the Communist Party.[20]

Just before Eisenhower returned to the United States, the two commanders met at a Soviet reception in Berlin on the 7th of November 1945, the anniversary of the October Revolution in 1917. They agreed, as Zhukov put it, that they had successfully cooperated in the Control Council, despite a number of contradictions and obstacles. He also added that more could have been achieved if all sides had fulfilled the obligations agreed on at the Potsdam Conference.

Zhukov and Eisenhower met again in Geneva in 1955. Eisenhower was then the president of the United States and Zhukov the Soviet minister of defense under Khrushchev. Zhukov reported that during that meeting Eisenhower spoke very differently than he had in 1945: he "firmly expressed and defended the policy of the imperialist circles of the U.S.A."[21] He might have added that by that time Eisenhower understood much better the role of Khrushchev and the Communist Party in setting Soviet policy.

President Eisenhower was interested both from a professional and a personal point of view in Zhukov's position in the Soviet hierarchy; he was particularly interested in Zhukov's role in setting Soviet disarmament policy. Because his son John had been a big hit with Zhukov in 1945, the president took him along in 1955 on the chance that Zhukov might say something to him that he might otherwise withhold. In Geneva, John accompanied his father to a stag dinner and in the course of one conversation, Zhukov told him that things were not what they seemed in Russia. What was meant by that remark either was never explained to the Eisenhowers or it has never been revealed. Both father and son found that Zhukov was not the same "cocky little rooster" they had known in Germany after the war. John believed that Zhukov was in Geneva as a member of the ruling group "only as a facade." The senior Eisenhower dismissed Zhukov as "window dressing" being used only as a possible bridge to the President.[22]

NOTES

1. Elena Rzhevskaia, "B tot den', pozdnei osen'iu" (That day in late autumn) in Smirnov, *Marshal Zhukov,* pp. 292–295. Zhukov, *Memoirs* 3: p. 271. *The New York Times,* 18 Sept. 1992, p. A10.
2. Zhukov, *Memoirs* 3: pp. 271–274. Eisenhower, *Crusade in Europe,* p. 427.
3. John R. Deane, *The Strange Alliance* (New York: Viking, 1947), p. 178.
4. Ibid., p. 180. Zhukov, *Memoirs* 3: p. 278. Mirkina and Iarovikov, *Marshal Zhukov: Polkovodets,* pp. 317, 318.
5. Volkogonov, *Triumf i tragediia,* book 2, part 2, p. 7.
6. Zhukov, *Memoirs* 3: pp. 279–288.
7. Ibid., pp. 311, 312.
8. Churchill, *Triumph and Tragedy,* pp. 573–581.
9. Zhukov, *Memoirs* 3: pp. 313–315.
10. Robert E. Sherwood, *Roosevelt and Hopkins* (New York: Harper, 1948), p. 914.
11. Eisenhower, *Crusade in Europe,* p. 472.
12. Ibid., pp. 472–473.
13. Ibid., p. 467.
14. Ibid., pp. 467–470.
15. Ibid., pp. 344–346.
16. Deane, *The Strange Alliance,* p. 151.
17. Zhukov, *Memoirs* 3: pp. 344, 345.
18. Eisenhower, *Crusade in Europe,* pp. 366, 367. Deane, *The Strange Alliance,* pp. 156, 157.
19. Zhukov, *Memoirs* 3: pp. 347, 348.
20. Walter Isaacson and Evan Thomas, *The Wise Men* (New York: Simon and Schuster, 1986), p. 318.
21. Ibid., p. 350.
22. John S. D. Eisenhower, *Strictly Personal* (New York: Doubleday, 1974), pp. 175, 176. Stephen Ambrose, *Eisenhower* (New York: Simon and Schuster, 1984), vol. 2, *The President,* pp. 262, 266.

XXI

CINC, SOVIET OCCUPATION FORCES, GERMANY, 1945-1946

In early June 1945 Zhukov, with Vyshinskii at his side, held a press conference on the veranda of his villa overlooking the Wannsee. In the words of Alexander Werth, a British correspondent who was in the Soviet Union during the war and who participated in the press conference, Zhukov's manner was simple and full of bonhomie. As Zhukov discussed the war and his role in it, he did not mention any other Soviet marshal or general and referred to Stalin only in passing. Werth observed in Zhukov a curious mixture of modesty and almost boyish boastfulness; he seemed to take credit for almost all of the victories the Red Army had won.[1]

Despite this press conference, Stalin shortly thereafter conferred on Zhukov one of his most satisfying postwar honors, selecting him to be the reviewing officer of the victory parade which was to be held on Red Square on 24 June. The CINC had proposed the ceremony in mid-May, but the question of who was to be the reviewing officer had been left open. A few days before the parade, Stalin casually asked Zhukov if he had forgotten how to ride. The CINC then told him that he was to review the parade. When Zhukov protested that the CINC should be the reviewer, Stalin said he was too old—he was then 65. Zhukov rode what the Soviets called a "white Arabian" that Budennyi had selected. Zhukov was to learn later from Stalin's son Vasilii that Stalin had intended to review the parade, but had tried to ride the horse and had been thrown from it.[2]*

*In Soviet Army practice, the senior officer "takes" (*prinimaet*) the parade. At that time, both the officer taking the parade and the commander of troops were mounted.

The parade itself was a masterpiece of allegory. Each of the ten Fronts in action against Germany at the end of the war was represented by a composite regiment, made up of its most decorated members led by the Front commander and his staff. They were aligned as they were when they finished the war, with the Karelian Front (the farthest north) on the right and the 4th Ukrainian Front (the farthest south) on the left, followed by a composite naval regiment and one representing the Moscow Military District. The weather precluded air force participation. When Zhukov was on the mausoleum with Stalin the rain was so heavy that he considered wiping the visor of his hat, but he noticed that Stalin made no move to wipe the streams of water from his visor. Zhukov decided to endure the minor discomfort.[3]

At an appropriate point in the ceremony, selected troops, accompanied by rolling drums, carried 200 Wehrmacht standards forward and cast them at the base of the mausoleum, just as Kutuzov's soldiers after the defeat of Napoleon had once thrown French standards and banners at the feet of Tsar Aleksandr I.[4]

Many years later Zhukov was asked what he considered to be the highlights of the parade. He responded that there were two: the first, when he rode through the Spasskie Gates on the Arabian to the music of his favorite Russian composer, Mikhail Glinka, *Slav'sia;* and the second, when the standards of the Nazi Wehrmacht were thrown on the ground before the mausoleum.[5]

In 1945, the parade seemed to represent the defining event in Soviet history. At enormous cost the Soviet state had rallied its forces and defeated the most powerful country in Europe. Soviet occupation troops were in Eastern Germany and in all of the states on the western borders of the Soviet Union. For Zhukov personally it was reasonable for him to expect to serve his remaining years in honor and with respect. St. George had slain the dragon.

In recent years, specially equipped open sedans are used for these officers. Those officials on Lenin's mausoleum are spectators, except for the reviewing officer who, after exchanging greetings with each major unit in the parade, dismounts, climbs up the steps to the top of the mausoleum, and gives a speech from there appropriate to the occasion. The troops then pass in review. There is no evidence that Stalin ever learned to ride.

Zhukov was so inspired by the Moscow parade that when he returned to Berlin, he proposed to the other Allied commissioners that a four-power parade be held in the area of the Reichstag and the Brandenburg Gate in September to celebrate the Allied victory. The necessary governmental approvals were obtained, but as the day of the parade approached, Zhukov learned that the other three high commissioners would not be able to attend and were sending deputies in their place. When Zhukov informed Stalin, the dictator attributed it to an attempt by the Allies to reduce the significance of the victory of the wartime coalition. He directed Zhukov to "take" the parade himself. For Zhukov, the parade was a success and accomplished its stated purpose.[6]

The parade also accomplished another purpose. It allowed the Soviets to show some of their latest model tanks and self-propelled guns to the senior Allied commanders who attended. The senior U.S. general present was George S. Patton, Jr. He met Zhukov but was not impressed. He wrote his wife, "He was in full-dress uniform much like comic opera and covered with medals. He is short, rather fat, and has a prehensile chin like an ape but good, blue eyes."[7] Patton's visceral dislike of the Soviets prevented him from acknowledging Zhukov as his military peer, even though Zhukov had in many respects a similar command style and at least as much military success. Patton's prejudice kept him from recognizing the physical power contained in Zhukov's compact frame, and he obviously received a bad impression from the Soviet military custom of wearing multiple copies of decorations. (It is the American practice to give oak leaf clusters in lieu of awarding the same medal a second or third time.) Even a chest as large as Zhukov's appeared overdecorated to Patton when it was covered with all the decorations he had received.* It is also unfortunate that Patton, a horseman, never saw Zhukov ride the Arabian.

---

*During his service Zhukov was awarded four Gold Stars of a Hero of the Soviet Union; six Orders of Lenin; two Orders of Victory; the Order of the October Revolution; three Orders of the Red Banner; and two Orders of Suvorov First Class; and thirty foreign decorations including the Knights Grand Cross of the Order of the Bath from Great Britain and the Order of the Legion of Merit (Commander in Chief) from the United States.

After Zhukov's return to Germany from the victory parade in late June, arrangements for the Potsdam Conference became one of his priority concerns. Potsdam was chosen because the former German Crown Prince's villa had survived the war intact and had available an adequate number of ancillary accommodations to house the numerous advisors and experts who would attend. Stalin arrived by train on the 16th—one day late. As he explained to President Harry Truman, whom he met the next day for the first time, he had been delayed by negotiations with the Chinese and because his doctors would not allow him to fly. Actually, Stalin did not want to fly because he had been terrified on his flight to Teheran in 1943 when his plane encountered air pockets. As the dictator became older, his fear of death grew stronger. The security arrangements for the special train that brought him to Potsdam were unprecedented. For the 1,923 kilometers the train travelled from Moscow, Beriia deployed 17,000 NKVD troops and 1,515 operational personnel. Each kilometer of the rail route had 6 to 13 guards on duty.[8]

In 1965, Zhukov told Elena Rzhevskaia, a writer, that Stalin had been shaken by the war and in 1947 had told him, "I am the most unfortunate person. I am even afraid of my own shadow."[9] Beriia, who recognized Stalin's phobia, used it to his advantage, frightening the dictator with reports of new plots against his life, thereby increasing the dictator's reliance on Beriia's security troops. Zhukov told Rzhevskaia that when Stalin rode in an automobile, his personal security chief always sat in front; Zhukov or any other passenger would ride in the back. Stalin sat in between. Thus an assassin firing from the front would hit the security man; from the back he would hit the passenger. The glass in the side windows was approximately 10 centimeters thick.[10]

Prior to his arrival in Potsdam, Stalin had told Zhukov that he did not want to be met by an honor guard (he probably did not trust one selected from the soldiers of the 1st Belorussian Front). Stalin's personal security officer, General Vlasik, was responsible for arrangements in the railroad station. Zhukov met the rail car and accompanied the CINC to his quarters, which formerly belonged to the German World War I general, Ludendorff. After reporting to Stalin on the status of the Soviet troops in Germany, Zhukov became an observer at the conference. Neither he nor the other Allied commanders in chief in Germany were official members of their country's delegation. Zhukov, however, attended the sessions and was present when Stalin returned from the meeting with Truman at which the president informed Stalin that the United States was going to drop a superpowerful bomb on Japan. In his memoirs, Zhukov characterized Truman's move as political blackmail. When Stalin told Molotov what Truman had announced, Molotov remarked, "They are raising their price." Stalin laughed and replied, "Let them. We'll have to talk to [Igor V.] Kurchatov [head of the Soviet nuclear program] today about speeding up our work." Zhukov understood that they were talking about developing an atomic bomb. He also commented in his memoirs that there was no military reason to drop bombs on the peaceful, heavily populated cities of Hiroshima and Nagasaki.[11]

Zhukov's description of the work of the conference, which ended on 2 August, was in the now familiar black and white terms of Soviet postwar propaganda. The Soviet delegation arrived with the firm intention of achieving an agreed policy on the regulation of postwar problems in the interest of establishing peace and security and preventing the rebirth of German militarism. The participants were limited by decisions made at Yalta, and the Soviet delegation managed to overcome the efforts of reactionary forces and achieve adoption of plans for the democratization and demilitarization of Germany. But at Potsdam, the efforts of the governments of the U.S.A. and England to use the defeat of Germany to strengthen their position in the struggle for world domination became much more obvious.[12]

Zhukov's appraisal of the Potsdam Conference and its achievements indicates that although he had direct, personal experience with the chronic injustices of the Communist system, he still believed in it and accepted its appraisal of its competitors.

With the achievement of victory over Germany and his own personal role in that victory, Zhukov would have been justified in assuming that there would be some relaxation of the scrutiny and surveillance of everything he did. He would soon find out that this was a false assumption. In late 1945, the Group of Soviet Occupation Forces in Germany received some uninvited guests. One of Beriia's deputies, Viktor Abakumov, arrived in Berlin and arrested some officers assigned to Zhukov's command. When he found out about it, Zhukov summoned Abakumov and demanded an explanation as to why he had not presented himself to the commander in chief and provided him with the grounds for the arrests. When Abakumov could not offer a satisfactory explanation, Zhukov released those arrested and ordered Abakumov to return to Moscow, threatening to have him returned under guard if he did not leave voluntarily. If Zhukov was not previously aware of it, he must have realized after this episode that he was not in Stalin's good graces and that it was now open season for Beriia and his operatives to build a case against him.

Stalin, in fact, had been accumulating such information for some time, and through the good offices of Lavrentii Beriia continued to do so. Some historians of the Soviet armed forces trace the beginnings of Stalin's efforts to disgrace Zhukov to his envy over the immense popularity that Zhukov enjoyed after the defense of Moscow in 1941. They cite Beriia's arrest in 1942 of V. S. Golushkevich, chief of the operations section of the Western Front (after he had been transferred to another Front), and the unsuccessful effort to gain from him information incriminating Zhukov. Then, as Zhukov's popularity continued to grow, the dictator in 1944 decided to get rid of Zhukov. First, he decided not to use him as representative of the Stavka. Second, he charged N. A. Bulganin, then a deputy commissar of defense, to find some error or omission that could be charged to Zhukov. With the aid of some officers of the General Staff, it was found that two artillery manuals had been approved by Zhukov without referring them to the Stavka. In an order distributed throughout the upper command echelons of the Soviet Army, Zhukov was warned not to be in haste when serious questions were being decided. In the fall of 1944, Stalin began to be more critical of the directions Zhukov was giving the commanders of the Fronts he was coordinating. Stalin also was irritated to learn that some of Zhukov's subordinates were referring to themselves as "Zhukovites." At the time, Zhukov did not pay much attention to these seemingly minor pinpricks.

During the Potsdam Conference, Stalin met his son Vasilii, an Air Force officer serving in the Group of Soviet Occupation Forces in Germany. Vasilii complained to him about the quality of Soviet military aircraft, saying they were far inferior to those of the United States. When Stalin returned to the Soviet Union, he immediately ordered the arrest of the leaders of the Soviet aviation industry and the leadership of the Soviet Air Force, including its commander in chief, Chief Marshal of Aviation A. A. Novikov. Beriia's operatives, using coercive measures, extracted incriminating information about Zhukov from Novikov.

In late 1945 at a meeting in the Kremlin, Stalin accused Zhukov of
ascribing to himself the credit for all the Soviet Army victories in the
war and understating the role of the Stavka. Stalin also discussed how
the various operations were planned and prepared, emphasizing the roles
of the field commanders, the General Staff, and the Stavka. Stalin then
asked for comments from the audience. All present felt duty bound to
give an opinion of Zhukov which supported that of the dictator. According to Admiral of the Fleet N. G. Kuznetsov, who informed Zhukov
of the meeting (when is not clear), the comments were sharp and often
unjust. The majority were cautious but in the same critical spirit as
those of the dictator. The dismantling of Zhukov's image had begun.[13]*
    Stalin's next move was to return Zhukov to Moscow, which he did
at the end of March 1946. In the beginning of the month Stalin had
called him in Berlin to discuss the plans for the postwar organization
of the armed forces. At that time Stalin still held the position of people's
commissar of defense and Bulganin was his first deputy. During the
conversation, Stalin noted that in the plan, apparently prepared by
Bulganin, Zhukov's name was not included among those who were to
occupy the top leadership positions and he professed to believe that
this was not right. That Zhukov was not listed for one of the top positions
was hardly surprising, since Bulganin would not have presumed that
Zhukov was to be recalled from Germany. Stalin, after saying that
Vasilevskii wanted to be chief of the General Staff, asked Zhukov if
he desired the post of commander in chief of the Ground Forces. Zhukov
gave the proper response, saying that he had not thought about it, but
was willing to serve wherever the Central Committee wanted him to
serve. Stalin continued, stating that he wanted Zhukov to come to Moscow
to work on the plan with Vasilevskii. Stalin, in this or a subsequent

---

*The text of the order dictated by Stalin criticizing Zhukov's haste in approving the
artillery field manual may be found in Shtemenko, *General'nyi shtab* 2: pp. 18–21.
In the same volume (p. 500) Shtemenko mentions a postwar meeting of the Supreme
Military Council (*Vysshii Voennyi Sovet*) at which Stalin presided and spoke about
modesty as a characteristic of good military leaders and the unacceptability of con-
ceit and delusions of grandeur. The issue was raised, according to Shtemenko, by a
letter written about one of the well-known but unnamed military leaders. Shtemenko
was undoubtedly referring to Zhukov and it may have been the same meeting that
Pavlenko described in which the opening rounds were fired against Zhukov.

conversation, also cited the fact that both Eisenhower and Montgomery had left Germany, asking if it were not time for Zhukov to return. Zhukov agreed. Within two or three days Stalin called Zhukov again and confirmed that he was to be the commander in chief of the Ground Forces.

Subsequently, Zhukov discussed the planned organization of the armed forces with Bulganin in Moscow. He soon found that he had serious differences with Bulganin over the authority of the commanders in chief of the armed services versus that of the first deputy minister. According to Bulganin's plan, the commanders in chief would deal directly with the first deputy and not with the minister of defense (Stalin). Bulganin justified his proposal by saying that it was necessary to lighten the enormous work load that the dictator was carrying. Zhukov's reply was that Stalin was the minister today but someone else might be tomorrow, therefore the plan should be written not for an individual but for the position.

Bulganin reported this conversation to Stalin in a distorted form and added his own self-serving supposition that Zhukov did not want to deal with him because he was not a Marshal of the Soviet Union. In a few days he was promoted to that rank. Stalin told Zhukov that the plan would have to be worked over. According to Zhukov, Bulganin was poorly informed about military matters and knew nothing about operational and strategic questions; he was intuitively clever, however, and had managed to insinuate himself into the dictator's confidence. Stalin also realized that Bulganin was not an ideal commissar, but he needed a clever diplomat who idolized him and would do anything he wanted.

After Zhukov turned over his duties in Germany to his deputy, V. D. Sokolovskii, and returned to Moscow, he began to work on a series of measures to bring the army back to what he considered its normal standards. The end of the war and the demobilization of the older-age cohorts had had a deleterious effect on discipline and effectiveness. The measures included a number of training exercises, which were contained in a draft order for combat training during 1946. It was sent to Stalin for approval with an information copy to Bulganin. Stalin, influenced by Bulganin, considered that Zhukov was proceeding independently and ignoring his deputy.

There followed what Zhukov described as a major and unpleasant conversation with Stalin, with Bulganin in attendance. The main sticking point was the provision in the order that units designated as "reserves of the High Command" would participate in combined field and command exercises with units of the Ground Forces. Bulganin warned the dictator that Zhukov wanted to concentrate all the reserves of the High Command under his authority, leaving the commissar and his deputy with nothing. The implication was that Stalin would be defenseless if Zhukov took them under his control. When Zhukov referred to Bulganin's comments as "a child's babbling," Stalin was clearly upset. He ordered the draft rewritten. When a second draft was also not approved, Vasilevskii speculated that Stalin wanted to issue the order himself. Vasilevskii was correct; the order to the Ground Forces was finally issued as an order of the commissar of defense.[14]

As time went on, relations between Zhukov and Bulganin and Stalin deteriorated. Zhukov felt that something unpleasant was brewing around him. In June, Zhukov was informed that he was to be present at a meeting the next day but he was not told the subject of the meeting. Late that night three young men came to his dacha. One of the men told Zhukov they were there to conduct a search, but could present no warrant or order authorizing them to proceed. Zhukov sent them on their way, threatening to use a weapon. He now knew that he would be the subject of the meeting the next day. He did not sleep for the rest of that night.[15]*

The forum the next day was an expanded session of the Main Military Council. Stalin presided and Shtemenko was the secretary. In addition, members of the Politburo Beriia, Lazar M. Kaganovich, and Bulganin were there and the following officers: Golikov, then chief of the Main Cadres Directorate of the Ministry of Defense; I. S. Konev, then first deputy to Zhukov; V. D. Sokolovskii, who had succeeded Zhukov as Soviet commander in Germany; K. K. Rokossovskii, then commander

---

*The organs of state security did not accept defeat passively. Soon after this fiasco, a group appeared at Zhukov's intown apartment with a search warrant and a uniformed armed guard looking for "valuables." They removed practically everything in the apartment, including nine-year-old Ella's doll. Zhukov was forced to stand by helplessly, wearing his uniform decorated with three gold stars of a Hero of the Soviet Union. The investigators then searched Zhukov's dacha at Sosnovka no. 5 and removed, among other things, his first efforts to record his experiences during World War II. Later, Stalin called him and told him to leave the writing of history to historians. N. N. Iakovlev, *Zhukov* (Moscow: Molodaia Gvardiia, 1992), pp. 427, 428.

of the Northern Group of Soviet Forces in Poland; P. S. Rybalko, then first deputy chief of Armored and Mechanized Forces; and A. V. Khrulev, chief of Rear Services.

Stalin started the meeting by handing Shtemenko a folder and asking him to read what was in it. Shtemenko found a typewritten letter in the folder signed by Chief Marshal of Aviation A. A. Novikov. According to the letter, Zhukov while with Novikov at the front discussed the actions of the Stavka and the government and often spoke in an unflattering way about Stalin. Marshal Konev, who has provided an account of this meeting, described the essence of the letter read by Shtemenko: Zhukov was unreliable politically, and was hostile to the Central Committee of the Communist Party and to the government. From evidence gathered from more than seventy arrested officers, including Novikov, Zhukov was accused of plotting against the Party, the government, and Stalin. To the marshals and the generals present it was clear that the objective of the meeting was to convince them that the evidence supported the charges so they would approve taking "repressive" measures against Zhukov.

When Shtemenko had finished reading the evidence, Stalin spoke first, in the same general vein he had used at the meeting at the end of 1945. He also added that officers around Zhukov had contributed to the problem by praising him excessively, praise to which Zhukov had not objected. Stalin closed by saying that Zhukov's conduct was intolerable. He asked the council to examine the case and decide what should be done.

Konev spoke next. He had been called to Moscow to participate in the meeting from a spa, Karlovy Vary, in Czechoslovakia, where he had been planning to take a long vacation. He noted that Zhukov was difficult to get along with, whether as a subordinate or as a neighbor at the front. He recalled the boundary problems that had arisen between them during the Berlin operation. But he rejected categorically the accusation that Zhukov was dishonest and lacked respect for the Central Committee. He also cited Zhukov's conduct at the front, constantly visiting the forward positions to assist commanders in carrying out the Stavka's orders. A dishonest person in a political sense would not have conducted himself that way.

Other officers present spoke of Zhukov in similar terms, with the exception of Golikov. Golikov, still smarting from his relief from command of the Voronezh Front in 1943, spoke from a notebook and according to Konev, poured much dirt on Zhukov's head, including various personal details. Prepared in advance, his testimony was designed to confirm Zhukov's unreliability. At one point when Golikov was complaining that Zhukov was responsible for his relief at Voronezh, Stalin broke in to say that he himself had ordered him relieved, but Golikov remained unconvinced.

The Politburo members spoke last. Their contributions all came down to the judgment that Zhukov was dangerous and that he had the ways of a Bonaparte.

Through it all Zhukov sat with his head down and alternately paled and flushed. When he was given the floor by Stalin, he denied Novikov's allegations. He admitted he did not have the character of an angel, but stated forcefully that he was a Communist who had responsibly fulfilled all that he had been given to do by the Party. He confessed that he had inflated his role in organizing the victory over the enemy.

Stalin then asked, "What shall we do with Zhukov?" The first decision was unanimous. Zhukov was to be relieved as commander in chief of the Ground Forces and replaced by Konev. Stalin again raised the question of Zhukov's future. The atmosphere was very tense; the speeches by the members of the Politburo had left the impression that they were leaning toward "repressive" measures. The resistance of the military members present, however, apparently convinced Stalin that this was unlike the Tukhachevskii case, in which the military had remained silent. The military had presented an almost united front against the accusation that Zhukov had plotted against the regime. Stalin proposed assigning him to command the Odessa Military District—a decidedly secondary military district. The decision was approved by the council.[16]

In December 1954, Novikov, who was rehabilitated after the death of Stalin, testified at the trial of Abakumov. He related the circumstances surrounding his letter denouncing Zhukov. Novikov had been arrested on the night of 22 April 1946. He soon realized that the condition of the Air Force was not the focus of his interrogation; Marshal Zhukov was. He was interrogated day and night from 22 to 30 April and from 4 to 8 May. At the end he was

broken morally, brought to desperation by the injustice of the accusation, sleepless nights. . . . You could not go to sleep, continuous

light in your eyes . . . not only because of the interrogations and
the nervous tension, excessive fatigue, apathy, indifference to
everything . . . only to be left alone. . . . therefore I signed . . .
cowardice, a broken will. They drove me to self destruction.

Abakumov was found guilty and shot on 19 December 1954.

When Zhukov left for Odessa, a *Krasnaia Zvezda* correspondent,
Lev Isaevich Slavin, gave him a book as a parting gift. Inside the front
cover he had written a short inscription, which can be roughly translated as follows:

You are always the same
And you can't be otherwise:
You don't get carried away by success
You don't bow to misfortune.
Remain that way to the end
As I knew you once:
Sincere as a wise man
And direct as a soldier.[17]

NOTES

1. Alexander Werth, *Russia at War: 1941–1945* (New York: Avon, 1965), pp. 897–901.
2. Zhukov, *Memoirs* 3: pp. 304–308.
3. Rzhevskaia, "B tot den', pozdnei osen'iu," in Smirnov, *Marshal Zhukov,* p. 300.
4. Isaac Deutscher, *Stalin: A Political Biography* (New York: Oxford, 1949), p. 549.
5. Evgenii Vorob'ev, "Kazhdaia piad' zemli" in Smirnov, *Marshal Zhukov,* p. 175.
6. Zhukov, *Memoirs* 3: pp. 308–309.
7. Ladislas Farago, *Patton* (New York: Obolensky, 1963), p. 804.
8. Volkogonov, *Triumf i tragediia,* book 2, part 2, pp. 10, 11.
9. Rzhevskaia, see note 3, p. 307.
10. Ibid., p. 308.
11. Zhukov, *Memoirs* 3: pp. 325, 335.
12. Ibid., p. 326.
13. Pavlenko, "Razmyshleniia" in *VIZh,* no. 12: pp. 30, 31.
14. G. K. Zhukov, "Korotko o Staline" (Briefly about Stalin) in *Pravda,* 20 January 1989, p. 3. This article was furnished for publication by Zhukov's youngest daughter, Maria Georgievna.
15. Pavlenko, see note 13, p. 31.
16. Konev, *Zapiski komanduiushchego frontom,* pp. 594–597. Vladimir Karpov, "Rasprava Stalina nad marshalom Zhukovym" (The reprisals of Stalin against Marshal Zhukov) in *Vestnik Protivovozdushnoi Oborony,* nos. 7–8, 1992, pp. 69–72. Quote is on p. 71.
17. David Ortenberg, "U Zhukova v Perkhushkovo" (With Zhukov at Perkhushkovo) in *KZ,* 3 December 1991, p. 41.

XXII

COMMANDER OF SECONDARY MILITARY DISTRICTS, 1946–1953

After this stunning reversal of fortune, Zhukov resolved that he would not reduce his personal standards one iota. Even if he had to command a secondary military district, he intended to remain true to himself. He knew that some in his command would expect that this bitter experience would make him more cautious in his drive for military and disciplinary perfection. He might have recalled the purges of 1937–38 in the Belorussian Military District, when commanders who were strict taskmasters were vulnerable to reports (*donosy*) on their political reliability from recalcitrant subordinates and were then called to account by the Party. In spite of the fact that his demanding command style was part of the case against him—and it soon became clear that Beriia and the organs of state security were continuing to search for or manufacture the evidence that would break him—Zhukov remained a commander who enforced strict discipline and required exact execution of orders.

Zhukov arrived in Odessa on 13 June 1946. After familiarizing himself with his new headquarters, he began to visit the units in his new command. At the end of World War II, the Soviet Union was divided into thirty-two military districts; these were consolidated over time into the sixteen that existed until the breakup of the Soviet Union and the formation of the Commonwealth of Independent States. The military district commander was responsible for the combat readiness, military and political training, and discipline of the units located on the territory of his district. The Odessa Military District, although it was a border district, was considered a secondary district because under the prewar mobilization plan the district headquarters would form an army headquarters while districts such as the Kiev, Leningrad, and Western (Minsk) would become Front headquarters. Normally, the Odessa Military District was commanded by a three-star general (*general polkovnik*). As a Marshal of the Soviet Union, Zhukov was the equivalent of a five-star general.

In the Odessa Military District in 1946, a number of the military units had fought with the 2d and 3d Ukrainian Fronts during the war. Training for these units was based on combat experience gained during the war. (While Stalin was alive the Soviet forces did not consider the effect that nuclear weapons would have on the battlefield.) At the same time, the troops were engaged in rebuilding the garrisons, training areas, and airfields damaged or destroyed during the war. The troops also rendered considerable aid to the local civilian economy as it struggled to recover from the war. For Zhukov, none of these tasks was new.

One of his aides, S. P. Markov, commenting on Zhukov's enthusiasm for visiting the troops, noted that he spent his fiftieth birthday, 2 December 1946, visiting troops in the field. In February 1947, he was travelling by train to an exercise in Tiraspol' when a heavy snowstorm halted the train. Rather than delay the exercise, the marshal ordered a light plane, an AN-2, to pick him up from a hastily dug-out strip; he then flew to the outskirts of Tiraspol', and the exercise proceeded as scheduled.[1]

Service in Odessa was not all work. In August 1946, he took his first postwar leave, which he spent with his family at Sochi, a resort on the Black Sea. He was joined there by Konstantin Konstantinovich Rokossovskii, on leave from his post in Poland, where he was commander in chief of the Northern Group of Forces. Unfortunately there is no record of what the two marshals discussed during the time they spent together.

While in Odessa Zhukov was not forgotten by those who were determined to stain the image of the country's most prominent war hero— even though he had been consigned to oblivion by the centrally controlled press. In June the Central Committee, in Party channels, reprimanded Zhukov for "incorrectly rewarding artists." Apparently Zhukov had authorized an award for some visiting artists while he was commander in chief of the Soviet Occupation Forces in Germany in 1945, which he was not authorized to do in peacetime. The occasion may have been the visit to Berlin of the singer Lidiia Andreevna Ruslanova to give a series of concerts. After one of her major performances, Zhukov had accompanied her on the accordion. Afterwards she commented that Zhukov did not play badly "for a marshal." On this occasion it was reported to Stalin, as was everything that might reflect negatively on Zhukov's character and performance, that Zhukov had rewarded the performer "too generously."[2]

In December 1947, Zhukov was summoned to Moscow urgently. After he arrived he was called to the Central Committee of the Communist Party. When the session reached a discussion of personnel matters, he found himself one of seven people whose removal from the Committee was proposed. Given the opportunity to speak, he refused, and as soon as the vote was taken he marched (*stroevym shagom*) out of the hall. Later, Khrushchev told him that his departure from the meeting room was a shock to all who were present.[3] There followed a period during which his future was uncertain, and he and those closest to him awaited a decision on his fate.[4] The uncertainty and tension arose because Zhukov's removal from the Central Committee at this time made him more vulnerable to exclusion from the Party and subject to arrest.

The organs of state security, apparently not satisfied with the results achieved in June 1946, continued to search for evidence of Zhukov's disloyalty. Officers who had served close to him in the past were special targets. The secret police found grounds to arrest them, and their interrogations soon reached the subject of the conduct of Georgii Konstantinovich Zhukov. Those who had been his generals for special assignments and adjutants such as Generals Miniuk, Varennikov, Kriukov, Filatov, and Lt. Colonel Semochkin had all been arrested by the end of 1947 and physically coerced into giving evidence against Zhukov. K. F. Telegin, former member of the Military Council of the Group of Soviet Occupation Forces in Germany, was still being beaten with rubber truncheons in 1948 to force him to provide additional incriminating information about Zhukov.[5]*

---

*Telegin apparently got into trouble with the "organs" by reporting to Zhukov while they were in Germany that the NKVD had shipped itself 51 trains loaded with "trophies." Telegin was forced to retire, tried, and sentenced to 25 years at hard labor. He was rehabilitated after the death of Stalin. N. L. Anisimov and V. G. Oppokov, "Eshelon dlinoi v chetvert' veka" (A train the length of a quarter of a century), in *VIZh,* no. 6, pp. 79, 89.

Some measure of the impact of Zhukov's disgrace on the Soviet officer corps may be gained from the transcript of a conversation between Col. Gen. V. N. Gordov and his wife on 31 December 1946. The transcript, obtained by a secret listening device, was furnished to Stalin three days later. Gordov, who had been relieved from his post as commander of the Volga Military District and retired at age 50 in November 1946, was overheard bemoaning his fate and criticizing Stalin. His wife, commiserating with him and recognizing the hopelessness of his situation, commented, "They have even broken such a spirit (dukh) as Zhukov." She continued, "And he [Zhukov] said, 'Excuse me. I will not be [that way] again' and went off to work. Someone else, with such convictions as you have, would have asked for retirement and walked away from all this." Gordov responded, "He could not do it, politically, he could not do it. All the same they would not release him. Now they only clean out those in whom Zhukov had the slightest confidence. They will keep Zhukov a year or two and then he will be in the soup and that will be all."

Gordov had been retired on the recommendation of a commission headed by Bulganin which included Golikov. The commission was investigating Gordov, his chief of staff, and G. I. Kulik because they had allegedly spoken out against political officers. Gordov, his wife, and the other officers were arrested in January 1947. They were tried, found guilty, and the officers were executed in August 1950. They were all rehabilitated posthumously in 1956. As of 1992, Gordov's son was still trying to find out where his father was buried.[6]

With his fate hanging in the balance, Zhukov suffered his first heart attack in early January 1948, a month after he turned fifty-one. He was hospitalized about a month before he departed on 12 February 1948 for his new assignment—command of the Ural Military District headquartered in Sverdlovsk (now restored to its former name, Ekaterinburg). Stalin had not been convinced by the new information collected by Abakumov and Beriia. Later, Zhukov learned that Abakumov had manufactured the entire case against Zhukov in 1947. The new assignment was in no way better than Odessa. Again he was replacing a three-star commander in a secondary military district. The weather on his arrival was −22° Fahrenheit, but he laughed and joked with those who met his train. He was soon engaged in his favorite command activity, visiting the troops of the district in their garrisons and training areas.

In 1950 Zhukov was elected a delegate to the Supreme Soviet after his candidacy was advanced by a local motorcycle factory. Although the high-level political influence of the Supreme Soviet was never great in the former Soviet Union, the fact that Zhukov's name was allowed to be placed in nomination suggested a certain mellowing toward him on the part of Stalin. In June the next year, he was permitted to attend the celebration of Polish National Day in Warsaw as a member of the Soviet government's official delegation. At that time Konstantin Rokossovskii was serving as Polish minister of defense, "at the request of the Polish government." The wartime comrades had another opportunity to exchange reminiscences.[7]

Konstantin Simonov related an even more positive indication that Zhukov's long period of disgrace and exile was ending. Sometime in late 1952, Stalin was discussing a Soviet novel about the taking of Berlin. He commented that the author, conscious of Zhukov's situation, had given the impression in the book that key decisions of the 1st Belorussian Front were made by the member of the Military Council. Stalin, who apparently approved of the novel otherwise, told Simonov that the Front was commanded by Zhukov and not by some member of the Military Council. Stalin suggested that, if it was not too late, the author should correct the false impression he had created. Unfortunately, several editions of the book had already been published and the change could not be made.

Zhukov was selected as a delegate to the Nineteenth Party Congress, held in October 1952. At the congress he was named a candidate member of the Central Committee, which meant he would attend committee sessions but would not have a vote. As Simonov noted, there was no doubt that this had occurred on Stalin's initiative; at that time, there could be no other explanation for the marshal's return to one of the Party's more significant bodies.

Simonov sat next to Zhukov at a dinner for foreign visitors to the congress and found him in excellent spirits; although Zhukov was somewhat restrained, Simonov sensed that the election to the Central Committee had been a surprise and that it had made a strong impression. Zhukov seemed pleased that a Simonov novel, based on the events at Halhin Gol, had just been published, the first in Soviet literature to be set in Mongolia in 1939. Zhukov was not named in the novel but the commander had been portrayed positively. Some of Simonov's colleagues had worried that the novel might have censorship problems, but it passed without difficulty—another sign, perhaps, that Zhukov was returning to the dictator's favor.[8]

In late February 1953, Zhukov was called to Moscow and may have been there on 1 March when Stalin suffered the stroke which killed him four days later. Stalin died as the fantastic real life drama known as the Kremlin "doctors' plot" was playing. In January, it had been announced that the organs of state security had discovered a terrorist group made up of doctors, whose aim was to cut short the active lives of certain public figures of the Soviet Union, including Marshals Vasilevskii and Konev and General Shtemenko. The doctors allegedly were members of two groups: an international Jewish organization, "Joint," established by American intelligence; and agents of British intelligence. One of the doctors was Stalin's personal physician. Many considered that the "doctors' plot" was the prelude to another purge.[9]

Stalin reviewed the status of the case with Beriia and other members of the Presidium (Stalin had renamed the Politburo at the Nineteenth Party Congress) during the last late night session at his dacha, which ended at 0400 on 1 March. He had instructed Beriia to prepare a public trial. When he failed to rise at the usual hour (1100), his servants became alarmed, but because they had no authority to disturb him he was not found until 2300—twelve hours later. Then, even though he was semiconscious and could not speak, he was not seen by a doctor until 0900 on 2 March. A government bulletin was issued some hours later. He died on 5 March.[10]

Not being a member of the inner group (Beriia, Malenkov, Molotov, Bulganin, and Khrushchev), Zhukov did not see the dictator in his last hours. He had no way of knowing what the attitude of these men toward him would be when the dictator died. Most of them had been among his accusers during the ordeal before the Main Military Council in June 1946. Stalin's heirs realized, however, that the name Zhukov could still inspire confidence among the people. He had not long to wait. Zhukov was named a first deputy minister of defense and commander in chief of the Ground Forces in the first announcement by the successor government, the same post he had occupied before his exile. He was no longer the commander of a secondary military district.

NOTES

1. S. P. Markov, "Poslevoennye gody" (Postwar years) in Mirkina and Iarovikov, *Marshal Zhukov: Polkovodets* 2: p. 22.
2. Smirnov, *Marshal Zhukov,* pp. 200, 374. Pavlenko, "Razmyshleniia" in *VIZh,* no. 12: p. 30.
3. Konev, *Zapiski komanduiushchego frontom,* pp. 594–599. Pavlenko, "Razmyshleniia" in*VIZh,* no. 12: pp. 31, 32. N.S. Svetlishin, "Krutye stupeni" (Steep steps), in Mirkina and Iarovikov, *Marshal Zhukov: Polkovodets,* pp. 245–253.
4. Markov, see note 1, pp. 22, 23.
5. Ibid. G. K. Zhukov, "Korotko o Staline" in *Pravda,* 20 January 1989, p. 3. Telegin's letter to Voroshilov reporting the beating is quoted in N. L. Anisimov and V. G. Oppokov, "Eshelon dlinoi v chetvert' veka" (A train the length of a quarter of a century), in *VIZh* no. 6 (1989): pp. 79, 89. Volkogonov, *Triumf i tragediia,* Book 2, part 2, pp. 214, 215.
6. *Izvestiia,* 17 July 1992, pp. 1, 7.
7. Markov, see note 1, pp. 23, 24.
8. Simonov, "Zametki" in *VIZh,* no. 7: pp. 49, 50.
9. Adam B. Ulam, *Stalin: The Man and His Era* (New York:Viking, 1973), p. 736.
10. Volkogonov, *Triumf i tragediia,* Book 2, part 2, pp. 191–199.

XXIII

RETURN TO MOSCOW, 1953

Zhukov returned to the Ministry of Defense in March 1953. He began to work with the new ten-man Presidium (replacing the twenty-five-man Presidium installed by Stalin at the Nineteenth Party Congress), which was formed immediately after the dictator's death. It included at least eight men with whom he had had direct contact during the war: Malenkov, Beriia, Khrushchev, Bulganin, Mikoyan, Kaganovich, Voroshilov, and Molotov. (The other two members, Saburov and Pervukhin, are not mentioned in Zhukov's memoirs.) These were men he had observed under pressure, men who had sat behind Stalin and had often, depending on how they assessed the dictator's mood, attempted to belittle Zhukov's proposals, men who were contributors to the indictment that resulted in his almost seven-year exile.

The senior military leaders at that time were the same men whom Zhukov advised, commanded, overawed, tutored, insulted, and evaluated during the war. Due to the purges and the wartime expansion of the armed forces, the Soviet military leadership had emerged from the war as a relatively young and high-ranking group. Zhukov was only fifty-six. V. D. Sokolovskii, the chief of the General Staff, was younger still. Vasilevskii, the first deputy minister of defense, was a year older. In March 1953, the military districts were commanded by Antonov, Bagramian, Gorbatov, Grechko, Luchinskii, Malinin, Malinovskii, Meretskov, Eremenko, Konev, Timoshenko, and Krylov. Chuikov was commanding the Group of Forces in Germany. Govorov, Golikov, S. S. Biriuzov, Moskalenko, and Zakharov were occupying posts in the Moscow area. Rokossovskii was now serving as minister of defense in Poland. There was no officer in this group whose professional experience, record of success, and prestige could match that of Zhukov.

During the next four years Zhukov and his colleagues were to be interested spectators and at times participants in the contest for political power which seemed to end with Khrushchev's victory over the anti-Party group in 1957.

The first obstacle to the stability of the post-Stalin political arrangements was Lavrentii Beriia. Immediately after Stalin's death, he had been made head of a ministry that combined all of the internal and external police and security functions. Khrushchev, by his own account, sensed the inherent danger in the man and his power. He began recruiting allies against Beriia even before Stalin had breathed his last. From March until June 1953 he found opportunities to approach the other members of the Presidium and to unite them against the secret police chief. Only Mikoyan, when approached by Khrushchev, was tentative, because he had closer ties to Beriia than the others.

The confrontation took place during a meeting of the presidium of the Council of Ministers to which all members of the presidium of the Central Committee of the Communist Party were invited. Because of the interlocking directorship which characterized the ruling bodies of the Soviet state, only Voroshilov, who was chairman of the presidium of the Supreme Soviet, required a special invitation. Malenkov, who was chairman of the Council of Ministers and first secretary of the Party, turned the meeting into a meeting of the Party Presidium.

Before the meeting, Khrushchev and Malenkov decided that army officers would execute the actual arrest. The conspirators had to proceed with extreme caution. The entire Kremlin armed security force was subordinate to Beriia, and the commander of the army troops in the Moscow Military District, P. A. Artem'ev, had been an NKVD officer before he was given command of the military district in 1941. Khrushchev and his allies did not trust him to participate in the arrest of Beriia. Also, most of the army troops normally stationed in and around Moscow were away in summer training camps. Since there were two divisions of internal affairs troops also subordinate to Beriia in the city, he had a clear advantage in available force over the other members of the Presidium. Khrushchev, who masterminded the plot, turned to General Moskalenko, whom he had known during the war and who was now commander of the Moscow Air Defense District, to select a group of reliable officers to make up the arresting party. Khrushchev claimed that Malenkov expanded the group to include Zhukov.[1]

One of the military participants in the arrest, Col. I. G. Zub, was head of the political directorate of the Moscow Air Defense District. On 26 June 1953 he was ordered to report to the minister of defense and to bring his personal weapon with him. When he was ushered into Bulganin's office, the minister was alone. He asked Zub how he felt, was he brave, did he have his weapon with him, and was he ready to execute a government assignment. Having answered these questions satisfactorily, Zub was told to wait in the reception room and to speak to no one. Soon other officers arrived in the reception room who were well known to Zub from the Moscow Air Defense District: the district commander, K. S. Moskalenko; his first deputy, P. F. Batitskii; the chief of staff, A. Vaksov; and Moskalenko's adjutant, Lt. Col. V. Iuferov. While they waited, trying to carry on casual conversations, Zhukov entered and left Bulganin's office several times. Zub noted that Zhukov was the only one of the group to appear nervous; as it turned out, his automobile, which was to be used in the operation, was in the repair shop and was not yet ready. The presence of Zhukov gave Zub confidence the mission he was about to undertake would be successful, even though he still did not know exactly what it was.

The group of six was then taken to the Kremlin in two automobiles (Bulganin's and Zhukov's, each of which had darkened windows), entering under the guise of attending a meeting. They were ushered into a waiting room, still not aware (with the exception of Zhukov) of what they were going to be called upon to do. The waiting room adjoined the room in which the Presidium was meeting. Eventually, Bulganin and Khrushchev came out of the meeting room and told them that they were there to arrest Beriia. Khrushchev gave them instructions: on a signal by Malenkov from within the meeting room, they were to enter in pairs by the three doors to the room, block any attempt by Beriia to escape, and arrest him. Khrushchev concluded with the warning that if the operation for some reason were to fail they would all be considered "enemies of the people." One wonders if Malenkov had considered that possibility when he included Zhukov in the arresting group. Zhukov had already been accused of being a plotter; now he and his accomplices could be caught red-handed if something unexpected were to happen.

On signal, Zhukov and Moskalenko entered one of the doors together. Some of the members of the Presidium, who were not fully informed as to what was happening, jumped from their seats in alarm. Zhukov told them to be calm and take their seats. Malenkov asked for a vote approving the arrest of Beriia and received unanimous approval, after which Zhukov ordered Beriia to stand and follow him. They took him to an anteroom off the meeting room, where he was held until it was decided what to do with the prisoner. Later, Zub was ordered to draw up a list of fifty reliable officers who were used to replace the Kremlin guards at the end of their watch. When the regular Kremlin guards had been replaced by the officers from the Air Defense Headquarters, Beriia was escorted out of the Kremlin by five of the arresting group. Zhukov's last contact with Beriia was to order the group to shoot him if he tried to escape. He was initially kept in a garrison guard house for a week, before being transferred to an underground location in the headquarters of the Moscow Military District. Beriia was tried by a special court, presided over by Marshal Konev, on 18 December 1953. He was found guilty, sentenced, and shot on 23 December. Like the verdict of the special court which had tried Tukhachevskii, the sentence was final and was not subject to appeal.[2]*

While the high command was watching the political drama with more than passing interest, its primary concern was with matters of national defense. Following Stalin's death, crisis conditions in Soviet agriculture had been revealed; Malenkov, as Party first secretary and prime minister, had advocated amelioration of the lot of the Soviet consumer at a time when what the Soviets were eventually to call the "revolution in military affairs" was beginning. The revolution was caused primarily by the development of nuclear weapons and long-range rockets, but it was also due to the adoption of modern technology in all areas of military activity. Malenkov's opposition to the costs in manpower and resources of reequipping the Soviet armed forces to meet modern

---

*One of the generals of the arresting group, Batitskii, was given the assignment of shooting Beriia. He told his wife that Beriia crawled on his knees begging for mercy before he was shot.

requirements is generally assumed to have been one of the issues that led to his resignation in February 1955—a move that was believed to have military support and approval. Malenkov was replaced as prime minister by Bulganin, while Khrushchev became Party first secretary and Zhukov became minister of defense.

The appointment of Zhukov as minister of defense was not greeted with enthusiasm by some senior members of the armed forces. Bulganin was given the mission of talking with some of the marshals and getting their opinions. Sokolovskii was alleged to favor Vasilevskii for the post. Rokossovskii responded professionally, saying that since the appointment had already been made it did not make sense for him to give his opinion. One who did make his opinion known was N. G. Kuznetsov, commander in chief of the Navy, who told Bulganin somewhat angrily that if Zhukov was going to be minister then he should be told to be more objective in his attitude toward the fleet. Zhukov was told about Bulganin's conversation with Kuznetsov the same day.[3]

After Malenkov's departure, during the 1955–1958 period the armed forces were sharply reduced from 5,763,000 to 3,623,000 men, a reduction of 2,140,000 men. These cuts were rationalized by citing a "certain reduction of tensions" caused by the Geneva summit talks in 1955 and by references to the enormous increases in firepower now available to the existing forces.

Meanwhile, the armed forces under Zhukov's leadership proceeded to study the impact of nuclear weapons on military doctrine, strategy, and tactics. During Stalin's last years the development of nuclear weaponry had proceeded at a rapid pace; the first atomic device was exploded in 1949, and a hydrogen bomb was exploded in 1953. Rockets were undergoing a parallel course of development beginning in 1947.[4] But Stalin had not permitted either theoretical or practical exercises in the use of the new weapons.[5] It was not until the beginning of 1954 that the armed forces began studying the new weapons and their effects on combat operations. In September of that year the first significant military exercise in which an atomic bomb was exploded was conducted at Totskoe in the southern Urals.[6]

Zhukov, as commander in chief of the Ground Forces, attended the exercise, but there is no available evidence of his reaction to it. With the advent of glasnost' dramatic articles concerning this explosion have appeared in the Soviet press,* the principal sources for which have been low-ranking participants or residents of villages in the exercise area. To correct some of the inaccuracies that appeared in those articles, the *Military Historical Journal* in December 1991 published an account by Col. Gen. B. P. Ivanov, who participated in the exercise as deputy division commander of the 12th Mechanized Division. His article, based on his own observations and on notes he made at the time, shows that the exercise was planned and conducted with what at the time was considered conservative regard for the personnel in the two-sided exercise and for the population surrounding the exercise area. The only quotation attributed to Zhukov in the article was "You have frightened people by your safety measures. Now it will be necessary to 'unfrighten' them."[7]

From General Ivanov's description, the Soviet exercise appears to have been similar to exercise "Desert Rock VI" conducted at Yucca Flat, Nevada, in 1955. There a composite armored force, positioned 3,000 meters from ground zero, experienced the detonation of a 30-kiloton nuclear device. The force began firing 30 seconds after the explosion and moved out eight minutes after the blast, skirting within 900 meters of ground zero. In the Soviet exercise, a nuclear weapon was air-dropped and detonated at an altitude of 285 meters at 0933. This was followed by a 30-minute artillery preparation. The first echelon of a motorized rifle regiment did not approach ground zero until 1200. Due to difficulty in ground orientation after the blast (an oak grove in the area had been obliterated for a radius of 1 kilometer from ground zero), no troops or vehicles approached ground zero closer than 500–600 meters.[8]

In the case of Desert Rock VI, the exercise provided a great show for news reporters, but a later official U.S. Army after-action report

*Such articles continue to appear. One officer who participated in the exercise eventually experienced the symptoms of radiation sickness. His subsequent treatment was hampered because all participants were required to sign an agreement to remain silent about the exercise for 25 years. Aleksei Khorev, *"Chernoe pepelishche"* (Black ashes) in *KZ*, 9 June 1992, p. 4.

called it "an unrealistic maneuver" devoid of tactical authenticity.[9] From General Ivanov's description one could draw a similar conclusion about the exercise at Totskoe.

In February 1955 Marshal V. D. Sokolovskii proclaimed publicly the need to revise Soviet military doctrine and reorganize the armed forces in accordance with modern requirements. Zhukov's order of May 1957, directing that the activity of military-scientific research institutions be broadened and vitalized, was still cited ten years later as having important significance in the development of Soviet strategy.[10] In August 1957 the Soviets announced the first successful tests of an intercontinental ballistic missile, and in October of the same year they used some of the new technology to place Sputnik in orbit.

For Zhukov, the pace of these events must have been exhilarating. His return to the center of military affairs during a period of exciting, revolutionary changes was a challenge to his experience and his capabilities. To solve the problems created by the introduction of new weapons, he turned to the laboratory he knew best—the field exercise. He also put heavy emphasis on physical training, because the demands of the nuclear battlefield would be more strenuous than the demands of a conventional battlefield. The questions of reequipping the armed forces and developing new tactical, operational, and strategic precepts had to be decided during an uneasy period of continuous international tension, including unrest in Eastern Europe, domestic economic and political change, and while serious manpower reductions were in progress in the armed forces. In many respects the situation may have resembled that which Zhukov faced when he became chief of the General Staff in February 1941, with the major difference that in the 1953–1957 period there was no one authority such as Stalin to decide all questions. It is not surprising that among his military colleagues in the high command, many of whom he had tutored during the war, Zhukov felt he had earned the right to make many of these decisions.

Possibly as a measure that had to be taken because of the severe personnel reductions that the armed forces were experiencing, and possibly as a result of a conviction Zhukov had formed early in his career that the political apparatus was bloated, inefficient, and maybe counterproductive, Zhukov took steps to reduce it in size and influence. Many political organs were liquidated, the number of students at the Military Political Academy and courses for preparing political workers were sharply reduced, and promotions for political officers were cut back. Zhukov's evaluation of the relative merits of physical and political training can be judged from the following complaint:

> In the order of the minister of defense defining positions to be manned by officers with higher education, it was pointed out that half of the leaders of physical education in a regiment must have a higher education and in divisions and corps all [physical education leaders] must have a higher education. At the same time the propagandist in the regiment was not required to have a higher education and only one quarter of the propagandists of political sections of divisions and corps had to have a higher education.[11]

Under the Zhukov administration the possibilities for political officers to advance in rank were also severely limited. The highest rank for a political officer with the troops was established as colonel for all political organs through the field army level.

In August 1955 a decision was made to eliminate the political officer at the company level. Allegedly, this was contrary to the opinion of the majority of commanders. To provide professional political workers at the battalion level a political organ was introduced, the staff of which depended on the numerical strength of the battalion. The maximum number would be three workers, the minimum one.[12]

Later these and other reductions in the number, rank, and activities of political officers would be used against Zhukov. The charge would be made that he attempted to "shrivel" the Party organizations in the armed forces and that certain proven forms of political work such as the Marxist-Leninist preparation of officer personnel, political training, and political information were undervalued. The ties between military and local Party organizations "began to be broken."[13] In answer to both of these charges, particularly the latter, it is possible that the question of training time was involved. In order to maintain ties with local Party organizations, joint meetings, with travel to and from the local garrison to the local Party meeting place and vice versa, would have to be arranged, and for Zhukov, the critical question was—with what practical result?

As the details of these steps are examined, it seems clear that Zhukov sought to streamline the professional Party apparatus in the armed forces.

He sought to do this in two ways: by reducing the numbers of political workers in the armed forces, and by discouraging those who were engaged in political work by limiting their functions and their opportunities for advancement. During a period of intense military activity in the face of reductions in personnel, the formula employed to solve the problem was consistent with Zhukov's entire previous career. In the course of the year 1943, about 122,000 political officers were transferred to command positions. The strength of the active army in the summer of 1943 was 6.4 million men. The 122,000 saved for line service was approximately 1.9 percent of that total. If a similar economy could have been achieved during the 1955–1958 period when the armed forces' strength reached 3.6 million men, a manpower economy of roughly sixty thousand men would have been achieved.

While Zhukov was wrestling with the overall question of manpower for the armed forces, Admiral of the Fleet Kuznetsov was attempting to obtain approval for his naval program. Khrushchev had formed a negative opinion of Kuznetsov when the admiral led the Navy during Stalin's regime, and he was in no hurry to launch an ambitious naval building program. Khrushchev procrastinated to the point that Kuznetsov became frustrated and told him so in no uncertain terms. Now Kuznetsov had made two powerful enemies for the fleet—Khrushchev and Zhukov. In May 1955 Kuznetsov suffered a heart attack, and the following month he asked to be relieved from his post. No action was taken on his request, which has been taken as a further indication of Zhukov's negative attitude toward him. Unfortunately for Kuznetsov, in October 1955 while he was still in command of the Navy, the battleship *Novorossiisk* hit a mine while in a small bay off Sevastopol'. The ship, which had been obtained as part of reparations from the Italians and renamed by the Soviets, sank with the loss of several hundred seamen.

This tragedy was the latest "ChP," *chrezvychainoe proisshestvie,* during the year 1955. (The term is used by the Soviet military to describe an accident or, in the extreme, a catastrophe involving heavy loss of life.) In most of the world's armed forces such an event calls for an investigation, and, depending on the findings, those responsible for the errors of omission or commission are penalized. In this case not only those directly involved were punished but also the commander of the Black Sea Fleet and the commander in chief of the Navy. Kuznetsov was reduced in rank two grades to vice admiral and retired. He was

51 years old. Kuznetsov recalled that on 15 February 1956 he was called into Zhukov's office, and in exceptionally crude form he was told of his punishment. There was no formal ceremony. A representative of the cadres directorate left the necessary separation papers at his quarters. Kuznetsov claimed he was never shown the reports that led to his reduction in rank and early retirement.[14] It seems clear that Zhukov had a key role in the decision to punish Kuznetsov and that it was hardly a noble one. Zhukov, as one Soviet historian has said, was "vindictive" (*zlopamiaten*).[15]

Zhukov was a candidate member of the Presidium at the Twentieth Party Congress, held in February 1956. It was at this Congress, the first since Stalin's death, that Khrushchev delivered his famous "secret speech" on Stalin's crimes. What became known as the de-Stalinization campaign began. According to Khrushchev, the question of how Stalin's heirs were to handle the rehabilitation of thousands of falsely accused, arrested, sentenced, and imprisoned victims of Stalin's purges and terror campaigns became acute after the arrest and investigation of Beriia. Initially, it was attempted to blame the crimes on Beriia and his collaborators in the secret police. Khrushchev admitted that he did not realize the falsity of this position until he attempted to defend it during a visit to Yugoslavia in 1955. There, the Yugoslavs "smiled scornfully and made sarcastic remarks."[16] An investigatory committee had been established in 1954 and 7,379 individuals had been rehabilitated by the time of the Party Congress, but this was only a small fraction of Stalin's victims. When Khrushchev discussed the problem in the Presidium and suggested further investigation, he encountered opposition from those former members of Stalin's Politburo who had been in positions to know the truth about Stalin's involvement and approval of Beriia's activities: Molotov, Malenkov, Voroshilov, Kaganovich, and Mikoyan. Khrushchev claimed that final approval of his speech was not given until he threatened, during a Presidium session held while the Congress was meeting, to speak without sanction if necessary. (The editor of *Khrushchev Remembers*, Strobe Talbott, casts doubt on Khrushchev's version of the genesis of this speech because of its length, the amount of detail presented, and the absence of negative information about Stalin in Khrushchev's general report, which he had given to the Congress in its early sessions.)[17]

Zhukov must have perceived the secret speech as a mixed blessing.

On the one hand, Khrushchev addressed the military purges of 1937–1938 forthrightly. He attributed Stalin's postwar attitude toward Zhukov to the dictator's desire that Soviet victories be credited to no one but himself. Khrushchev also stated that Stalin had planned military operations on a globe and gave his own version of his role in the operations around Khar'kov in 1942, which reflected negatively on Vasilevskii. He invited the military to give their version of Stalin's negative influence on World War II operations. What Khrushchev wanted was an indictment of Stalin's wartime leadership from the military, especially Zhukov and Vasilevskii, who were so intimately involved in the wartime operational decisions and their execution, but neither man was prepared to furnish one. It was not accidental that neither Zhukov nor Vasilevskii published his memoirs until after Khrushchev had been deposed in 1964.[18]

The secret speech was circulated to the Communist parties of all the Warsaw Pact states, which to some degree or other had governments patterned after the one in the Soviet Union. In two of the states, Poland and Hungary, the similarities went further. In Poland, Stalin had approved the arrest and imprisonment of Wladyslaw Gomulka and others in the Polish Communist Party in July 1951. Gomulka was released in 1954. After the Polish party first secretary, Bierut, died in March 1956, the successor leadership was incapable of coping with the disorders and demonstrations that broke out in Warsaw and other cities in October, many of which were anti-Soviet in tone. There were also demonstrations in favor of a new leadership to be headed by Gomulka. Khrushchev decided to go to Warsaw and evaluate the situation, taking with him Marshal Konev, then commander in chief of the Warsaw Pact forces.

After being briefed at the Soviet Embassy in Warsaw, Khrushchev ordered Konev to move Soviet troops closer to the capital. Included in that move were several Soviet divisions stationed in East Germany along the Polish–East German border. Presumably the orders to move those divisions to the east came on instructions from the minister of defense, Zhukov. This crisis came to an end when Gomulka persuaded Khrushchev that the people of Warsaw were prepared to defend themselves if Soviet troops entered the city. The Soviet troops halted and eventually returned to their garrisons in East Germany. The Soviet delegation approved the selection of Gomulka as first secretary of the Polish

Communist Party. Marshal Rokossovskii, who had been serving as the Polish minister of defense, returned to the Soviet Union for reassignment.[19]

Toward the end of October 1956 a similar situation arose in Hungary. What Khrushchev referred to as a mutiny had arisen as a result of Stalin's abuse of power and the discontent provoked by Stalin's man in Budapest, Matyas Rakosi. He was replaced in July and exiled to the Soviet Union. His successor was no improvement. On 23 October a massive demonstration frightened the discredited group around Rakosi's successor, Erno Gero, and they asked for Soviet help. Iurii Andropov, then Soviet ambassador to Budapest, conferred with Gen. P. N. Lashchenko, commander of the corps of Soviet troops stationed in Hungary. Lashchenko would not move a single soldier without an order from the minister of defense, Zhukov. The order from Zhukov was received that evening, and Lashchenko's "Special" Corps began to move into Budapest. In the meantime Imre Nagy had assumed the leadership of the Hungarian government on 24 October. On 25 October, a division of Soviet troops stationed in Romania moved into the city and suffered heavy losses in street fighting. The continued unrest in the country caused the introduction of two armies from the Carpathian Military District to cover the Hungarian border to prevent any possible aggression from the west and secure the rear area of the troop operation in Budapest.

On 30 October, the Soviet government announced that it was ready to enter into discussions with the government of the Hungarian People's Republic and the governments of other member states of the Warsaw Pact. On 3 November two discussions were held. No representatives of the other Warsaw Pact states were present at the first meeting. The second discussion was held late at night, and the Hungarian representatives were arrested by an operations group of the KGB headed by General Serov. On 4 November, the troops of the Special Corps entered Budapest for the second time. That decision was made by Khrushchev after it became clear that the former ruling party in Hungary had lost its authority, a multiparty system had been proclaimed, and the exit of Hungary from the Warsaw Pact had been announced. Marshal Konev ordered Lashchenko's corps, now reinforced with artillery and airborne troops, to begin its operation on 4 November. The operation lasted seven days. When it was over the resistance was broken, the government of Imre Nagy was overthrown, and Janos Kadar became leader of the new government.

Zhukov had no direct role in these operations, but the reinforcement of the Special Corps in Hungary and the movement of two armies into Hungary required the coordination of the Ministry of Defense and the General Staff. The tragic mission was accomplished. Hungarian casualties were 2,000 killed and 19,000 wounded. Soviet casualties have never been officially announced, but according to one Soviet participant at least 2,000 were killed.

Charles E. "Chip" Bohlen, the United States Ambassador to the Soviet Union from 1953 until 1957 and a Russian speaker, encountered Zhukov several times at diplomatic receptions during these crises. He gained the impression that Zhukov had urged military action against the Poles but was overruled when the Soviet political leadership became convinced that the Polish armed forces could not be counted on to support the Soviet Army. After the settlement in Warsaw that allowed Gomulka to remain at the head of the Polish state and returned Marshal Rokossovskii to serve in the Soviet Army, Zhukov told Bohlen that there were adequate forces in East Germany, Poland, and Belorussia to have forced a settlement on Soviet terms. He added, "They could have crushed them like flies." "They" obviously referring to the Soviet Army, "them" being the Polish protestors.

During the Hungarian crisis, Bohlen passed the essence of a message from Secretary of State Dulles to Zhukov, Khrushchev, and Bulganin that the United States did not look on Hungary or any of the Soviet satellites as potential military allies. The message was sent in the hope that the Soviets would allow the Hungarians to withdraw from the Warsaw Pact, remove their troops from Hungary, and allow the Hungarians to proceed on an independent course of development outside the Soviet bloc. Bohlen believed that Zhukov, in his response, mixed untruths and half-truths with some real facts. Bohlen found Zhukov to usually be honest, but was certain that on that occasion Zhukov told him several outright untruths: He denied that Soviet reinforcements had been sent to Hungary, he said that there had been no firing by Soviet troops in the last 48 hours, and he said that Soviet troops in Budapest were not under his command but that of the Hungarian minister of defense. Zhukov also attempted to make a "foreign connection" between the insurgents and outside forces, mentioning that large quantities of American rifles and German artillery had been captured.

In his conversations with Bohlen, Zhukov was undoubtedly playing his Party role. He was also contributing to the screen of deception by which the Soviets attempted to conceal their decision to crush
the Hungarian opposition. As a Russian patriot and a believer in the
Party's precepts, he probably believed that lying to a capitalist ambassador was meritorious and hardly a sin. In addition, Zhukov, like
other Soviet citizens, undoubtedly felt a strong sense of betrayal on
the part of those Poles and Hungarians who had apparently forgotten
the enormous price the Soviet Union had paid to "liberate" them from
the Germans.[20]

On Zhukov's 60th birthday, 2 December 1956, he was awarded his
fourth gold star medal of a Hero of the Soviet Union. Usually the award
of a medal on the "round date" anniversary of an individual's birth is
the Order of Lenin; the higher award suggested that the political leadership
was more than satisfied with the performance of the armed forces during
the Polish and Hungarian crises. Published with the announcement of
the award was a warm letter to Zhukov, "our friend and comrade," signed
by the Central Committee and the Council of Ministers.[21]

NOTES

1. Strobe Talbott, *Khrushchev Remembers: The Last Testament* (Boston and Toronto: Little, Brown, 1974), pp. 322–337.
2. S. Bystrov, "Zadanie osobogo svoistva" (A mission with a special attribute), in *KZ,* 18, 19, 20 March 1988. N. Zhusenin, "Neskol'ko episodov odnoi prestupnoi zhizni" (Some episodes from one criminal life), in *Nedelia,* no. 8, (22–28 February 1988): pp. 11–12. *Nedelia* is a weekly supplement of *Izvestiia.*
3. V. Chernavin, "Slovo ob avtore" (A word about the author) in N. G. Kuznetsov, *Nakanune. Kursom k pobede* (On the eve. Course to victory) (Moscow: Voenizdat, 1991), p. 720.
4. Zakharov, *50 let,* pp. 482, 504.
5. See criticism of Stalin's attitude in Sokolovskii and Cherednichenko, "Nekotorye voprosy" (Certain questions), in *VIZh,* no. 3 (1965).
6. Zakharov, *50 let,* p. 502.
7. B. P. Ivanov, "Atomnyi vzryv u poselka Totskoe" (The atomic explosion near the village of Totskoe) in *Vizh,* no. 12 (1991): p. 79.
8. Ibid., pp. 80, 85. A. J. Bacevich, *The Pentomic Era* (Washington: National Defense University Press, 1986), pp. 110–113.
9. Bacevich, *The Pentomic Era,* p. 112.
10. Zakharov, *50 let,* p. 521.
11. Iu. P. Petrov, *Stroitel'stvo politorganov partiinykh i komsomol'skikh organizatsii armii i flota (1918–1968)* (The structuring of political organs of Party and Komsomol organizations of the army and fleet, 1918–1968) Moscow: Voenizdat, 1968, fn. 1, p. 436.
12. Zakharov, *50 let,* p. 521.
13. Ibid., note 2, p. 436.
14. Chernavin, see note 3, pp. 719–721. Pavlenko, "Razmyshleniia" in *VIZh,* no. 12: pp. 33, 34.
15. V. M. Kulish in a conversation with the author.
16. Talbott, *Khrushchev Remembers,* pp. 343, 344.
17. Ibid., pp. 346–350.
18. The text of the speech may be found beginning on p. 559 of *Khrushchev Remembers.*
19. Talbott, *Khrushchev Remembers,* pp. 179–183, 196–205.

20. V. Fomin, "Budapesht, osen' 56-go" (Budapest, autumn of '56), in *KZ,* 5 November 1991, p. 3. Charles E. Bohlen, *Witness to History 1929–1969* (New York: W. W. Norton, 1973), pp. 409, 413–415.
21. *KZ,* 2 December 1956, p. 1.

XXIV

THE YEAR 1957:
ZENITH AND NADIR OF A CAREER

With his career in an ascendant stage and his personal prestige at home and abroad at a high level, Zhukov began the year 1957 on what appeared to be a confident note. He was listed among the Party and government leaders attending a reception in the Kremlin to celebrate the new year, and a brief announcement in *Krasnaia Zvezda* noted that he had accepted an invitation to visit India. An editorial on the same page that carried this information exhorted the Soviet armed forces to improve their combat capabilities in the coming year and pointed out that success in this task would be

> linked directly with the improvements in political work among the troops. Explanation of the internal and external policies of our party and government, [and] the problems confronting the Soviet people and its armed forces, arms Soviet soldiers with conscious responsibility for matters entrusted to them.[1]

The front page of the military newspaper early in the new year set the tone for the next ten months: a strong emphasis on military matters, heavy coverage (by Soviet standards) of the activities of the minister of defense, but, at the same time, attention to Party work in the armed forces and acknowledgment of the importance of this work.

Zhukov's departure for India was front-page news, including a large photograph showing him walking toward his plane—a new Tu-104, the first Soviet jet airliner—with a group of marshals and generals in the background, including Konev, Malinovskii, Rokossovskii, Moskalenko,

Meretskov, and Vershinin.[2] The visit to India was covered on a daily basis in succeeding issues, with frequent photographs. On 9 February it was announced that Zhukov had accepted an invitation to visit Burma from 10 to 15 February. On his return to Moscow on 17 February he was met by virtually the same group that had seen him off.[3]

While he was gone an important plenary session of the Central Committee had been held (13, 14 February), but Zhukov, although a member, was not called back. Although he had risen high in Party circles, Zhukov was not a key member of the ruling group. The long, independent trip abroad was a first for a Soviet postwar military leader, but although it seemed to enhance Zhukov's personal image, the trip was also in accord with Soviet policies of the period. Soviet diplomacy was breaking out of the self-imposed isolation of the Stalin era, and the gesture of sending a soldier of Zhukov's stature to a country engaged in a military confrontation with Pakistan—a SEATO (Southeast Asia Treaty Organization) ally of the United States—was nicely calculated.

After Zhukov returned, a series of articles reviewed the visit to India and provided additional details about various places he had visited. Among the comments Zhukov made in India was an extended one at the Indian Staff College on the character of future war, in which he appeared to be exceeding the limits of ministerial authority and substituting personal opinion for official doctrine. His statement was modest, but even so, probably not officially correct for a Soviet leader speaking in a public forum. When asked whether nuclear and thermonuclear weapons would be used in a future war and what role ground, naval, and air forces would play Zhukov responded: "nuclear and thermonuclear weapons will unquestionably be used in warfare between coalitions of the big powers because [these weapons] are ingrained in their armaments and organization." He then made a plea for prohibition of tactical nuclear weapons, pointing out that these weapons would in future years be introduced into the arsenals and tables of organization (*shtaty voysk*) in place of conventional weapons. "This is known from the boasting declarations of various spokesmen of the USA and other countries; it is also known from the decisions of NATO."[4]

Zhukov also commented that, in spite of the new weapons, the Soviet armed forces had a balanced structure, since victory in future wars could be achieved only by the coordinated efforts of all types of armed forces and branches of the service. This posture was in sharp contrast to that of the United States which was proclaiming a policy of "massive retaliation" against any aggressor. In light of what was to come, it is interesting that Zhukov also told the Indian officers that one of the deciding factors in Soviet officer training and selection was "the ability to independently and creatively decide questions of the organization and conduct of combat action, the ability to display wise initiative."[5]

There was nothing in Zhukov's statements that had not been discussed in the Soviet military press. What was remarkable was the absence of any reference in the extended quotations to Party guidance or of a collegial solution of such complicated problems as the nature of future war involving the great powers, and the absence of institutional references such as "Soviet military doctrine considers . . ." or "Soviet military science teaches . . ." Even the use of the first person plural seemed editorial rather than literal.[6]

As these remarks were being published, *Krasnaia Zvezda* reported that a military-scientific conference was being held at the Frunze Military Academy, devoted to questions of contemporary combined-arms combat. Zhukov's remarks in India were not mentioned in the article.[7] However, it would have been obvious to the participants in the conference that the minister of defense had resolved certain aspects of the problems of contemporary war.

Zhukov's activities during the months of April, May, and June were busy but routine. He travelled to Bucharest in April and to Budapest in May with Foreign Minister Andrei A. Gromyko to sign status-of-forces agreements with those governments, covering the presence of Soviet troops "temporarily" stationed in those countries. Gromyko later recalled his conversations with Zhukov on those occasions. The war and Zhukov's role in it were the primary topics of their conversation and Gromyko remembered that Zhukov credited the steadfastness of the Soviet soldier as an important factor in the achievement of victory. He also recalled that Zhukov had been "forceful" in defending the harsh disciplinary measures that had been invoked during the war, especially during its closing phases. Gromyko thought that Zhukov's statements were prompted by the fact that "he personally had a hand in some very stringent acts, directed toward maintaining the high level of discipline of the Soviet soldier."[8]

During their conversations Zhukov touched on the successful tests of new Soviet rocket weapons and the efforts of Washington politicians and strategists to achieve and maintain military superiority over the Soviet Union. For them and their efforts Zhukov had some "very sharp words." Gromyko also queried him on his popularity among the people and received a straightforward answer: he had done all he could but it was not up to him to judge. Possibly, not everyone was pleased that the people valued his work. He recalled that his relations with Stalin were uneven, but in difficult moments the dictator always found the right words to address him. Gromyko was impressed favorably by the sober thoughts of the "renowned soldier."[9]

Gromyko also observed that Zhukov seemed more relaxed when he was not around Khrushchev. He also noted that Zhukov never mentioned Khrushchev in discussions of the preparation or execution of military operations. According to Gromyko, Khrushchev often liked to recall his visits to the front and his contacts with certain military leaders, giving Gromyko the impression that he was trying to acquire vicariously a reputation for competence in military affairs. On the other hand, Gromyko could not recall any statements by Zhukov that could be considered critical of Stalin's wartime leadership. In fact he quoted Zhukov as saying, "I acknowledge the enormous services of Stalin as the Supreme Commander in Chief."[10]

In their discussions of the responsibility for the unpreparedness of the country at the start of the war, Zhukov disclaimed the responsibility of the military leadership. He acknowledged that Soviet rearmament was very tardy, but was firm in his belief that the political leadership should be blamed for the delays. Zhukov also recalled with bitterness the enormous harm Stalin's purges had inflicted on the military leadership on the eve of the war. But Gromyko observed, however, that Zhukov did not express himself in this vein in the presence of former members of [Stalin's] Politburo.[11]

The discussions that Gromyko chose to recall mark very clearly the time in which his article was published, even though the publication date is not given. Sometime after the downfall of Khrushchev in October 1964, it was decided that the denigration of Stalin had proceeded far enough, and during this period favorable comments in print about Zhukov were again permitted. But there was a limit to what could be printed and what the old soldier would be permitted to do and say.

Gromyko did not choose to mention that Zhukov's visit to Bucharest in April 1957 was not without incident. While the drafters of the text of the agreement were awaiting the arrival of the Soviet ministers Gromyko and Zhukov to complete the formal signing of the document, Zhukov did not appear. The Romanian defense minister and the local Soviet troop commander became very concerned, waiting for information from Moscow about Zhukov's arrival time. At the last moment, the Romanian minister ran in and breathlessly announced that Zhukov had arrived; he had flown across the Romanian border without receiving clearance from Romanian air traffic control. All present, Romanians and Soviets, were stunned. No apologies were offered for this border violation and it alarmed the Romanians. Later, in conversations with Soviet military and diplomatic personnel, the Romanians stressed the necessity for the Soviet Union to honor the state sovereignty of Romania.

A witness to this incident, Ambassador A. Nikolaev, saw in the episode the complicated and contradictory character of Georgii Konstantinovich. Nikolaev did not attempt to determine who was at fault in failing to notify the Romanian authorities of the border crossing, but attributed the border violation to an arbitrary decision of Zhukov's. If this were so, Zhukov was in effect showing his disdain for the agreement and the Romanians.[12] He was also acting at cross purposes with the policy of his own government, which was trying to present and promote the Warsaw Pact organization as one made up of sovereign nations.

An illustration of the increasing scope of Zhukov's authority in the government was a short announcement that an Iranian government delegation, in Moscow to sign a border agreement with the USSR on behalf of their government, had been received by Chairman of the Council of Ministers Bulganin and Defense Minister Zhukov.[13] During Stalin's era the green-hatbanded Soviet border troops had been under the control of one of the security organs: the NKVD or its successor the MVD. Zhukov's participation in this meeting indicated that the border troops were now within his competence as minister of defense.[14]

On 24 June, the Yugoslav secretary of defense, Ivan Gosniak, arrived in Moscow for an official visit and was pictured with Khrushchev, Bulganin, Zhukov, Konev, Sokolovskii, and General Antonov. Gosniak's departure on 26 June was also noted. What was not announced to either the Soviet public or the world at large was that from 22 to 29 June 1957, a contest for supreme power was taking place in a plenum of the Central Committee between Khrushchev and his supporters and the "anti-Party group" of Malenkov, Molotov, Kaganovich, and Shepilov. Zhukov decisively supported Khrushchev during this crisis. At some point in the debate the anti-Party group had a majority in the Presidium on a proposal to remove Khrushchev from his Party and government posts. Khrushchev succeeded in postponing the decision in order to place the question before the entire Central Committee, which was rapidly assembled with Zhukov's help, and the decision was reversed. In the heat of the polemics exchanged between the two contending groups, Zhukov warned the Malenkov-Molotov group: "The army is against that decision [to remove Khrushchev] and not one tank will move from its place without my order." Khrushchev later recalled that remark, interpreting it as a manifestation of Zhukov's "Bonapartism," even though it was uttered to support him.[15]

Writing of this period, Konstantin Simonov recalled that after the Twentieth Party Congress and Khrushchev's de-Stalinization speech in February 1956, Zhukov was very concerned with restoring the good name of those who had spent long years as German prisoners of war after being captured in 1941 and 1942. He was bitter that Lev Z. Mekhlis, at that time Chief of the Main Political Directorate and deputy commissar of defense, in 1941 had devised the formula that anyone who was captured was a traitor to the fatherland. Mekhlis felt that a Soviet officer or soldier threatened with capture and unable to avoid it should commit suicide. Those who did not were considered to be cowards and were subject to further imprisonment when they returned to friendly lines or home after the war. This formula was part of the rationale for the early Soviet defeats; the other part was the accusation that some officers in the Soviet high command had been traitors. Zhukov considered it his duty to do everything he could to restore dignity and freedom to all the soldiers and officers who had suffered under these Draconian policies.

A year later Simonov was present at one of the stormiest meetings of the Central Committee, when Zhukov in his speech sharply reminded two or three of those seated on the dais behind him of their direct responsibility for the events of 1937 and 1938. One of those accused interrupted Zhukov, saying that the times were such that certain documents had to be signed willy-nilly, and that if one dug, one could find the signature of Zhukov on some of the documents of that era. Zhukov turned to his accuser and said, "No, you won't find anything. Dig! You won't find my signature."[16] Simonov was probably describing the plenum at which the "anti-Party group" was defeated in its bid for power. Molotov, Malenkov, Kaganovich, and Voroshilov[17]* were all vulnerable to Zhukov's charge that they, by their signatures on "documents" that in many cases were death warrants, had condemned Soviet Army and Navy officers at all levels of command. There was never any doubt where Zhukov's sympathies were in the contest with Stalin's old guard.

Zhukov's challenge to dig into his record was not answered during his lifetime. But sometime prior to 1988, while Dmitrii Volkogonov was researching the archives of the Ministry of Defense for his biography of Stalin, he found a letter to the then commissar of defense, Voroshilov, signed by a G. Zhukov, which was an accusation (*donos*) against A. I. Egorov, former chief of the General Staff (1935–1937). Volkogonov did not name Zhukov in his work, stating only that the letter was sent by a former colleague of Egorov's who subsequently became an important military commander. The letter was brought to Voroshilov's attention on 26 January 1938. Volkogonov saw fit to add that by that time Egorov's fate had already been decided.[18]

The same document was also cited reluctantly by the writer V. V. Karpov in a magazine article in which he named Georgii Konstantinovich as the author of the letter. Karpov attempted to remove some of the tarnish to Zhukov's name by writing that Egorov by that time in 1938 had already been arrested and had perished.

Amazingly, as has been convincingly demonstrated by Gen. Anatolii Khor'kov in a scathing article in *Pravda* in January 1992, the internal evidence in the document clearly shows that the G. Zhukov who reported on Egorov in 1938 could not have been Georgii Konstantinovich. Khor'kov also pointed out that Egorov's fate had not been decided in January of that year (he died or was executed in February 1939). Additionally, he revealed that Zhukov's oldest daughters, Era and Ella, after being rebuffed in an attempt to have Volkogonov or Karpov review

---

*Voroshilov had been minister of defense from October 1925 until May 1940 and could not avoid a share of responsibility for the military purges of 1937 and 1938. It was to develop later that he was initially in opposition to Khrushchev during the June plenum.

the accusation against their father, had the signatures of the two Zhukovs compared by handwriting experts. The conclusion was that Georgii Konstantinovich had not signed the letter. It has now been established that the letter was signed by Georgii Vasil'evich Zhukov, who served briefly with Georgii Konstantinovich during the Civil War.[19]

On 4 July 1957, it was announced that Zhukov had been selected by the plenum for membership in the fifteen-member Presidium of the Central Committee and that Malenkov, Molotov, Kaganovich, and Shepilov had been voted out. Zhukov was the first professional soldier ever to be elected to the highest policy-making body in the Soviet Union. His selection was clearly a reward for the support he had given Khrushchev. The next day, Zhukov and other senior military leaders, including Konev and Malinovskii, were quoted in *Krasnaia Zvezda* as speaking in support of the decisions of the plenum; the headline read: "Communists of the Ministry of Defense and the Moscow Garrison unanimously approve and support the June plenum of the CC CPSU [Central Committee of the Communist Party of the Soviet Union]."[20]

Between 13 and 15 July, Zhukov was in Leningrad for ceremonies connected with Soviet Navy Day. According to press accounts, Zhukov gave three speeches in support of what became known as the decisions of the June plenum. In these speeches he attacked the anti-Party group for opposing Khrushchev's proclaimed effort to overtake the United States in per capita production of meat and dairy products, for opposing Khrushchev's policy of broadening contacts with the outside world, for opposing his proposal to decentralize the economic decision-making process, and for continuing to press for the liquidation of the personality cult (the de-Stalinization campaign). Some believed that Zhukov, in an effort to force the Party leaders to broaden the indictment of Stalinism, in his references to de-Stalinization went further than Khrushchev did in his "secret speech."[21]

Spread across the bottom of the first page of the 16 July issue of *Krasnaia Zvezda* was a heroic photograph of Zhukov giving his Navy Day address on the banks of the Neva with a new Soviet cruiser, suitably decorated, in the background. Also in the background were Frol Kozlov, first secretary of the Leningrad Party organization, and General of the Army M. V. Zakharov, the Leningrad Military District commander.[22]

On 24 September it was announced that Marshal Zhukov had accepted the invitation of Yugoslav Secretary of Defense Gosniak to visit

Yugoslavia on 8 October, and what appeared to be a repetition of the coverage of his visit to India began in *Krasnaia Zvezda* on 5 October with an article and news photo of his departure from Moscow. A new Soviet cruiser, the *Kuibyshev*, was used to transport him to Yugoslavia from Sevastopol' and he arrived on schedule. Daily press coverage of the visit followed.[23]

In retrospect, Zhukov said he was put on guard by the timing of his foreign excursion, which coincided with an exercise in the Kiev Military District. He raised the question directly with Khrushchev, who was in Kiev. The first secretary directed him to complete his state mission, telling him that the exercise could be conducted without him. Zhukov's foreign mission was in fact an important one because at that time the Soviets were wooing the Yugoslavs, attempting to repair the Tito-Stalin split of 1948. And, as was to be revealed later, Zhukov had a similar mission in Albania. Zhukov later learned that Khrushchev used the occasion to canvass the military leaders assembled for the exercise on their opinion of the minister of defense and to insinuate the idea among them that Zhukov was a dangerous man.[24]

While Khrushchev was masterminding his downfall at home, Zhukov appeared to enjoy his first sea voyage. The Soviet Navy had taken every precaution to ensure that the minister of defense had a pleasant trip. A commission headed by the first deputy to the commander in chief of the Navy inspected the ship in advance of Zhukov's boarding. The ship passed a rigorous inspection, and the crew was warned that if anything went wrong it would go badly for someone. The extreme caution displayed by the high command of the Navy derived from their experience with Zhukov. They had witnessed the punishment that those in the chain of command had suffered in the *Novorossiisk* tragedy. In recent inspections of the Baltic and the Northern Fleets, the minister had personally demoted and relieved from active duty 273 officers. No wonder the Navy "feared rather than respected" Zhukov.

Early in the voyage, the closest thing to a *ChP* (extraordinary incident) occurred. Zhukov's hat was almost blown overboard by a gust of wind. It was saved by an agile sailor. For wear on deck a Navy beret was altered to fit the marshal's outsized head. In addition to being struck by the sailor's quick response in the hat incident, Zhukov was impressed by the complexity of navigating a modern warship through the Bosphorus in conditions of poor visibility and rough seas. The *Kuibyshev*'s commander, then Captain First Rank V. V. Mikhailin, took advantage of Zhukov's proximity to tell him of a Soviet captain who had been relieved of command because his ship had run into a buoy the week before in these waters under similar weather and sea conditions. When Zhukov's aide confirmed Mikhailin's story and told him that the relief had been ordered by Zhukov himself, the minister ordered the relief cancelled. Whether or not the relief order really was cancelled is uncertain.

The *Kuibyshev* also encountered units of the U.S. Sixth Fleet (a carrier, a cruiser, two frigates, and several destroyers), which rendered the customary ship to ship courtesies and sent greetings to the Soviet minister of defense. The crews of the U.S. ships were on deck, in whites, at attention, and ruffles and flourishes were played. Zhukov received the honors in ill-humor, muttering, "Even here they feel as if they are in their own backyard (*votchina*)." A one-word response was sent from the Soviet ship to the Americans, "*Blagodariu*" (I thank you).[25]

Captain Mikhailin had learned that Zhukov had a weakness for the music of the *baian,* a large accordion with a complex system of keys, which Zhukov had learned to play during the war. During a shipboard concert, 32 sailors played the instrument while performing an intricate routine in which they appeared on deck through a hatch from below like "bees coming out of a hive." Zhukov was delighted and participated on the baian in the concert's last number.[26]*

The *Kuibyshev* arrived at Zadar, Yugoslavia, on 8 October. There Zhukov was met by the commander of the Yugoslav Navy; as he left the Soviet cruiser he told Captain Mikhailin to proceed to Split where he would rejoin the ship for an official visit to Albania. Later the ship was ordered back to Sevastopol' without the minister of defense, arriving there on 17 October.[27]

Zhukov's activities in Yugoslavia were overshadowed in the Soviet and world press by the announcement on 6 October that the Soviet Union had successfully placed an artificial satellite in earth orbit. On 10 October Khrushchev disclosed, in an interview with James Reston of the *New York Times,* that the Soviet ambassador in Washington had attempted

---

*The baian is named for a poet of ancient Russia who is mentioned in the "Song of Igor's Campaign."

to follow up on an off-hand remark by President Eisenhower to the effect that a meeting between United States Secretary of Defense Charles E. Wilson and Defense Minister Zhukov would be useful, but that Secretary of State Dulles had said Eisenhower had not been correctly understood.[28] The implication was that Khrushchev and the Soviet political leadership were in favor of the idea of a Zhukov visit to the United States. Considering what was under way behind the scenes, it seems clear that Khrushchev had misled Mr. Reston.

Another event receiving continuous attention in the Soviet press was a threatening crisis in the Middle East involving Turkey and Syria. The United States was, in the Soviet view, urging the Turks to take military action against Syria and at the same time pressuring the Syrians to yield.[29] The Soviet Union was supporting the Syrians, and as evidence of this support, Marshal Rokossovskii, well known from his service in World War II and as former minister of defense of Poland, was sent to take command of the Transcaucasian Military District, which borders Turkey.[30]*

With international tension increasing, it was reported on 18 October that Zhukov would also visit Albania. Coverage of his stay there continued until his return to Moscow by air on 26 October. The same issue of *Krasnaia Zvezda* that announced his return to Moscow also announced that R. Ia. Malinovskii had been designated minister of defense and that Zhukov had been relieved of his duties.[31]

---

*This device was to be used again during the Berlin crisis in 1961 when Marshal Konev was sent to East Germany to command the Group of Soviet Forces, Germany, and General Batov to command the Southern Group of Forces in Hungary.

NOTES

1. *KZ,* 3 January 1957, p. 1.
2. Ibid., 24 January 1957, p. 1.
3. Ibid., 25, 26, 27, 29, 30, 31 January; 1, 17 February 1957.
4. Ibid.
5. Ibid.
6. Ibid. However egocentric Zhukov's remarks may have seemed in retrospect they were nevertheless reprinted in book form shortly after Zhukov returned from India. L. M. Kitaev and G. N. Bol'shakov, *Vizit druzhby* (Visit of friendship) (Moscow: Voenizdat, 1957).
7. *KZ,* 24 March 1957, p. 2.
8. A. A. Gromyko, "Georgii Konstantinovich Zhukov" in Mirkina and Iarovikov, *Marshal Zhukov: Polkovodets* 2: p. 13. Judging by the internal context this article was published sometime after Khrushchev was removed from office in October 1964.
9. Ibid., pp. 12, 13.
10. Ibid., p. 16.
11. Ibid., p. 17.
12. A. Nikolaev, "Marshal Zhukov protiv Zhukova?" (Marshal Zhukov against Zhukov?) in *Armiia,* no. 15 (1991): p. 65.
13. *KZ,* 9 May 1957, p. 3.
14. Cf. Raymond Garthoff, *Soviet Strategy in the Nuclear Age* (New York: Praeger, 1962), pp. 30, 31, which lists responsibility for the border troops as part of the "concessions" that Zhukov sought following the June 1957 plenary session of the Central Committee.
15. Pavlenko,"Razmyshleniia" in *VIZh,* no. 12 (1988): p. 34. The sentence is found in Captain 1st Rank S. Bystrov, "V oktiabre 1957-ogo" (In October 1957) in *KZ,* 19 May 1989, p. 4. Zhukov's aid in assembling the members of the Central Committee is reported in Vladimir Karpov, "Tainaia rasprava nad marshalom Zhukovym" (The secret reprisals against Marshal Zhukov), in *Pravda,* 17 August 1991, p. 4.
16. Simonov, "Zametki" in *VIZh,* no. 7 (1987): pp. 33, 34.
17. *XXII S'ezd Kommunisticheskoi Partii Sovetskogo Soiuza* (Twenty-second Congress of the Communist Party of the Soviet Union),

Stenographic account, vol. 2 (Moscow: State Publishing House of Political Literature, 1962), pp. 589, 590.

18. Volkogonov, *Triumf i tragediia,* Book 1, part 2, pp. 271, 272.

19. Major General Anatolii Khor'kov, "Ten' na marshala Zhukova" (A shadow is cast on Marshal Zhukov) in *Pravda,* 16 January 1992, p. 6. Major General of Reserves Akon Dadaian, "Kak Georgii Zhukov donos pisal" (How Georgii Zhukov wrote an accusation) in *Situatsiia,* no. 12 (1992): p. 6.

20. *KZ,* 4 and 5 July 1957, p. 1.

21. Wolfgang Leonhard, *The Kremlin since Stalin* (New York: Praeger, 1962), pp. 249, 250, and 256. *KZ,* 14, 18 July 1957.

22. *KZ,* 18 July 1957.

23. Ibid., 24 September 1957, p. 1; 5, 6, 8, 9, 10, 11, 12, 13, 14, 16, 17, 18 October 1957.

24. Pavlenko, "Razmyshleniia" in *VIZh,* no. 12, p. 34.

25. Bystrov, "V oktiabre 1957-ogo" in *KZ,* 20 May 1989, p. 4.

26. Ibid.

27. Ibid., 21 May 1989, p. 4.

28. *KZ,* 10 October 1957.

29. Ibid., 19 October 1957, p. 4.

30. *Pravda,* 25 October 1957.

31. *KZ,* 27 October 1957, pp. 3, 4.

XXV

THE OCTOBER PLENUM—
THE SECRET REPRISALS

It was not until 3 November 1957 that the Soviet public and the world at large were given the rationale for the replacement of the minister of defense. All major Soviet papers printed a resolution (*postanovlenie*) of the plenum of the Central Committee, which announced the removal of Zhukov from the Presidium and the Central Committee. The heading noted that at the end of October a plenum had been held on the subject of improving Party political work in the armed forces. The plenum had adopted a resolution and expelled Comrade Zhukov from the Presidium and from the Central Committee.

The resolution, which was an indictment against Zhukov, included the following principal charges:

1. Attempting to "shrivel" Party organizations, political organs, and the Military Councils, leading toward liquidation of Party and government control of the armed forces;
2. Encouraging the creation of his own personality cult, including inflating his role in the Soviet victories in World War II;
3. Being inclined to adventurism both in the foreign policy of the Soviet Union and in his leadership of the Ministry of Defense; and
4. Having insufficient *partiinost'* (party spirit) and therefore incorrectly understanding the high evaluation of his services by the Party and the government.

Partiinost', used here in an ethical sense, was applied to all spheres of Party activity. In general *partiinost'* demanded that Party members be alert to sense the implications of any theory or action from the point of view of the Party's current "line" and that the "truth" of any theory or the value of any action was determined on the basis of whether or not it contributed to the Party's program. In accusing Zhukov of having insufficient *partiinost'*, the Plenum was alleging a lack of modesty on Zhukov's part, a failure to give sufficient credit to the Party and the people for the awards and promotions he received.[1]

Krasnaia Zvezda that same day reported that the decisions of the plenum were being discussed and approved at meetings of Party activists in many military districts and fleets throughout the country.[2]

Some idea of how these discussions proceeded and how they were received outside of Moscow can be judged from Captain Mikhailin's (the captain of the *Kuibyshev*) account of his participation with the activists of the Sevastopol' Naval Base. Soon after he returned from Yugoslavia he was ordered to attend a meeting at the base officers' club. As he entered the club, the club officer came up to him and reported alarmedly that he had been ordered to remove all of the photographs of the recent voyage of the *Kuibyshev* (which featured its important passenger prominently) from the foyer of the club. He wondered what had happened. Mikhailin had no answer.

When Mikhailin in anxious puzzlement entered the hall of the club he found that the subject of the meeting was the resolution of the Central Committee and the discussant was to be Aleksandr I. Kirichenko, Khrushchev's successor in the Ukraine and a member of the Presidium. Kirichenko spoke for about an hour, mostly about shortcomings in Party work in the army and the fleet. Only toward the end of his speech did he mention Zhukov critically, without naming his position. The discussion that followed was not in the tone the convenors expected; mostly, according to Mikhailin, because the discussants had not been properly prepared. The speech of the political member of the Military Council of the Fleet, N. Torik, was more to the point. He cited Khrushchev's speech of 22–23 October in the Kremlin in which he said that he esteemed Zhukov and would always protect him, but that there had to be a limit to his abuses.

Despite quotations from Khrushchev's speech, the responses of the activists of the Black Sea Fleet were restrained. Torik warned his colleagues that they should think about this problem, because in Zhukov's conduct could be seen the beginnings of a new personality cult. Mikhailin recalled that he and his colleagues were surprised at the way the overthrow of the war hero was accomplished, and that it did not evoke any acceptance among the officers of the Black Sea Fleet.[3] One can speculate that other units outside the capital found the proceedings against Zhukov just as puzzling.*

Pravda, the central organ of the Communist Party, on 3 November contained, in addition to the charges outlined above, a quoted statement by Zhukov in which he admitted his political errors, saying the criticisms were basically correct, and stating that the plenum had been for him a great Party school. However, Zhukov denied charges made by certain speakers at the plenum that he had also been wrong when he was expelled from the Central Committee in 1946. This he said he did not admit in 1946 nor would he now.[4]

Pravda also published a stinging article signed by Marshal I. S. Konev, Zhukov's first deputy minister of defense, which accused Zhukov of limiting the role of Party organizations in the armed forces to a purely educational and enlightenment function and not permitting them to share in the overall direction of the military units of which they were a part. The article accused Zhukov of trying to decide all questions of leadership by himself. Without providing details, Konev accused Zhukov of attempting to substitute administrative measures—a euphemism for punitive measures—for the education and training of young officers, who should be cared for "as a golden resource of the country." Under Zhukov's administration, according to the article, an attempt was made to keep armed forces Party organizations separate from local Party organizations. He was also condemned for criticizing current Soviet field manuals which he said played a negative role in the training of commanders and did not promote initiative. This portion of Konev's article was summed up with the statement that these were not separate errors but an entire system of errors, and that Zhukov had a tendency to consider the armed forces as his patrimony (*votchina*).[5]

---

*In late 1957, while the author was serving with the U.S. Military Liaison Mission to the Soviet Forces in East Germany, he expressed surprise at seeing a large portrait of Zhukov prominently displayed in a Soviet *komendatura.* The *komendant* responded by saying that the Soviet Army still had enormous respect for Zhukov.

Konev's article then launched into a criticism of Zhukov's wartime role, assigning him a share of responsibility for the initial Soviet defeats, diminishing the importance of his contribution to the counteroffensive at Stalingrad, and ascribing to him various errors of omission and commission during other phases of the war. Konev also declared flatly that the basic weight of organizing operations lay on the shoulders of the Front and army commanders and their staffs during the war, thereby setting the tone of military historical literature for the next seven years.

The article also produced some specific instances of Zhukov's attempts to inculcate his personality cult: by editing a film on the Battle of Stalingrad, and by having a portrait of himself on a white horse before the Brandenburg Gate in Berlin hung in the Central Club of the Soviet Army in Moscow. This portrait was likened to a frequently copied icon of the Russian Orthodox Church—St. George on horseback, slaying the dragon. Since Georgii is Zhukov's given name, the analogy was hardly subtle.[6]

It cannot be said at this time how much assistance Konev received in writing the article. Col. Gen. A. S. Zheltov, chief of the Main Political Administration, claims that when he first raised the issue of Zhukov's attitude toward the Main Political Administration with Khrushchev (Zhukov was conveniently in Yugoslavia), the latter called in Konev and Malinovskii to hear Zheltov's charges; both men said that Zheltov was simply trying to settle accounts with Zhukov. In other words, neither Konev, whose principal duty was that of commander in chief of the Warsaw Pact forces, nor Malinovskii, who was commander in chief of the Soviet Ground Forces, had noticed any of the problems that were causing Zheltov to say he could not work under the existing conditions. On the other hand, members of the Presidium, who were also present, including Kozlov and Brezhnev, said they had been hearing reports about Zhukov's attitude toward the political administration and his leadership of the armed forces; they suggested that the situation should be investigated in the field. It was decided to send the members of the Presidium to the military districts and the fleets. When they returned there was a second meeting to which more than 15 military leaders were invited. It was then decided to convoke a plenum of the Central Committee.[7]

In the period that Zhukov was absent from Moscow, Konev was acting minister of defense and was in a position to collect the necessary supporting materials for the case against Zhukov. Ironically, the photograph that accompanied the announcement of Zhukov's departure for Sevastopol' shows Zhukov talking to Konev as they walked toward a waiting plane. One could imagine that Zhukov was passing on last-minute instructions about matters that might arise in his absence.

The most detailed indictment of Zhukov is contained in the first of two histories of political work in the Soviet armed forces written by Iurii P. Petrov, the acknowledged historian of the structure and activities of Party organizations in the military forces. A comparison of this book, signed to the press in February 1964 (before the removal of Khrushchev), with the second history, published in 1968 under the Brezhnev regime, provides an illuminating example of how the Party "line" concerning Zhukov changed.[8]

The account published during the Khrushchev period attempts to show that Zhukov's aberrations were a continuation of practices that had developed during Stalin's regime. To find a documentary basis for what Petrov calls "the incorrect views of Stalin on the armed forces of a socialist state"[9] two quotations from his collected works are produced, one from January 1921 and the other from December 1923. The error demonstrated in these quotes is Stalin's belief that coercion was the accepted manner of leading any army, which he classified as a closed organization directed from the top. According to Petrov, this approach concealed the radical differences between the armed forces of a socialist state and the armies of capitalist states. In the latter the principle of coercion was indeed characteristic, but in the former the elements of conviction, high political activity, and creative initiative of personnel prevail. Stalin's incorrect views led to his underestimation of the value of Party leadership of the Army, the role of the Party organizations, and Party political work in the Soviet military forces as a whole. This was reflected in general by the substitution of formal bureaucratic procedures for politico-educational work and by ignoring the creative initiative of Communists.[10]

To support this criticism of Stalin's view of the Soviet Army, Petrov cited a wartime regulation under which the personal cases of Communists accused of offenses were, depending on the rank of the individual, reviewed at higher Party echelons, thereby reducing individual responsibility to the primary Party organization and limiting inner-Party democracy. The absence of instructions to the Party organizations of the armed forces from 1934 until 1957 was also cited as leading to a general loss of orientation among Party activists in the armed forces. Because of these factors, military training often lost contact with political training and "the main method of strengthening Soviet military discipline—measures of persuasion—was not adequately used."[11]

In the course of overcoming the harmful effects of the personality cult of Stalin, according to Petrov, the Party encountered opposition from Zhukov, who not only did not liquidate the shortcomings of Party work in the armed forces but aggravated them by ignoring Party organizations. This conduct of Zhukov's led to a situation in which the Central Committee had to take measures.

Petrov's 1964 book provided the fullest public account of the indictment against Zhukov as it was presented to the expanded plenum on 28 and 29 October. The report to the plenum was delivered by Mikhail A. Suslov, a member of the Presidium and a secretary of the Central Committee in charge of ideology. Zhukov's "line" was criticized as being "anti-Party" and specifically included the following acts and policies:

1. Insisting on liquidating the Supreme Military Council;
2. Prohibiting Communists in the armed services from appealing to the Central Committee;
3. Limiting the rights of the Military Councils of military districts, groups of forces, fleets, armies, and flotillas and turning them into consultative organs;
4. Insisting that the composition of the Military Councils be approved by an order of the minister of defense even though civilian Party members were included in their membership; according to the indictment, Zhukov's purpose in this was to remove full-time military political workers from the position of "member of the Military Council";
5. Ignoring and depreciating the role of the Party-political work among the troops and converting it to "narrow" enlightenment;
6. Slighting the Main Political Directorate, forbidding it to inform the Central Committee of the condition and activity of the forces;
7. Limiting the rights of Party organizations and their independence of action, removing them from participation in deciding questions of combat training, and strengthening military discipline. For criticism of shortcomings in training and service, Communists were called into strict account, including discharge from the armed forces;

8. Abolishing tested forms of political work including Marxist-Leninist preparation of the officer corps and political instruction for privates and sergeants which was converted to a one-hour session on current questions, during off-duty hours;
9. Implanting naked administrative measures and crudity with subordinates, warping the essence of Soviet military discipline, the basis of which is personal conviction;
10. Inculcating a Zhukov personality cult in the armed forces, inflating his role in the war, and depreciating the inspirational role of the Communist Party.

In the discussion which followed Suslov's report, twenty-seven persons were reported to have spoken. The military speakers listed included: P. I. Batov, S. S. Biriuzov, S. G. Gorshkov, A. S. Zheltov, I. S. Konev, R. Ia. Malinovskii, K. K. Rokossovskii, N. Torik, and V. I. Chuikov.[12] Of the texts of these speeches, only the newspaper article signed by Konev, mentioned above, has been published.

In the revised indictment against Zhukov which was published in 1968, the specific charges that Zhukov was inclined to adventurism in foreign and domestic affairs and that he tried to create his own "personality cult" in the armed forces were dropped. The charge against him was summed up in one sentence:

At meetings of the Party aktiv, the Presidium, and the plenum of the CC of the Party, it was pointed out that G. K. Zhukov, being minister of defense, underestimated Party leadership of the Soviet Army and Fleet.[13]

Some details of how Zhukov "underestimated" that leadership were discussed in Chapter 23. It seems these actions could have been defended easily on the grounds of efficiency in a period of sharp cutbacks in personnel. Restrictions on the career prospects of the senior officers in the Main Political Administration were another matter but one which could have been corrected. Zhukov's personal behavior toward senior officers reflected a personality trait for which he had been criticized in 1946 and which hardly befitted an officer in his position. But his personality and command style could hardly have been a surprise to those who had returned him to Moscow and used his direct support to deal with their own opponents. In addition, his style of command reflected the prevailing culture which permeated the Soviet military high command. Soviet commanders were not expected to be "uncles" to their subordinates. Soft-spoken, controlled commanders such as Rokossovskii and Shaposhnikov were the exception rather than the rule. There had to be some more weighty grounds for the severity with which Khrushchev and his colleagues dealt with Zhukov.

The conditions of glasnost' have permitted the publication of excerpts from the "strictly secret" transcript of the October 1957 plenum of the Central Committee. Vladimir Karpov, an author and member of the Central Committee, after almost a year's effort gained access to the document in June 1991. It revealed the other, and possibly the main, reason for the reprisals against Zhukov. Zhukov and General Shtemenko, then head of the Main Intelligence Directorate (GRU), had commenced the formation of a school of saboteurs with more than 2,000 students and had not informed the Central Committee.[14] Khrushchev told the plenum that he had been warned by Malinovskii in October 1954 to watch out for Zhukov who was "a growing Bonaparte," a dangerous person who would stop at nothing.[15] Khrushchev had heard Zhukov tell the "anti-Party" group that he would use the army if they did not reverse their decision to remove Khrushchev; now he was forming a secret group of highly trained special-forces troops whom he could use to overthrow any leadership that did not suit him. Khrushchev knew that the Soviet leadership before him—those of Lenin and Stalin—had been installed by extra-legal actions. One of the main events in his own accession to power was his coup against Beriia. Without Zhukov's support he would not have prevailed against Malenkov, Molotov, Kaganovich, and Voroshilov in June. Zhukov had to be removed and the potential threat of this "secret" organization neutralized.[16]

The formation of special-forces units by the Soviet Army could have been easily justified in 1957. The U.S. Army had created such units, whose mission in event of hostilities was to include insertion behind the enemy's lines to disrupt his communications, to incite civil disorder, and to destroy selected targets including rocket-launching positions. The physically fit troops selected for this training were given parachute jump instruction and trained in languages, hand-to-hand combat, demolition, and sabotage techniques. Given the level of political hostility between the members of the Warsaw Pact and NATO, it would have been surprising if the Soviet Army had not created a similar force.

Also, there was nothing inherently sinister in keeping this entire program under the tightest secrecy controls. Soviet concepts of what should be concealed from potential enemies traditionally have been more stringent than those of the West, and Khrushchev himself was known to get carried away in a debate and reveal more than his associates wished him to divulge. The very nature of the special-forces missions seemed to demand that their existence, numbers, and capabilities be held closely.

When Zhukov was permitted to speak in his own defense before the plenum (a fact that was not reported in either the press or Petrov's 1964 book), he accepted full responsibility for his personal behavior toward senior officers. But he asked those present, particularly the military, if the armed forces, during his service as minister of defense, had not become more disciplined, better organized, in better order, with fewer *ChP*s (extraordinary incidents). He also contended that Soviet commanders who were Communists could also lead and direct Party work in the armed forces and that political activities should not be conducted by professional political officers but by the Party organizations that existed throughout the armed forces.

Zhukov recalled for the group that three weeks before, when he was preparing to leave for Yugoslavia and Albania, he had conferred with many members of the Central Committee and had said goodbye to them as he would have with close friends. They had offered him no complaints on his performance as minister of defense. Then he had found out while he was in Yugoslavia (he said he was not certain of the date) that a meeting of the Presidium was in progress. He believed that he should have been recalled, inasmuch as his conduct was the subject of the meeting.

At the plenum Zhukov apparently did not make any direct rejoinder to the accusation that he was a potential Bonaparte. Later, he thought long about why Malinovskii had made such a provocative statement to Khrushchev. He could only conclude that it was inspired by deeply personal considerations. In this context he recalled that in 1945 Beriia and Abakumov had presented Stalin with a fabricated case, accusing Zhukov of being disloyal to Stalin; years later their case was shown to be the deliberate slander of careerists and traitors.[17] If Zhukov brought this thought to its logical conclusion, then Zhukov believed Malinovskii to have been either a careerist or a traitor.

Zhukov apparently provided no explanation as to why he had not informed the Central Committee of the formation of the special-forces unit. Karpov did relate that as a former intelligence officer he had been offered a key position at the "school." According to him, the school was to become a special forces division and each military district was to have a company which eventually would be expanded into a brigade. Therefore Karpov believed that the school could hardly have been a secret organization in the sense that Khrushchev had attempted to depict it.

Following Suslov and Zhukov, the transcript provides the list of speakers in order (parentheses contain Karpov's comments on the individual): General Zheltov (representing the "offended" political workers); Brezhnev (the solid and loyal friend of Khrushchev); Marshal Biriuzov (offended very much by Zhukov, which is obvious from the words Zhukov allegedly said to him, "Who are you [using the familiar *ty*]? Who knows you? I'll take off your marshal's shoulderboards."); Kalberzin (the first secretary of the Latvian Communist Party); Admiral Gorshkov (an old "sworn friend" of Zhukov); Furtseva (a very big expert in military affairs) [she was the Minister of Culture and was reportedly having an affair with Khrushchev]; Kirichenko (member of the Presidium); Marshals Sokolovskii, Timoshenko, Konev, and Eremenko. As Karpov remarks, each person, either by request of Khrushchev or in an attempt to please him, bore a grudge against Zhukov.

Eremenko, who continually strove to don the laurels of the victor at Stalingrad, spoke so long that Brezhnev, who was temporarily in the chair, had to tell him that what he was saying was marvelous material for military history, but to keep to the agenda. One can speculate that Eremenko was relating how he and his staff had defended the city and originated the plan for the counterattack.

Khrushchev summed up the case against Zhukov. He said that the question had arisen because the people around the minister of defense had began to fear him, and were worried, and that it had begun to "smell bad" around him. When Zhukov at this point interjected that those were "whisperings," Khrushchev responded, "Comrade Zhukov! Maybe you think that English intelligence informed us? He thinks that we are battling each other: Khrushchev and Zhukov." Khrushchev was emphasizing that this was a corporate affair and not a personal matter between him and his defense minister. He went on to characterize Zhukov's conception of his role as minister: Zhukov believed that everything that pertained to the troops must pass through him, but go no further. Actually, as Karpov reminds us, why *should* matters pertaining to the Ministry of Defense go further?

Khrushchev was, of course, leading to the question of the school for saboteurs. He claimed that only Zhukov and Shtemenko knew the school was being organized. It was not accidental that Zhukov had brought Shtemenko back* to head the intelligence directorate; apparently Shtemenko was needed for dark business. Khrushchev then dealt Zhukov the unkindest cut of all: he recalled that Beriia had a group of saboteurs working for him, and before his arrest had assembled a group of cutthroats in Moscow—if he had not been exposed no one could say whose head would have flown. Here, of course, Khrushchev provided perhaps the strongest defense for Zhukov's actions, but one he could not or would not advance. The army needed to have such a force available to counterbalance the "cutthroats" of the secret police, even though the security organs had allegedly been reorganized and reformed after the Beriia affair.[18]**

---

*When Khrushchev said that Zhukov had brought Shtemenko back to be the head of the Main Intelligence Directorate (GRU) he was referring to the peregrinations of Shtemenko's career in the General Staff. He was chief of the Main Operations Directorate at the end of World War II and was chief of the General Staff from November 1948 until June 1952. In 1952 he was sent out of Moscow and demoted because Stalin allegedly suspected him of having connections with Beriia. When he returned to Moscow to become head of the GRU is uncertain. He was demoted and again returned to the field after the October 1957 plenum when it was discovered, after an intense investigation, that he had informed Zhukov through GRU channels while he was in Belgrade that Khrushchev was preparing a case against him. He returned to Moscow in 1962 as deputy CINC of Ground Forces. He finished his career as chief of staff of the Warsaw Pact Armed Forces. Konstantin Simonov, "Besedy s marshalom Sovetskogo Soiuza A. M. Vasilevskim" (Conversations with Marshal of the Soviet Union A. M. Vasilevskii) in *Znamia*, no. 5 (1988), pp. 94, 95. Karpov, "Tainaia rasprava nad marshalom Zhukovym" in *Pravda*, 17 August 1991, p. 4. Author's conversation with Dr. V. M. Kulish.

**It is instructive to note that during the August 1991 *Putsch* attempt, according to Boris Yeltsin, a special group called Group Alpha of the KGB's Seventh Directorate was to storm his office and capture or kill him. Group Alpha refused to execute this command, forcing the plotters to postpone and finally cancel the attack. Serge Schmemann, "Yeltsin Says Elite K.G.B. Unit Refused to Storm His Office," in *The New York Times*, 26 August 1991, p. 1.

In the more complete version of Khrushchev's memoirs serialized in the magazine *Voprosy Istorii* (Questions of History), Khrushchev claimed that in a discussion of the case against Zhukov "in a smaller group of people [than the Central Committee plenum]," Moskalenko accused Zhukov of an inclination to seize power. Zhukov responded to him, saying, "You yourself more than once said to me: 'What are you looking for? Take power in your hands, take it!' " Moskalenko had no reply to Zhukov, and Malinovskii proposed removing Moskalenko from his post. At that time Moskalenko was commanding the Moscow Military District—a dangerous position to entrust to anyone advocating a military putsch. Khrushchev claimed he told the members of the Central Committee that Moskalenko should be forgiven this episode because of the role he played in the arrest of Beriia.[19] Of course Zhukov had also played a key role in the arrest, but he was a threat to the leadership in Khrushchev's eyes and had to be neutralized if not eliminated.

Here it should be noted that Khrushchev, writing in the last years of his exile, did not have access to archives and his memory of events has often proven to be faulty and self-serving.

As Khrushchev reminds us in his recollection of the episode with Moskalenko, the accusation that Zhukov was plotting against the regime was a criminal offense. As in 1946, when Stalin tried to bring similar charges against him, not one of the senior military officers present would support the charge that Zhukov had created the school for saboteurs with the intention of overthrowing the regime. It is not known whether Khrushchev ever had the intention of bringing criminal charges against his defense minister, but it is not clear from the transcript that the military leaders would have supported more drastic punishment of Zhukov. Khrushchev probably was content to neutralize the man he considered a potential political rival and simply used the school for saboteurs to fortify an otherwise weak case.

Zhukov was removed from the Presidium and the Central Committee. He was replaced as minister of defense and in March the next year was retired.[20] Fedor Burlatskii, who served in the central Party apparatus during the Khrushchev regime and often accompanied him on his trips abroad, wrote that the reason for the removal of Zhukov was traditional—"fear of a strong man."[21]

NOTES

1. M. Rozental' and P. Yudin, eds., *Kratkii filosofskii slovar'* (Short philosophical dictionary), 4th ed. (Moscow: Politizdat, 1955), pp. 358–600. Cf. Raymond A. Bauer, *The New Man in Soviet Philosophy* (Cambridge: Harvard University Press, 1953), pp. 103–106. P. A. Kurochkin, ed., *Osnovy metodiki voenno-nauchnogo issledovaniia* (The bases of the method of military-scientific research) (Moscow: Voenizdat, 1969), p. 31.
2. *KZ,* 3 November 1957, p. 2.
3. Bystrov, *"V oktiabre 1957-ogo"* in *KZ,* 21 May 1989, p. 4.
4. *Pravda,* 3 November 1957, p. 2.
5. Ibid., p. 3.
6. Ibid., pp. 3, 4.
7. Bystrov, *"V oktiabre 1957-ogo"* in *KZ,* 21 May 1989, p. 4.
8. The two histories are in many respects identical except in the way they describe the Zhukov case. *Partiinoe stroitel'stvo v Sovetskoi armii i flote 1918–1961* (Party structuring in the Soviet army and fleet 1918–1961) (Moscow: Voenizdat, 1964) and by the same author *Stroitel'stvo politorganov partiinykh i komsomol'skikh organizatsii armii i flota 1918–1968* (Structuring of the political organs of Party and Komsomol organizations of the army and the fleet 1918–1968) (Moscow: Voenizdat, 1968) (hereafter *Stroitel'stvo politorganov*); the quotations attributed to Stalin are from J. Stalin, *Sochineniia* (Works) (Moscow: OGIZ, 1947) v. 5; pp. 5, 6, and 375.
9. Petrov, *Partiinoe stroitel'stvo,* p. 451.
10. Ibid., pp. 450, 451, and n. 2, p. 450.
11. Ibid., p. 461.
12. Ibid., pp. 461–464.
13. Petrov, *Stroitel'stvo politorganov,* p. 434.
14. Karpov, *"Tainaia rasprava"* in *Pravda,* 17 August 1991, p. 4; 19 August 1991, p. 4.
15. G. Feizullaev, *"Slovo o nepobedimom"* (A word about the unconquerable) in *Pravda,* 2 December 1991.
16. Karpov, *"Tainaia rasprava"* in *Pravda,* 17 August 1991, p. 4; 19 August 1991, p. 4.

17. G. Feizullaev, "*Slovo o nepobedimom*" in *Pravda,* 2 December 1991.
18. Karpov, "*Tainaia rasprava*" in *Pravda,* 17 August 1991, p. 4; 19 August 1991, p. 4.
19. *Memuary Nikity Sergeevich Khrushcheva* (The memoirs of Nikita Sergeevich Khrushchev) in *Voprosy Istorii,* no. 9/10 (1991); pp. 88, 89.
20. S. P. Markov, "*Poslevoennye gody*" (Postwar years) in Mirkina and Iarovikov, *Marshal Zhukov: polkovodets,* v. 2, p. 31.
21. Fedor Burlatskii, *Khrushchev: shtrikhi k politicheskomy portretu* (Khrushchev: details for a political portrait), in *Literaturnaia Gazeta,* 24 February 1988, p. 14.

XXVI

The Last Exile, 1957–1974

Reflecting on his life and career, Zhukov found a pattern in its low points. In 1937 he had avoided the purges; in 1947 he had felt the tightening noose of Beriia and Abakumov closing on him; and in 1957 he had fallen from the pinnacle of the Soviet military profession without much hope of being restored to the honor and dignity he had merited by his service. He told Konstantin Simonov that as he returned home after the plenum that had removed him from the Presidium and the Central Committee, he firmly resolved not to break, not to lose his willpower, not to become apathetic, no matter how difficult his situation became. His solution to overcoming his initial distress, his internal conflicts, and his anger was to take a sleeping pill, eat when he awoke, and then repeat the procedure. He found, however, that while sleeping he argued, tried to prove his case, and became more distressed. After fifteen days he went fishing. After that he applied to the Central Committee for permission to recover at a resort.[1]

Zhukov spent most of his final "exile" in the dacha Stalin had placed at his disposal at Sosnovka no. 5 in the Kuntsevo suburb of Moscow. The two-story dwelling was furnished with government-issue furniture and it was to be returned to the government on Zhukov's death. General N. A. Antipenko, who served as Zhukov's chief of Rear Services with the 1st Belorussian Front, recalled Zhukov describing the occasion when Stalin had given him lifetime use of the dacha. Zhukov had been called back to Moscow from the Western Front in January 1942. On arrival, he was directed to go to see Stalin directly, even though he was unshaven and in need of a wash after a four- or five-hour

automobile trip from the front. When he arrived and had attended to
his military business with Stalin, the dictator asked him how he rested.
Zhukov replied that he had dozed while on the road to Moscow. Stalin
did not have that kind of rest in mind. He asked if Zhukov had a dacha.
Stalin told him the war was going to be a long one, and that he had
to learn how to restore his energy. Stalin then had his chief personal
bodyguard take Zhukov and show him a large dacha with various modern
conveniences. When he returned, Zhukov told Stalin that it was too
grand and he could not accept it. Stalin overruled him, gave him the
key, and told him he could keep it as long as he lived.[2]*

While Zhukov in his exile would enjoy personal comforts (including a chauffeur-driven limousine, an old ZIS that resembled a 1930s
Packard) that would have been the envy of the overwhelming majority of the Soviet people, Khrushchev was taking steps to ensure that
his professional life and his influence on the country's military, domestic, and foreign policies were ended. One commentator has referred
to Zhukov's situation at Sosnovka during the Khrushchev regime as
that of a "state criminal."[3] In early 1958, Khrushchev appointed Zhukov's
nemesis, Filip Ivanovich Golikov, to be head of the Main Political
Directorate. Golikov had been pursuing Zhukov since the days of the
purges in 1937 and 1938. Then, as member of the Military Council
of the Belorussian Military District, he had been prepared to give credence
to charges that Zhukov was politically suspect. In 1943, he had blamed
his relief as commander of the Voronezh Front on Zhukov. In 1946,
Golikov had testified against him before Stalin during the process that
led to Zhukov's exile to the Odessa and Ural Military Districts. In 1957,
when he learned of the cabal against Zhukov, Golikov was commanding
what eventually was named the Malinovskii Military Academy of Armored
Troops in Moscow. He wrote Khrushchev that the entire command,
staff, and student body supported him in the actions he and the Central Committee had taken against Zhukov.

Golikov's career was a model illustrating the principle that in the
Soviet armed forces the rewards of military service were more likely

---

*According to V. Anfilov, Khrushchev attempted to take the dacha back from Zhukov
but somehow was thwarted and Zhukov retained the use of it until he died. Anfilov,
"U Zhukova, v Sosnovke."

to go to those who followed the Party line, even though it would eventually prove to be incorrect, than to those who opposed it, even though that might eventually prove correct. Golikov was in complete accord with Stalin's view that Hitler would not attack in 1941 and he denigrated all intelligence reporting that did not support his superior's thesis. As head of the Main Intelligence Directorate in June 1941, Golikov had refuted reports of the Soviet military attaché in Berlin that the Wehrmacht had assembled 170 divisions and was preparing to attack the Soviet Union. He also thought that Richard Sorge, the Soviet spy in Tokyo who reported when Germany would attack the Soviet Union, was a double agent.[4]

Golikov, after commanding the 10th Army in the counteroffensive before Moscow in 1942 and failing before Sukhinichi, was relieved of command of the Briansk Front in June 1942. At Stalingrad in 1942, Golikov was directed to remain in the city as liaison to Chuikov's 62d Army as the Front headquarters relocated on the eastern side of the Volga. According to Khrushchev, a look of terror came over his face and he begged not to be left behind. Later he was reported to have gone off his head, and he had to be evacuated from the city. In 1943 he was relieved of command of the Voronezh Front. For the last two years of the war he served as chief of the Main Cadres Directorate. In 1944 he was also in charge of securing the repatriation of Soviet citizens who had been taken abroad to perform forced labor for the Nazis. Since many of those Soviet citizens were opposed to returning to the Soviet Union after the war, they received little sympathy or understanding of their plight from Golikov. For this service he was given the nickname of "transferred marshal" (*peremeshchennyi marshal*). In Golikov, a loyal, unquestioning member of the Party and a declared enemy of Zhukov, Khrushchev had found the almost perfect watchdog for Zhukov. Golikov's only shortcoming was that he had also been a perfect Stalinist.[5]

Golikov's influence on the daily life of the disgraced war hero was soon felt. Military acquaintances avoided contact with Zhukov. He was not allowed to belong to the Party organization in the armed forces, which would have brought him into contact with military Party members. Instead, he was enrolled in the Party organization of a local factory. In March 1958 he was retired as a Marshal of the Soviet Union. That this step took over four months to arrange suggests that there was no precedent for it. Marshals of the Soviet Union were not supposed to retire; when they reached an inactive stage they were transferred to the "group of inspectors," where they were available to perform limited tasks as required. By not being retired, the marshals retained their active-duty perquisites. Special regulations were required for the pay and privileges of a retired marshal, one of which specified that he was required to do without the services of an aide-de-camp. During the initial years of his disgrace, in addition to his family, Zhukov's most frequent visitors were Marshals Bagramian, Vasilevskii, and Rokossovskii, Marshal of Aviation A. A. Novikov, and Generals Antipenko, Kozhedub (a World War II flying ace), and Miniuk (who had served with him as general for special assignments). His other acquaintances avoided him. He spent his days hunting, fishing, reading, ice skating in winter, and he soon began working on his memoirs, although he did not have a publisher until 1965. According to his last aide, who was required to leave him in March 1958, Zhukov requested that he obtain a list of the times and places he had been at the front during the war. He intended to write what the war was like for the army and the Soviet people, in the hope that some archivist would know the truth about the great struggle of the Red Army and the Soviet people.[6]

Outside of Sosnovka no. 5 there was a brief but intense campaign in the armed forces to find those who commanded in the "Zhukov style" and bring them to account. The "school of saboteurs" was dissolved, and the officers connected with it were transferred to the reserve without pensions, regardless of their age and length of service.[7] The question of the size of the political apparatus and the rank and qualifications of its key members was resolved by April 1958. More than 500 political worker positions were restored in the armed forces, "a significant portion of which had been baselessly reduced," and in February 1958 sixty-nine political workers were promoted to the rank of general or admiral.[8]

After these and other measures to strengthen the political apparatus and invigorate political activity in the forces, Golikov was promoted to Marshal of the Soviet Union in 1961. Zhukov's reaction to this promotion can only be surmised. The promotion to the highest rank in the Soviet armed forces for purely political expediency, as opposed to outstanding military performance, was not unprecedented—witness the fact that Stalin had given Kulik, Bulganin, and Beriia that rank. It was also not to be the last time that the rank was cheapened in the eyes of the military. Leonid Brezhnev was promoted to Marshal of the Soviet Union in 1976.

In 1962, the year after his promotion to marshal, Golikov was replaced as chief of the Main Political Directorate by A. A. Epishev. Epishev, who had been the Soviet ambassador to Yugoslavia, was recalled and given the rank of General of the Army. Golikov's fall has been attributed to the complaints of the Leningrad Party organization, which objected to seeing Golikov on Lenin's mausoleum during the military parades on May Day and on the anniversary of the revolution, 7 November. Golikov had been a member of the commission which descended on Leningrad in 1948, during the so-called Leningrad Affair, and had conducted a Stalinist purge. Golikov, if his career had been examined, could have been recognized as a confirmed Stalinist. He had finally been called to account. Golikov also suffered a mental seizure of some type [similar to the one he suffered at Stalingrad?] at about this time, which may have been the ostensible reason for his relief.[9]

In the summer of 1964, Khrushchev reportedly contacted Zhukov, "for old times' sake," and attempted to restore their relationship, saying that he had been misled in 1957. Zhukov did not believe him, because he knew for certain that Khrushchev had personally tried to convince certain of the military of his guilt.[10] Perhaps Khrushchev had begun to sense his own vulnerability and wished he had someone with Zhukov's integrity and popularity standing behind him.

In October 1964, Nikita Khrushchev was replaced in a coup that resembled the one he had engineered against Zhukov. It took place while he was vacationing in the Crimea. When he returned to Moscow he was informed that he had been deposed. The new leadership, headed by Leonid Brezhnev, modified the Party line, muting criticism of Stalin and his policies while denigrating Khrushchev and most of what he stood for. These circumstances gave reason to believe that Zhukov might soon be rehabilitated.

In 1965, Zhukov was invited to be present at a festive meeting marking the twentieth anniversary of the victory over Germany. On that occasion, when his name was announced among those of other renowned marshals and generals, Konstantin Simonov, who was also there, reported that a spontaneous ovation ensued. Zhukov was applauded with such strength and unanimity that Simonov felt in that day and hour, historic justice had been restored.

Later that evening, Zhukov and some of the other wartime military leaders met with writers in the House of Writers. Even though he was the guest in whom the writers were most interested, Zhukov's short speech contained no references to himself. Simonov considered that Zhukov's speech was a lesson for the writers, who in their enthusiasm for Zhukov and his presence had lost their sense of proportion and were ignoring the other famous soldiers.[11] The next day he joined his high-ranking colleagues on top of Lenin's mausoleum to review the victory parade.

That summer, the editors of the press agency *Agenstvo Pechati Novosti* (Novosti press agency—APN) received a telegram from their bureau in Paris informing them that a French publisher wanted to publish a series of twenty books on the most important Soviet military and political figures of the Second World War. One of the names on the list was Georgii Konstantinovich Zhukov. The reaction of the editors to this request provides an indication of Zhukov's political health at that moment: he was still someone of whom you spoke with caution. Somehow the editors found the courage to embark on the enterprise, perhaps because the request had come from abroad. Anna Davidovna Mirkina was designated the editor of the project.

A Western reader will be surprised to learn that the editors of a fully sanctioned news agency such as Novosti did not know how to get in touch with Zhukov. Someone remembered that his daughter Ella worked for the All-Union Radio Committee, and it was eventually through her that a meeting was arranged with the disgraced war hero. Mirkina met the old soldier in his dacha and eventually arrived at a contract with him, which was signed on 18 August 1965. Zhukov insisted that the book be published first in the Soviet Union. The manuscript was to be delivered in March 1966. It was delivered on time which gives some idea of Marshal Zhukov's sense of obligation and also the amount of work he had already done on his life story. The manuscript was 1,430 typed pages. Zhukov wrote in longhand. We don't know who typed the manuscript.

Preparation of the first edition took three years. Mirkina thought that the editing process might have been shorter if a special editor could have been found to deal with the military aspects of the book. But no military officer would take on the assignment, fearing, Mirkina speculates, that it would be a risk to his career. There were two major objections to its publication: first, a general objection to publishing the work of a person who had been relieved of all of his duties by a plenum of the Central Committee; and second, a specific objection to the author's thesis that the Soviet Union had not been sufficiently prepared for the German onslaught. The all-knowing, all-wise Party leadership had difficulty admitting that Party policies were ever wrong. Only certain individuals who did not fulfill the Party's expectations might occasionally make errors, often because they had been bought by foreign interests.

The principal opponent to publishing the book was M. A. Suslov, the Party's guardian of ideological purity. Suslov had been the keynote speaker at the October 1957 plenum and was probably the first to object to allowing Zhukov to publish. In regard to the second objection, Mirkina reminds us that the issue of the country's preparedness for war with Germany had already been addressed by the Soviet historian Nekrich, who in his book *June 22, 1941* had argued that the country was not prepared. The book had undergone heavy criticism and the author had been attacked personally, to the point where he left the Soviet Union. There was also the new, softer Party line on Stalin. The result of this opposition, criticism, and the shift in the Party view of Stalin was an endless stream of attempts to find compromises that could be accepted by both Zhukov and the Party censors.

Zhukov, perhaps wearied and discouraged by what must have seemed irritating delays in the publication of his work, suffered a second severe stroke in late December 1967 while resting at a sanatorium at Arkhangel'skoe outside of Moscow. He did not return to Sosnovka no. 5 until the end of the summer the next year, after spending six months in a hospital and time in a sanatorium at Barvikha. At home he continued his rehabilitation under the supervision and care of his second wife Galina Aleksandrovna,* who was a doctor, and with the aid of

---

*Zhukov married Galina Aleksandrovna in 1966 according to N. N. Iakovlev. Presumably, he divorced his first wife around that time. N. N. Iakovlev, *Zhukov* (Moscow: Molodaia Gvardiia, 1992), p. 456.

his cousin, M. M. Pilikhin, who with his wife had lived in one of the outbuildings on the estate since 1965.

Zhukov had recovered sufficiently by February 1968 to write to Leonid Brezhnev and Aleksei Kosygin to complain about the unexplained delay in the publication of his memoirs. Some time later, probably after Zhukov's letter was received, Zhukov and Mirkina were given to understand that Brezhnev wished to be mentioned in Zhukov's book. Unfortunately, they had never encountered each other during the war. The solution was to write that when Zhukov had visited the front before Novorossiisk in 1943, he had wanted to consult with Colonel Brezhnev but Brezhnev was forward in the bridgehead and was not available. When Zhukov made this insertion he smiled bitterly and said, "The wise will understand." They would understand that marshals of the Soviet Union rarely had a need to consult with colonels who were political officers, and if they did the colonels would make themselves available.

One night in late 1968, the editors of Novosti received word that Brezhnev wanted to see the draft. Zhukov was given one final look at the latest version, and the next morning at 0900 it was available for the general secretary's perusal. By noon, permission was received to publish the book. In March 1969, Zhukov received his copy of the book and it reached the book stores in Moscow at the end of April. The book was an immediate commercial success but, perhaps more importantly for Marshal Zhukov, his Soviet readers responded with over 10,000 letters between publication of the first and second editions. They were, in effect, the reviewers of the first edition, and their comments, corrections, and questions assisted in the preparation of the second edition. The success of the book was also a tonic for its author. Mirkina believed that the old marshal looked younger after its success.

Even before the book appeared, the Main Directorate for the Preservation of State Secrets in the Press had issued secret instructions to all of its subordinate directorates that no reviews, commentaries, or excerpts from Zhukov's book were to be published. The directive was issued on instructions from the Propaganda Department of the Central Committee on 10 April. Presumably the Party did not wish to encourage discussion of the book and thereby boost its sales.[12] Despite this effort the first edition sold out immediately and the prohibition was eventually lifted.

The book's success did not change the old Communist world in which the revitalized marshal was living. The appearance of the book may have suggested to members of the Party organization to which Zhukov belonged that he was now fully rehabilitated. In any event, he was elected a delegate to the Twenty-fourth Party Congress, which was to be held in Moscow in March 1971. For the Communist Party of the Soviet Union, the Party Congress was a periodic event at which approximately five thousand elected delegates from all over the Soviet Union assembled to hear reports on the state of the Party from its top leaders, to elect a new Central Committee which in turn would elect a new Politburo (a title restored to favor by the Brezhnev regime), and to renew acquaintances and socialize with old comrades.

It is not difficult to imagine the anticipation of Zhukov, who had long been excluded from these opportunities to see and be seen by his Party comrades. He had a new uniform jacket tailored, bought new shoes, and sought to mobilize his strength. Then his wife was refused a guest pass to the Congress. She immediately called Brezhnev. Citing Zhukov's health problems, he urged her to discourage him from attending. When she argued that Zhukov's appearance at the Congress would be an unambiguous signal of his rehabilitation in the eyes of the Party, Brezhnev replied that the fact of his selection as a delegate was acknowledgement enough. After this conversation, the Zhukovs were visited by a phalanx of doctors and minor Party officials, all of whom advised against the old marshal's attendance at the Congress. The Zhukovs got the message: Marshal Brezhnev did not want the competition of the popular war hero at his Congress. Mirkina, who saw Zhukov shortly after he had accepted that his presence at the Congress was not desired, saw tears in the old man's eyes for the first and last time.

Characteristically, Zhukov soon returned to work on the second edition of his autobiography. He derived solace from the continuing flow of appreciation and support he received from readers from all walks of life who had various memories of what the Russians continue to call the Great Fatherland War. But fate had another blow in store for him. Galina Aleksandrovna became seriously ill in 1973; she died on 13 November at the age of forty-six. She was buried with the military honors due a lieutenant colonel of medical service in the cemetery of the Novodevich'ii Monastery. Georgii Konstantinovich could only attend a civilian memorial service in the suburb of Kuntsevo, supported by his two old comrades, Marshal Bagramian and General I. I. Fediuninskii.

One event in these last years gave the aging marshal a measure of satisfaction. Vasilii Peskov, a journalist who had developed an admiration and friendship for Zhukov following an interview in 1970, reported that Zhukov told him Marshal Konev had visited him to apologize. The two men apparently recalled the wartime events in which they both played so large a part and also the postwar events. Konev was "disarmingly sincere," Zhukov told Peskov. Zhukov told Konev to forget what had happened after the war, that it was minor compared to what they had accomplished. Unfortunately, Zhukov did not share the details of Konev's "confession" with Peskov.

Georgii Konstantinovich Zhukov died on 18 June 1974. He did not live to celebrate his 78th birthday, nor did he live to see the second edition of his memoirs, which were signed to the press in July of 1974. He was given full military honors, including a Red Square parade. The principal address at the ceremony was given by the Minister of Defense, A. A. Grechko. Marshal of Aviation Rudenko, who had commanded the air armies of several of the Fronts Zhukov had commanded, also spoke. His ashes were placed in the Kremlin wall, where they now rest between those of S. S. Kamenev, commander in chief of the Red Army during the last years of the Civil War, and his comrade and father-in-law of one of his daughters, A. M. Vasilevskii, who died in 1977.

Zhukov was survived by three daughters, Era, Ella, and Maria. Era and Ella were daughters by his first wife, Aleksandra Dievna, whom he married in 1920. Maria (Masha) was his daughter by his second wife, Galina Aleksandrovna. Both Era and Ella have written about their father and mother in loving terms. Era, the oldest, born in 1928, has described their nomadic family life in the years between the World Wars. She emphasizes the support Aleksandra Dievna gave their father as he moved up the command ladder, making a home for the family in the harsh conditions of pre-war garrisons and working with him to improve his Russian. As an army child, Era attended eleven schools in ten years. She has also described her mother's concern when her husband was suddenly called to Moscow in 1939, in the years when such unexplained summons often meant death or prison. It was only later that she found out Zhukov had been sent to Mongolia, to Halhin Gol. After the victory there, the entire family stayed with him in Ulan Bator.

One of the highlights of the older girls' young lives was their brief visit to the headquarters of the Western Front at Perkhushkovo* to be with their father to celebrate the coming of the New Year 1942. The family was flown to Perkhushkovo from Kuibyshev, where they had been since their evacuation from Moscow in 1941. They did not return to Moscow from Kuibyshev until 1943. Both girls recalled that they could count on their fingers the number of times they saw their father during the war, even though he was in Moscow often on official business. He did keep in touch with notes, reporting in general terms on the progress of the war and his health, while inquiring about their school work. In the last years of the war, telephone service was available and family information could be exchanged in minutes.[13]

Ella, who was born in Slutsk in 1935, has described her father's interest in reading and her regret that she did not catalogue their domestic library, which totalled some 20,000 books. Zhukov preferred the works of Russian authors and constantly urged his daughters to read such authors and poets as Pushkin, Ostrovskii, Tolstoi, Turgenev, and Chekhov. He also, of course, read works by such foreign military writers as Clausewitz, Schlieffen, Fuller, and Liddell Hart. On one occasion he had his daughters read a translation of *Seven Days in May,* an American novel about an attempted putsch by the military. Although he had urged them to read it, he laughed at the plot because he did not believe the authors understood the psychology of the professional military officer.[14]

His daughters found Zhukov to be completely Russian. He loved the Russian countryside, and his passion for hunting and fishing was a manifestation of his inner longing to be part of the natural world of Russia. He enjoyed Russian classical and folk music, dancing, and art, especially that depicting Russian flora and fauna. He relished Russian food. Era compared him in these respects to the great Russian bass, Fedor Shaliapin.[15]

Both daughters were convinced that those who described his professional demeanor as stern, harsh, cruel, demanding, and somber either

---

*As an example of some of the pettiness that continued to surround Zhukov's activities even after his "rehabilitation," the Main Political Administration refused to allow an interview with Marshal Zhukov to be filmed at Perkhushkovo for a film about the Battle of Moscow.

did not understand him as a man, or did not understand the limitless demands that winning the war placed on the shoulders of the soldiers, officers, high commanders, and people of the Soviet Union. Those demands were so great that they could only be met through an unreconcilable attitude toward slackers and cowards.[16] The reaction of Zhukov's daughters to the erroneous accusation that Georgii Konstantinovich had sent an accusatory letter about Marshal Egorov is a demonstration of the fervor with which they are prepared to defend his honor and his reputation.

Zhukov's youngest daughter, Maria, was 16 at the time of his death in June 1974. She and her maternal grandmother were living at Sosnovka at the time and were required to return the dacha to the government.[17] Her education and subsequent career were a worry to the old soldier as he felt his end approaching, but she finished an institute and subsequently married.[18] Maria has also been active in maintaining her father's reputation and keeping his memory alive. She has preserved and provided her father's previously unpublished manuscript materials to the press and was acknowledged by APN for materials she supplied for the tenth edition of *Vospominaniia i razmyshleniia*. She has also been an honored guest at memorial ceremonies commemorating wartime events in which her father played a leading role.[19]

NOTES

1. Simonov, "Zametki" in *VIZh,* no. 12: p. 46.
2. A. D. Mirkina, *"Ne skloniv golovy"* (With head unbowed), in Mirkina and Iarovikov, *Marshal Zhukov: Polkovodets* 2: p. 49. N. A. Antipenko, "My znali drug druga 25 let" (We knew each other for 25 years), in Ibid., 1: pp. 328, 329.
3. G. Feizullaev, "Slovo o nepobedimom" (A word about the unconquerable) in *Pravda,* 2 December 1991, p. 6.
4. Evgenii Vorob'ev, "Kazhdaia piad' zemli" (Each inch of land) in Smirnov, *Marshal Zhukov,* pp. 157, 158.
5. Golikov's official biography can be found in *SVE* 2: p. 585. His actions at Stalingrad are found in Talbott, *Khrushchev Remembers,* pp. 194, 195. His performance as chief of the Main Intelligence Directorate can be inferred from P. I. Ivashutin, "Razvedka bila trevogu" (Intelligence sounded the alarm) in *KZ,* 2 February 1991, p. 5. Information about Golikov's letter to Khrushchev was provided to the author by two Soviet historians, Drs. V. V. Larionov and V. M. Kulish.
6. S. P. Markov, "Poslevoennye gody" (Postwar years) in Mirkina and Iarovikov, *Marshal Zhukov: Polkovodets* 2: p. 31.
7. Karpov, "Tainaia rasprava" in *Pravda,* 19 August 1991, p. 4.
8. Petrov, *Stroitel'stvo politorganov,* p. 453.
9. Conversations of the author with Soviet military historians Larionov and Kulish in October, 1991.
10. Feizullaev, see note 3.
11. Simonov, "Zametki," in *VIZh,* no. 7: p. 34.
12. The directive was displayed in the exhibit "Revelations from the Russian Archives," held at the Library of Congress, Washington, D.C., 17 June–16 July 1992. Exhibit no. A28.21.
13. Era Zhukova, "Otets" (My father), in Mirkina and Iarovikov, *Marshal Zhukov: Polkovodets* 1: pp. 30, 38, 39, 43, 45.
14. Ella Zhukova, "Interesy otsa" (My father's interests) in Ibid., pp. 48, 49.
15. Era Zhukova, "Otets," Ibid., p. 35.
16. Ibid., p. 46.

17. Mirkina, "Ne skloniv golovy," Ibid., p. 49.
18. Markov, see note 6, p. 34.
19. "El'nia pomnit" (El'nia remembers), in *KZ,* 19 September 1991.
    Maria G. Zhukova, "Korotko o Staline" (In short about Stalin) in
    Pravda, 20 January 1989, p. 3. Feizullaev, see note 3.

XXVII

CONCLUSION

The collapse of the Soviet Union has exposed for all to see the flaws in the economic, political, legal, military, and moral systems that undergirded a state which had risen to the status of military superpower in the seventy years or so of its existence. Some of those flaws were clearly evident in the way that system dealt with Georgii Konstantinovich Zhukov. And some of them are obvious in the personality of Zhukov himself. A major shortcoming in the state was the structure of its leadership, which had seized power conspiratorially and retained it through a ruthless police machinery. The leadership never developed a method of legitimizing itself nor did it provide an accepted system of periodic rejuvenation. The leadership to its very end in 1991 was, or should have been, continually looking over its shoulder, on guard against the next coup.

Zhukov rose through the ranks in this system, accepting its ideological premises, during the period 1925–1940 when the "Stalin style" of leadership was the norm, a norm that was to persist in the Soviet bureaucracy long after Stalin's death. Aleksandr Solzhenitsyn has depicted that style in another context:

Knorozov was proud that he never budged from what he said. As formerly in Moscow the word of Stalin was not changed or revoked so in this *oblast'* the word of Knorozov was still even now not changed or revoked. And while Stalin was long gone Knorozov was still there. He was one of the best known representatives of the "strong-willed style of leadership" and considered this his greatest service. He did not imagine that one could lead in some other manner.[1]

K. K. Rokossovskii, who first met Zhukov in 1924, has provided a thoughtful impression of this aspect of Zhukov's character, concluding that:

High exactingness is a necessary and most important trait of a military leader. But his iron will must always be combined with sensitivity to his subordinates and the ability to be guided by their intelligence and initiative. Our commander [Zhukov] in those difficult days did not always follow that rule. He would be unjust, as they say, in the heat of anger.

Rokossovskii also noted his self-esteem: "He was exceptional in everything—talent, energy and confidence in his power."[2]

The role of Stalin in the formation of Zhukov's command style seems to have been overlooked by Rokossovskii, who was himself one of Stalin's victims. Stalin was not just a model for Soviet leaders; in Zhukov's case he was always looking over Zhukov's shoulder. And not only did Stalin scrutinize his every action and order, but he was assisted by a system of police informers who were reporting to Beriia, and a system of political reporters, whose reports on morale, loyalty, and discipline could be on the desk of the dictator in a matter of hours, if not minutes. The pressure on Zhukov to perform, particularly in critical situations, is difficult to describe adequately. As Zhukov passed triumphantly through one military crisis after another and became a national hero, the megalomaniacal envy of the "boss" boiled until it exploded in 1946.

Even after escaping the fate of Tukhachevskii, in 1946 and 1947 Zhukov remained true to himself, knowing all too well that, paradoxical as it might seem, the disciplinarian in him was at risk. The Party aktiv could call him to account and might at any time be encouraged to do so. When Zhukov returned to Moscow in 1953, his initial successes, his role in the arrest of Beriia, and the defeat of the anti-Party group reinforced his confidence that the leadership style he had maintained during his exile was still effective and still necessary. But he failed to reckon with the bureaucratic infighting skills of the military political apparatus, the depth of the wounds he had inflicted over time on his professional colleagues in the high command, and the fear he evoked in a political leadership that was never confident of its own legitimacy.

While Zhukov's outbursts may have been pardonable in the context of the desperate battles that marked the war on the eastern front during World War II, there seems to be no excuse for his reported treatment of Admiral Kuznetsov and Marshal Biriuzov and others of the senior leadership while he was minister of defense. The 1946 plenum and his subsequent seven years in exile should have taught him how counterproductive his uncontrolled anger was. The pressures on him as minister of defense were intense, but they could not compare to those of 1941, and he certainly did not have the same respect for (or fear of) Khrushchev that he had for Stalin.

Zhukov's use of abusive language toward his senior subordinates seemed to be almost chronic. It may have been intended to test the mental resilience of the target of his wrath, to see if the individual would respond and how. As minister of defense he was nicknamed "*marshal troichatki*" (a translation could be "the triple-threat marshal") after what were said to be his three principles of disciplinary action: relief from assignment; reduction in rank; relief from active duty. However, those who withstood his verbal assault remembered that Zhukov, who was himself very straightforward, valued subordinates who would stand up to him in the interest of getting the job done.[3]

At the time, the prevailing view outside the Soviet Union of the Zhukov episode was that it was related to the fundamental question of the subordination of the armed services to Party control. As Timothy Colton wrote in 1977:

A revised understanding of the Zhukov affair would emphasize his character, personal history, and peculiar position in the Soviet leadership; it would deemphasize elements of institutional conflict.[4]

The information that has become available with glasnost' has not seemed to change this conclusion.

In the years since the removal of Zhukov from the inner councils of the Soviet state, the Party and the military reached a consensus on the military policy of the state, a consensus based on a common view of the external threats to national security. A common program was adopted to meet those threats. There appeared to be no convincing voices warning of the ultimate costs of that program to the economic well-being of the state as a whole. When the growing stagnation could not be overcome by repeating the old slogans, glasnost' was invoked to show the population just how bad the situation was. It worked to the extent that it became obvious that the entire ideological basis of the state had to be rebuilt in order to find an escape from the current morass.

On the ninety-fifth anniversary of Zhukov's birth in 1991, as the Russian people struggled through another time of troubles, Zhukov was being held up as an icon representing the genius of the Russian people to provide a leader to save them in extreme circumstances. Zhukov, the embodiment of Russian honor and valor, the symbol of Russian victory, Russian sovereignty, and the Russian spirit, is being portrayed as the inspiration for the next Russian revolution.[5] A person with the positive attributes of Zhukov's character and national prestige, and commitment to the national well-being may well be found, but, it is hoped, not astride a white horse.

However the quest for a new leadership is resolved and whatever may be discovered in the archives about Zhukov's political intentions, nothing is likely to erase or tarnish the image of the man on the white horse who did so much to bring his country to its shining hour. Surely these words of Pindar, written in praise of an earlier hero, fit the doughty marshal:

> Glory is the reward of the valiant . . .
> He who in that hurricane that is war,
> fighting for his country, shields her from
> bloody hail and goes out, carrying death
> into the enemy camp; that man so increases
> the glory of his fellow citizens that it reaches
> heaven itself, by his life or his death.[6]

NOTES

1. A. Solzhenitsyn, "Dlia pol'zy dela" (For the sake of the matter), in *Sochineniia* (Works) (Frankfurt/Main: Possev, 1964), p. 202.
2. Rokossovskii, 5th edition, pp. 89, 90, 92.
3. Arsenii Vorozheikin, "*Po shpiony ogon' ne otkryv*at' " (Don't open fire on the spy), *KZ*, 5 August 1992, p. 3.
4. Timothy J. Colton, "The Zhukov Affair Reconsidered" in *Soviet Studies* 29, no. 2 (April 1977): p. 185.
5. Feizullaev, "Slovo o nepobedimom," *Pravda*, 2 December 1991.
6. Pindar, *Isthmians* 7: 26–30, cited in Nicole Loraux, *The Invention of Athens* (Cambridge, Mass.: Harvard, 1986), p. 51.

Selected Bibliography

Books and Pamphlets in English

Bacevich, A. J. *The Pentomic Era*. Washington, D.C.: National Defense University Press, 1986.

Bohlen, Charles E. *Witness to History 1929–1969*. New York: W. W. Norton, 1973.

Chaney, Otto P., Jr. *Zhukov*. Norman, Oklahoma: University of Oklahoma Press, 1971.

Deane, John R. *The Strange Alliance*. New York: Viking, 1947.

Deutscher, Isaac. *Stalin: A Political Biography*. New York: Oxford, 1949.

Eisenhower, Dwight D. *Crusade in Europe*. New York: Doubleday, 1948.

Eisenhower, John S. D. *Strictly Personal*. New York: Doubleday, 1974.

Farago, Ladislas. *Patton*. New York: Obolensky, 1963.

Guderian, Heinz. *Panzer Leader*. New York: Ballantine, 1961.

Liddell Hart, B. H. *The German Generals Talk*. New York: Morrow, 1948.

Manstein, Erich von. *Lost Victories*. Chicago: Regnery, 1958.

Talbott, Strobe, trans. and ed. *Khrushchev Remembers*. Boston and Toronto: Little, Brown, 1970.

———. *Khrushchev Remembers: The Last Testament*. Boston and Toronto: Little, Brown, 1974.

Ulam, Adam B. *Stalin: The Man and His Era*. New York: Viking, 1973.

Werth, Alexander. *Russia at War: 1940–1945*. New York: Avon, 1965.

Zhukov, Georgii. *The Memoirs of Marshal Zhukov*. New York: Delacorte, London: Jonathan Cape, 1971. An English translation by Novosti of the first edition of *Vospominaniia i razmyshleniia*.

Ziemke, Earl F. *Stalingrad to Berlin: The German Defeat in the East*. Washington, D.C.: U.S. Government Printing Office, 1968.

Ziemke, Earl F., and Magna E. Bauer. *Moscow to Stalingrad: Decision in the East*. Washington, D.C.: U.S. Government Printing Office, 1987.

Books and Pamphlets in Russian

Anfilov, Viktor A. *Nachalo Velikoi Otechestvennoi Voiny* (The Beginning of the Great Fatherland War). Moscow: Voenizdat, 1962.

Batov, Pavel I. *B pokhodakh i boiakh* (In campaigns and battles). Moscow: Voenizdat, 1st ed. 1962, 3d ed. 1974.

Chuikov, Vasilii I. *Legendarnaia 62-ia* (The legendary 62d). Stalingrad: Knizhnoe Izdatel'stvo, 1958.

Eremenko, Andrei I. *Stalingradskaia bitva* (The Stalingrad battle). Stalingrad: Knizhnoe Izdatel'stvo, 1958.

———. *Stalingrad* (Stalingrad). Moscow: Voenizdat, 1961.

Golikov, Filip I. *V Moskovskoi bitve* (In the Moscow battle). Moscow: Nauka, 1967.

Grechko, Andrei A. *Bitva za Kavkaz* (The battle for the Caucasus). Moscow: Voenizdat, 2d ed. 1969.

Grechko, Andrei A., et al, eds. *Istoriia Vtoroi Mirovoi Voiny, 1939–1945* (History of the Second World War, 1939–1945). 12 vols. Moscow: Voenizdat, 1973–1982.

Ivanov, Semen P. *Shtab armeiskii, shtab frontovoi* (Army staff, Front staff). Moscow: Voenizdat, 1990.

Kapusto, Iuliia. *Poslednimi dorogami generala Efremova* (The last roads of General Efremov). Moscow: Politizdat, 1992.

Kazakov, Mikhail I. *Nad kartoi bylykh srazhenii* (Over the map of bygone battles). Moscow: Voenizdat, 1st ed. 1965, 2d ed. 1971.

Kitaev, L. M., and G. N. Bol'shakov. *Vizit druzhby* (Visit of friendship). Moscow: Voenizdat, 1957.

Konev, Ivan S. *Sorok piatyi* (Forty-five). Moscow: Voenizdat, 1966.

———. *Zapiski komanduiushchego frontom* (Notes of a Front commander). Moscow: Voenizdat, 1991.

Kuznetsov, Nikolai G. *Nakanune. Kursom k pobede* (On the eve. Course to victory). Moscow: Voenizdat, 1991.

Mirkina, Anna D., and Viktor S. Iarovikov. *Marshal Zhukov: Polkovodets i chelovek* (Marshal Zhukov: Great captain and man). Moscow: Novosti, 1988.

Moskalenko, Kirill S. *Na Iugo-zapadnom napravlenii* (On the Southwestern Axis). Moscow: Nauka, 1969.

Peresypkin, Ivan T. *Sviaz' v Velikoi Otechestvennoi Voine* (Communications in the Great Fatherland War). Moscow: Nauka, 1973.

Petrov, Iurri P. *Partiinoe stroitel'stvo v Sovetskoi armii i flote 1918–1961* (Party structuring in the Soviet army and fleet 1918–1961). Moscow: Voenizdat, 1964.

———. *Stroitel'stvo politorganov partiinykh i komsomol'skikh organizatsii armii i flota 1918–1968* (Structuring of the political organs of Party and Komsomol organizations of the army and the fleet 1918–1968). Moscow: Voenizdat, 1968.

Pospelov, P. N., chmn. ed. comm. *Istoriia Velikoi Otechestvennoi Voiny Sovetskogo Soiuza 1941–1945* (The History of the Great Fatherland War of the Soviet Union 1941–1945). 6 vols. Moscow: Voenizdat, 1961–1965.

———. *Velikaia Otechestvennaia Voina Sovetskogo Soiuza 1941–1945: Kratkaia istoriia* (The Great Fatherland War of the Soviet Union 1941–1945: Short history). Moscow: Voenizdat, 1967.

Rokossovskii, Konstantin K. *Soldatskii dolg* (A soldier's duty). 5th ed. Moscow: Voenizdat, 1988.

Rotmistrov, Pavel A. *Tankovoye srazhenie pod Prokhorovkoi* (The tank battle near Prokhorovka). Moscow: Voenizdat, 1960.

Samsonov, Aleksandr M. *Stalingradskaia bitva* (The Stalingrad battle). Moscow: Nauka, 1st ed. 1960, 4th ed. 1989.

Shtemenko, Sergei M. *General'nyi shtab v gody voiny* (The General Staff in the war years). Moscow: Voenizdat, 1968.

Simonov, Konstantin. *Zhivye i mertvye* (The living and the dead). 3 vols. Moscow: Sovetskii pisatel', 1972.

Smirnov, S. S. *Marshal Zhukov: Kakim my ego pomnim* (Marshal Zhukov: As we remember him). Moscow: Politizdat, 1988.

Solzhenitsyn, Aleksandr I. *V kruge pervom* (In the first circle). New York: Harper Colophon, 1969.

Sovetskaia voennaia entsiklopediia (The Soviet military encyclopedia). 8 vols. Moscow: Voenizdat, 1976–1980.

Vasilevskii, Aleksandr M. *Delo vsei zhizni* (The business of an entire lifetime). Moscow: Voenizdat, 5th edition, 1984.

Volkogonov, Dmitri A. *Triumf i tragediia: Politicheskii portret I. V. Stalina* (Triumph and tragedy: A political portrait of J. V. Stalin). 2 books, 4 parts. Moscow: Novosti, 1989.

Volkov, Fedor D. *Vzlet i padenie Stalina* (The rise and fall of Stalin). Moscow: Spektr, 1992.

Zakharov, Matvei V., chmn. ed. comm. *50 let Vooruzhennykh Sil SSSR* (50 years of the Armed Forces of the USSR). Moscow: Voenizdat, 1968.

Zhukov, Georgii K. *Vospominaniia i razmyshleniia* (Reminiscences and reflections). Moscow: Novosti, 1st ed. 1969, 2d ed. 2 vols. 1974, 10th ed. 3 vols. 1990.

Public Documents in Russian

Izvestiia TsK KPSS (News of the Central Committee of the Communist Party of the Soviet Union). This publication providing official accounts of the activities of the Central Committee from 1919 until 1929 resumed publication in 1989.

Articles in English

Colton, Timothy J. "The Zhukov Affair Reconsidered." *Soviet Studies* 29, no. 2 (April 1977), pp. 186–213.

Tarleton, Robert E. "The Life and Fate of the Stalin Line, 1926–1941." Unpublished seminar paper submitted to Professor Donald W. Threadgold, University of Washington, June 1991.

Ziemke, Earl F. "Operation Kreml: Deception, Strategy and the Fortunes of War." *Parameters* 9, no. 1, (September 1979), pp. 72–83.

Articles in Russian

Anfilov, Viktor. "Rukoi Marshala Zhukova" (By the hand of Marshal Zhukov). *Krasnaia Zvezda,* 24 January 1992.

———. "U Zhukova, v Sosnovke" (With Zhukov at Sosnovka). *Krasnaia Zvezda,* 24 April 1992.

Bystrov, S. "V oktiabre 1957-ogo" (In October 1957). *Krasnaia Zvezda,* 19, 20, and 21 May 1989.

———. "Zadanie osobogo svoistva" (A mission with a special attribute). *Krasnaia Zvezda,* 18, 19, and 20 March 1988.

Eliseev, V. "Pobeda pod Moskvoy: Lozh' i pravda" (The victory before Moscow: The lie and the truth). *Krasnaia Zvezda,* 18 February 1992.

Isaev, S. I. "*Vekhi frontovogo puti*" (Markers of a frontal journey). *Voenno-istoricheskii Zhurnal,* no. 10, 1991.

Ivanov, B. P. "Atomnyi vzryv u poselka Totskoe." (The atomic explosion near the village of Totskoe), *Voenno-istoricheskii Zhurnal,* no. 12, 1991.

Ivanov-Skuratov, Anatolii. "Napadenie lzhe-Suvorova na Rossiiu" (The attack of the false-Suvorov on Russia). *Na Boevom Postu,* nos. 8/9, 1992, p. 30.

Ivashov, L., and Iv. Rubtsov. "V proryv idut shtrafnye batal'ony" (Into the breakthrough go the penal battalions). *Krasnaia Zvezda*, 25 December 1991.

———. "Vyzhit' shtrafniky bylo bol'shim schast'em" (To survive in a penal unit was great [good] luck). *Krasnaia Zvezda*, 19 March 1992.

Karpov, Vladimir. "Marshal Zhukov, ego soratniki i protivniki v gody voiny i mira" (Marshal Zhukov, his comrades in arms and opponents in the years of war and peace) in *Znamia*, nos. 9, 10, and 11, 1989.

———. "Tainaia rasprava nad marshalom Zhukovym" (The secret reprisals against Marshal Zhukov). *Pravda*, 17 and 19 August 1991.

———. "Rasprava Stalina nad marshalom Zhukovym" (The reprisals of Stalin against Marshal Zhukov). *Vestnik Protivovozdushnoi Oborony*, nos. 7-8, 1992.

Khor'kov, Anatolii. "Ten' na marshala Zhukova" (A shadow is cast on Marshal Zhukov). *Pravda*, 16 January 1992.

Okorokov, V. *"Pravda o pokoinom marshale i pogibshem generale"* (The truth about the deceased marshal and the fallen general). *Syn Otechestva*, 12 April 1991, p. 10.

Ortenberg, David I. "U Zhukova v Perkhushkovo" (With Zhukov at Perkhushkovo). *Krasnaia Zvezda*, 30 November 1991.

Pavlenko, N. G. "Razmyshleniia nad o sud'be polkovodtsa" (Reflections on the fate of a Great Captain). *Voenno-istoricheskii Zhurnal*, nos. 10, 11, and 12, 1988.

Simonov, Konstantin M. "Zametki k biografii G. K. Zhukova" (Notes for a biography of G. K. Zhukov). *Voenno-istoricheskii Zhurnal*, nos. 6, 7, 9, 10, and 12, 1987.

———. "Besedy s marshalom Sovetskogo Souiza A. M. Vasilevskim" (Conversations with Marshal of the Soviet Union A. M. Vasilevskii). *Znamia*, no. 5, 1988.

Vorozheikin, Arsenii. *"Po shpiony ogon' ne otkryvat' (Don't open fire on the spy). Krasnaia Zvezda*, 5 August 1992.

Zakharov, M. V. "Nakanune vtoroi mirovoi voiny" (On the eve of the Second World War). *Novaia i Noveishaia Istoriia*, no. 5, September–October, 1970.

Russian Language Newspapers and Periodicals

Kommunist
Krasnaia Zvezda [KZ]

Na Boevom Postu
Pravda
Russkaia Mysl'
Syn Otechestva
Vestnik Protivovozdushnoi Oborony
Voenno-istoricheskii Zhurnal [*VIZh*]
Znamia

Index